KNOWSLEY LIBRARY SERVICE

Knowsl@y Council

Please return this book on or before the date shown below

You may return this book to any Knowsley library
For renewal please telephone
Halewood - 486 4442   Housebound Service - 443 4223
Huyton/Mobile - 443 3734/5   Kirkby - 443 4290/89
Page Moss - 489 9814   Prescot - 426 6449
School Library Service - 443 4202
Stockbridge Village - 480 3925   Whiston - 426 4757
http://www.knowsley.gov.uk/

THIS IS A CARLTON BOOK

Published in 2008 by Carlton Books Limited
20 Mortimer Street
London W1T 3JW

10 9 8 7 6 5 4 3 2 1

Text © 2008 Steve Turner
Design © 2008 Carlton Books Limited

The right of Steve Turner to be identified as the author of this work has been asserted by him in accordance with the Copyright, Designs and Patents Act 1988

A CIP catalogue record for this book is available from the British Library.

ISBN 978-1-84442-037-7

Printed in Dubai

Editorial Manager: Lara Maiklem
Art Director: Lucy Coley
Designer: Barbara Zuniga
Picture Researcher: Paul Langan
Production: Claire Hayward

PREVIOUS PAGE
1959: royal photographer Norman Parkinson photographed Cliff in Chelsea for Vogue

BELOW
December 17, 1999: Cliff performs at Birmingham's NEC in one of his last concerts of the twentieth century

CONTENTS PAGE
1960: Cliff and the original Shadows' line-up. From left to right: Bruce Welch (rhythm guitar), Jet Harris (bass), Hank Marvin (lead guitar), Tony Meehan (drums)

CLIFF RICHARD
THE BACHELOR BOY

STEVE TURNER

CARLTON
BOOKS

The publishers would like to thank the following for their kind permission to reproduce the pictures in this book.

Malcolm Addey's private collection: 52
Alamy: /Popperfoto: 97t
Joan Bosse: 45b, 58, 59, 60, 61
Vincent Bridgewater: 14, 18
Camera Press: /Heilemann: 119; /Peter Kain: 212; /Ken Rake: 217t; /David Stern: 92b
Cheshunt Weekly Telegraph: 27, 29, 32
Gerald Coates: 176, 210
Corbis: /Bettmann: 113; /Terry Cryer: 91t; /Norman Parkinson Limited: 1; /Derick A. Thomas: 188t
Joyce Dobra: 15, 16, 17, 19
Stan Edwards: 54
Royston Ellis: 112t, 219b
EMI: 53b
Ronnie Ernstone: 86t
John Foster: 57
Getty Images: /Mike Barnes: 137t; /Dave Benett: 209; / Margaret Bourke-White/Time & Life Pictures: 20c; /Michael Buckner: 218; /Central Press/Hulton Archive: 147; /Martin Dilger/Scoopt: 114; /John Drysdale/Keystone Features/Hulton Archive: 74; /Fox Photos: 156, 157; /Tim Graham: 179b, 197t, 204; /Charles Hewitt: 48b; /Hulton Archive: 46, 139, 155; / Peter Hustler/Central Press: 116, 124; /Cambridge Jones: back endpaper; /Keystone Features: 20t, 65, 98; /Mike Lawn/Fox Photos/Hulton Archive: 140t; /McCabe/Express: 102t; /Stan Meagher/Express: 90; /John Minihan/Evening Standard: 148; /S. O'Meara: 138; /Michael Ochs Archives: 51, 71, 88t, 134; /Frank Pocklington/Picture Post: 33; /John Pratt: 44, 77b; /Sasha: 49; / ShowBizIreland: 219t; /Graham Stark/Hulton Archive: 130; / George Stroud/Express: 100t; /Wesley/Keystone: 118b
Janice Goring: 35
David Hawley Collection: 6, 10t, 10b, 11t, 12, 13, 67, 75, 77t, 79, 82, 86b, 91b, 92t, 94, 95, 97b, 99t, 101, 102b, 103, 104, 105b, 110b, 112b, 126, 128, 137b, 140b, 141, 143, 165t, 168, 222l, 222c, 222r, 223l, 223c, 223r
Cindy Kent: 129
London Features International: /David Koppell: 164

Mary Evans Picture Library: 20b
Aleksander Mezek: 206
Mirrorpix: 9, 63, 121t, 125, 198
Norman Mitham: 25, 37
PA Photos: 2, 135, 197b; /Cruisepictures: 208; /Toby Melville: 214; /Yui Mok: 213b; /Stefan Rousseau: 193; /Ian West: 207
Larry Peterson: 47
Pictorial Press: 50, 85, 105t
Redferns: /BBC Photo Library: 72, 145, 149, 192t; /Fin Costello: 158; /Gab Archives: 127, 175; /Rick Hardy: 41, 68b; /Beverly Lebarrow: 34, 55, 70, 83, 84; /Gered Mankowitz: 144, 159; / David Redfern: 189; /Rick Richards: 73
Retna: /Monitor Picture Library: 93, 107, 109, 136, 170t
Rex Features: 7, 177, 186t, 190, 196, 199, 215; /Action Press: 192b; /Peter Brooker: 167, 182, 184; /Mauro Carraro: 174; / Silver Clef: 152; /Carolyn Contino/BEI: 194b; /Andre Csillag: 142, 161; /Clive Dixon: 11b; /Andrew Dunsmore: 8t; /Juergen Hasenkopf: 205; /Dezo Hoffmann: front endpaper, 8b, 39, 42b, 64, 66, 69, 100b, 106, 108, 146, 224; /Nigel Holland: 166; / Robert Hunt Library: 163t, 163b; /Cliff Kent: 187t, 211, 213t; /George Konig: 30, 110c; /David Levenson: 160; /Alisdair Macdonald: 68t; /Ilpo Musto: 179t; /News UK Ltd: 181; /Bill Orchard: 122, 150; /Palmer & Nutley: 178; /Sipa Press: 186b, 200; /Snap: 28; /Dennis Stone: 201; /Webb: 110t; /Richard Young: 153, 171b, 180, 194t, 195, 216: /24/7 Media: 202
Ripley and Heanor News: 43
Ian Samwell: 4-5, 31, 38, 87
Topfoto.co.uk: 42t, 88b, 89, 96, 120, 203; /Arena PAL: 118t, 188b; /Pro Sport: 169
Steve Turner: 170b, 171t, 172, 173
Steve Turner Collection: 23, 36, 40, 45t, 53t, 62, 115, 121b, 165b, 187b, 217b
Tyne Tees Television: 133
V&A Images: /Harry Hammond: 48t, 78
Delia Wicks: 99b
Dorothy Willis: 22t, 22b
Mark Wynter: 81

Contents

LEFT
*Cliff and The Shadows perform
"I Love You" on "The Cliff
Richard Show", November 1960.
This was Cliff's first dedicated
TV series and ran until 1963*

Preface

This is an oral history of the life and career of Cliff Richard. Instead of narrating his story as in a biography, I've collected the accounts of as many people as I could find who have lived, worked, played, travelled, recorded and performed with Cliff over the past 68 years. I'm hoping that the collage of voices, with their different accents, adjectives and perspectives, build as accurate a picture of Cliff as possible.

The earliest of these interviews was done in 1974 and the most recent in 2007. I have been fortunate not only to interview Cliff many times in many different locations, but also to see him at home, in church, on the road in Britain and America, at supper parties and in the recording studio. I first met him at a party in 1970. I was researcher and interviewer on a series of BBC documentaries in 1980, co-wrote a song that he recorded in 1982 ("Now You See Me ... Now You Don't") and became his biographer in 1993.

During these times I got to meet many of those who'd been most intimately involved in his life and began interviewing them in 1982 in the knowledge that they wouldn't always be around to tell their side of the story. Thirty-six of my interviewees are no longer alive. Some of the interviews were done when I was researching *Cliff Richard: The Biography*, but I was unable to use all the information in the book because I had to keep the story on track. That meant leaving out a lot of interesting anecdotes and little-known facts.

In the case of Cliff himself I have used quotes from unpublished interviews I conducted with him both before and after the publication of the biography, but have refrained from using material given to me by him specifically for that project. I've supplemented this material of mine with quotes Cliff gave to newspapers, magazines and radio stations throughout his career. I have identified these quotes by adding the dates they were given.

Almost all the other quotes come from interviews I conducted personally, with the exception of a handful of people I hadn't interviewed about Cliff but who were already dead. What interests me about all these voices is that, although they don't always agree with each other, the very clash of opinion creates an arresting and more realistic portrait of the man.

You don't have to love Cliff's music to acknowledge that he's had a remarkable career. When he had completed one year in the music business, it was noted in the music press as a career landmark, because rock 'n' roll was thought to be a short-lived phenomenon. For almost all of his contemporaries it was just that. They went into acting, disappeared from the charts or went and found "proper jobs".

For Cliff, there was a fifth anniversary and then a 10th celebrated with the release of the album *Established 1958*. By the time it got to 25 years and the release of the *Silver* album, most people realized that, like the Queen Mother, he was here for the long haul. In 1998 he published the book *Cliff Richard: A Celebration*, subtitled *The official story of forty years in show business*.

What is even more remarkable about his career is that it hasn't survived by simply reliving his early moments of glory but by continually attempting to stay relevant. Although he hasn't been without his down times, he has had hits in all five decades of his career. He's also excelled in other areas of show business. He's been a star of film, television and stage, in that order, and has acted in straight theatre, produced albums and singles for other artists and written songs for himself.

Key to his success is his unwavering determination. Although he's proud of his past achievements he doesn't wallow in them. He is totally focused on the present and wants to be better than whoever's considered best at the moment. Although the singles charts have become increasingly irrelevant as a guide to what people are listening to, he still eyes it with the keenness of someone who came into the music business when the hit parade was the guide to your artistic well-being. He still remembers all his chart positions and has been angered by the refusal of certain radio stations to play his singles over the past decade.

The one ambition he has never been able to fulfil has been conquering America. He has had hits there; he has toured there; but he has never been a name to reckon with. Even in his late sixties he hasn't entirely given up, and as he spends more time in Barbados, New York and Florida he's no doubt thinking how he could succeed on that side of the Atlantic.

BELOW
Few artists of Cliff's vintage perform unaccompanied in public. During a rainstorm at Wimbledon in 1996, Cliff spontaneously entertained the crowd with a rendition of "Congratulations"

I think this book shows that, although Cliff is often dismissed as "bland" and "uninteresting", he is a far more complex person than he might seem. He remains mysterious even to those close to him because he's unlike anyone else they've ever known. He doesn't fit the normal categories. He sings love songs to women but has never been married or lived with a woman. He visits the poor in Bangladesh and Haiti yet owns at least six properties around the world. He urges people to go to church and yet doesn't go himself. He's generous and yet appears to be self-obsessed.

These memories and reflections by those who've known him best are unlikely to unravel that mystery completely, but they will explain a few things. As Cliff has said in recent interviews, "There are some secrets I'll take to the grave with me."

Steve Turner

Interviewees

Tony Blackburn – Veteran radio DJ voted 'King of the Jungle' on TV's *I'm a Celebrity Get Me Out of Here* in 2002.

Alan Blows – Pupil at Cheshunt County Secondary School who acted in the school production of *A Christmas Carol* (1956).

Derek Bodkin – Chauffeur who married Cliff's mother in June 1966. The couple divorced in 1982.

Joan Bosse – Holidaymaker who photographed Cliff and The Drifters at Butlins, Clacton-on-Sea, in 1958.

Franklyn Boyd (1925–2007) – Music publisher and former singer who managed Cliff briefly between 1958–59.

Vincent Bridgewater (1913–92) – Brother of Cliff's maternal grandmother.

Terry Britten – Guitarist in Cliff's band during the 1970s who wrote many songs for him, including "Devil Woman" and co-produced the album *Rock 'n' Roll Juvenile*.

Roger Bruce – Cliff's dresser on the musical *Time* and later personal assistant.

David Bryce – (*Right*) Former employee of agent Leslie Grade, he became Cliff's tour manager in 1966 and later his professional and recording manager. He retired in 2001.

Tito Burns – Cliff's manager 1959–61.

Mel Bush – British concert promoter who mounted "The Event" at Wembley Stadium in 1989.

Pete Bush – Pupil at Cheshunt County Secondary School and Cliff's friend.

Stu Calver (1947–2000) – Backing vocalist.

Freddy Cannon – US pop star, best known for his hit "Palisades Park", who had three top-10 hits and was a headline act on Cliff's first (1960) tour of America.

Ron Cass (1923–2006) – Writer and composer who, with Peter Myers, wrote the screenplays for *The Young Ones* (1961) and *Summer Holiday* (1963).

Steve Chalke – Christian leader, activist, TV presenter and founder of Oasis Trust, who has worked with Cliff on several projects, including "Fanfare for a New Generation", an effort to revitalize the British church at the turn of the twenty-first century.

Dave Clark – Drummer with The Dave Clark Five (1964–70) who went on to produce the musical *Time*.

Jill Clarke – Former girlfriend of Bill Latham, Cliff's mentor and adviser; Sue Barker's flatmate.

Malcolm Addey – EMI studio engineer who worked on Cliff's records 1958–68.

Anthony Andrews – Actor who played the role of Hugo Flaxman in the film *Take Me High* (1973). Best known for his part in the TV adaptation of *Brideshead Revisited*.

Surinder Arora – Former wine waiter who became a property developer and is now one of the UK's leading hoteliers.

Sue Barker (*Above*) – British tennis player who reached the Wimbledon semifinal in 1977, retired in 1984 and became a popular sports presenter on TV. Romantically linked to Cliff 1982–84.

Lionel Bart (1930–99) – Wrote Cliff's 1959 hit "Living Doll". Began his songwriting with Tommy Steele ("Rock with the Cavemen", 1956) and composed the hit musical *Oliver!*

Brian Bennett – Replaced Tony Meehan as the drummer in The Shadows in 1961.

Janice Berry – Pupil at Cheshunt County Secondary School who acted alongside Cliff in the school's plays 1954–56. After leaving school she became Cliff's first serious girlfriend.

Tony Clark – Engineer at EMI who started as a tape operator in 1964. He worked on several of Cliff's records before leaving EMI in 1986.

Betty Clarke – Member of The Quintones, the first group Cliff sang with (1956), and briefly his girlfriend.

Frank Clarke (1924–2007) – Session musician (bass) who played "Move It", Cliff's debut single.

Joyce Clarkson (1915–2003) – Sister of Cliff's father, Rodger Webb.

Gerald Coates – The founder and leader of Pioneer, a network of charismatic evangelical churches, one of which (Cobham Christian Fellowship) Cliff attended in the early 1980s. He has been a friend and spiritual mentor.

Mike Conlin – Cliff's tour manager from 1961–66.

Jess Conrad – Pop star and actor whose career began at the same time as Cliff's.

Brian Cooke – Friend and classmate from Cheshunt County Secondary School.

Dave Cooke – Played keyboards on many of Cliff's tours from the 1980s onwards.

Carol Costa – Once married to Shadows' bass guitarist Jet Harris, Costa had a brief affair with Cliff in 1960.

John Davey – Schoolteacher who got to know Cliff through the Crusaders Christian organization and became part of a close-knit all-male group that holidayed together.

Terry Dene – Rock 'n' roll star of the late 1950s who was briefly touted as Britain's "answer to Elvis." He met Cliff in 1958 at Soho's 2 I's Coffee Bar.

Vincent Dickson – Cliff's mother's half-brother, who was living in Carshalton when Cliff and his family arrived in England in 1948.

Graham Disbrey – Art teacher at Cheshunt County Secondary School who was involved with the Crusaders Christian organization. One of the first to argue religion with Cliff.

Joyce Dobra – Cliff's cousin from the Webb side of the family.

Yolande Donlan (*Below right*) – American actress who played Dixie Collins in *Expresso Bongo* (1959), Cliff's second film.

Chris Eaton – British songwriter partly based in Nashville who has written over a dozen songs for Cliff since 1981, including the Christmas hit "Saviour's Day". He helped organize the "writer's camp" that produced the songs for the album *Something's Goin' On* (2004).

Stan Edwards – A Redcoat at Butlins, Clacton, who befriended Cliff in 1958 and made an amateur recording of one of his rehearsals.

Royston Ellis – British poet and journalist who gained a reputation as a teen pundit in the late 1950s. Interviewed Cliff with DJ Steve Race for BBC radio in 1960 and ghost-wrote the books *Driftin' with Cliff Richard* and *The Shadows by Themselves*. He left Britain in 1963.

Ronnie Ernstone – Friend of Cliff's between 1958–60. Holidayed in Italy with Cliff and Tony Meehan in 1959.

Phil Everly – Half of The Everly Brothers, one of Cliff's original inspirations. Met Cliff in Britain in the early 1960s, appeared on stage with him at Hammersmith in 1981 and recorded "All I Have to Do is Dream" with him in 1994.

Paul Field – Musician, songwriter and performer whose group Nutshell performed with Cliff on gospel tours. Co-author of the controversial "Millennium Prayer" in 1999 and "All That Matters," Cliff's contribution to the *Diana Princess of Wales Tribute* CD (1997).

Vic Flick – Played with The Vic Allen Quintet at Butlins, Clacton, in 1958 where he met Cliff. Provided the guitar sound on the classic James Bond theme music.

Mark Forster – Agent working for promoter Arthur Howes who booked Cliff on The Kalin Twins UK tour of 1958.

Dave Foster – Director of Eurovangelism, the organization that mounted Cliff's first gospel concert tour in 1968.

John Foster – Ex-sewage-farm worker who discovered Cliff in a Hertfordshire pub, got him a gig at the 2 I's Coffee Bar in London

and was his manager between 1958–59.

Mrs Foster – Mother of John Foster, Cliff's first manager.

George Ganjou (1901–88) – Cliff's first agent, who discovered him at the Shepherd's Bush Gaumont in 1958 and introduced him to Norrie Paramor of EMI. Prior to being an agent, Russian-born Ganjou had been part of the *adagio* act The Ganjou Bothers and Juanita (1931–56).

William Gaunt – British stage and television actor who appeared with Cliff in Peter Shaffer's play *Five Finger Exercise*, when it ran at the New Theatre, Bromley, in 1970.

Rita Gillespie (1929–94) – Director of the "Oh Boy!" TV shows that were produced by Jack Good in 1958 and 1959.

Alan Godson – Anglican vicar and director of British organization Christians in Sport who was responsible for introducing tennis star Sue Barker to Cliff.

Jack Good – Oxford graduate who produced Britain's first innovative rock 'n' roll TV show, "Oh Boy!", and launched Cliff's career by featuring him on it when he was an unknown. He coached him in style and presentation and raved about "Move It" in his weekly column for the music paper *Disc*.

Nigel Goodwin – TV and stage actor who encouraged Cliff to remain in show business after his conversion to Christianity. Appeared in the film *Two a Penny* (1967) and founded the Arts Centre Group, of which Cliff became a patron, in 1970.

Peter Gormley (1921–99) – Australian-born manager who steered Cliff's career from 1961 onwards, officially retiring in the early 1980s but continuing to offer advice.

Billy Graham – American evangelist at whose Earl's Court appearance in 1966 Cliff chose to reveal his Christian conversion. Frequently had Cliff to sing at his rallies in Europe and had him appear in two evangelistic films, *Two a Penny* (1967) and *His Land* (1970).

Peter Graves – University lecturer who met Cliff through the Crusaders and was involved in the early days of the holiday gang.

Olive Gregory (1922–95) – Cliff's maternal aunt.

Mark Griffiths –Guitarist in Cliff's band 1980–86.

Barrie Guard – Cliff's chief arranger and musical director during the 1970s.

Val Guest (1911–2006) – British-born director of *Expresso Bongo* (1959) and husband of its lead actress, Yolande Donlan.

Cliff Hall – Keyboard player who first toured with The Shadows in 1978, and also toured with Cliff for six years.

Eric Hall – Head of promotion for EMI in the 1970s, when Cliff recorded *I'm Nearly Famous*. Later became a football agent.

Terry Harness – Singer that Cliff replaced in The Dick Teague Skiffle Group in 1957 when he was called up to serve in the army.

Kenneth Harper (1913–98) – Producer of *The Young Ones* (1961), *Summer Holiday* (1963), *Wonderful Life* (1964) and *Take Me High* (1973).

Terence "Jet" Harris – Bass player with The Drifters, then The Shadows 1958–1962.

Charles Haswell – Businessman and tennis-playing friend of Cliff's since the mid-1980s.

Melvyn Hayes – British stage, film and television actor who starred in *The Young Ones* (1961), *Summer Holiday* (1963) and *Wonderful Life* (1964).

Bob Hellyer (1943–96) – Lighting technician who worked on Cliff's shows in the 1970s, '80s and early '90s.

Bob Henrit – Lived next door to Cliff in Waltham Cross in the early 1950s. Drummer for Adam Faith's backing group, The Roulettes (1963–67), Unit Four Plus Two (1967–68), Argent (1969–76) and The Kinks (1984–96).

Patricia Henrit – Bob Henrit's sister.

Garth Hewitt – Church of England curate whose albums *I'm Grateful* (1978) and *Did He Jump?* (1979) were produced by Cliff. Since 1985, Garth has been director of Amos Trust, an organization committed to bringing hope and justice to forgotten people around the world.

George Hoffman (1933–92) – Founder and director of Tearfund (The Evangelical Alliance Relief fund), who travelled with Cliff to several parts of the developing world, including Bangladesh, Uganda and Haiti.

Christine Holmes – Former children's TV presenter and singer who wrote the lyrics to "Devil Woman".

Ritchie Howells – London-based photographer who took the earliest EMI promotional shots of Cliff.

Liz Hutchison – Nurse working for Tearfund in Dhaka, Bangladesh, who escorted Cliff around refugee camps in 1973.

Jackie Irving – Dancer from Blackpool who was Cliff's "steady date" 1960–63. In 1967 she married Cliff's old professional rival, singer Adam Faith.

Derek Johnson – *New Musical Express* journalist 1957–86 who first saw Cliff at Butlins, Clacton-on-Sea.

Paul Jones – Singer with Manfred Mann who was known in the 1960s for his atheistic views. Later became a Christian.

Sonya Jones – Backing vocalist who worked on the *Time* show and appeared at "The Event".

Hal Kalin (1934–2005) – One-half of pop duo The Kalin Twins, who had a huge hit with "When" in 1958 and had Cliff Richard and The Drifters as a support act on their first UK tour. The other half of the duo was Herb Kalin, Hal's identical twin.

Cindy Kent –Singer with folk group The Settlers that toured with Cliff on his first gospel dates.

Ron King (1927–2000) – Driver of the bus on Cliff's first UK tour in 1958, later tour manager and then personal assistant. He retired from Cliff's service in 1988.

Tony King – VP of Elton John's Rocket Records label in America when it released "Devil Woman". Accompanied Cliff on a promotional tour of America in 1976.

Gerry Kitchingham – Manager and chief recording engineer for the independent Wimbledon studio R. G. Jones when Cliff recorded *Always Guaranteed* (1987). The studio shut down in 2001.

David Kossoff (1919–2005) – British actor who appeared in the *Stars in Your Eyes* show at the London Palladium with Cliff and The Shadows in 1960.

Bill Latham – Former schoolteacher at Cliff's old school who played a significant role in guiding Cliff to the Christian faith. Introduced him to the Crusaders organization and became his spiritual mentor as well as closest friend and charity affairs manager. Ghost-wrote Cliff's books, conducted many public interviews with him especially in church venues and shared homes with him 1965–99.

Linda Lauezzari – Childhood neighbour who lived in Hargreaves Close, Cheshunt, and was younger than Cliff.

John Lennon (1940–80) – Founder member of The Beatles.

Sally Lewis – Former girlfriend of songwriter Dave Townsend, who wrote "Miss You Nights" for her during a time of separation.

Paul Lincoln – An Australian-born wrestler "Doctor Death", who managed the 2 I's Coffee Bar in Soho's Old Compton Street, London's rock 'n' roll Mecca.

Phil Lloyd – Worked in EMI's international division in the 1970s. Manager of Patch, a record label developed for Cliff to produce Christian recording artists.

Brian "Licorice" Locking – Worked as the bass player for The Shadows April 1962– September 1963.

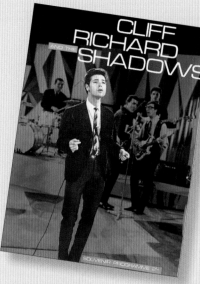

Jerry Lordan (1934–2005) – Songwriter, musician and singer who toured with Cliff in 1960 and wrote the instrumental hits "Apache" and "Wonderful Land" for The Shadows. Also wrote for Cliff.

Dave Mackay – An Australian who produced Cliff's album *31st of February Street* (1974).

Ray Mackender (1933–97) – Manager of pop singer Mark Wynter. Friend and adviser to Cliff in the 1950s and '60s.

Wolf Mankowitz (1924–98) – Wrote *Expresso Bongo* as a West End play based on Tommy Steele's rise as a British rock 'n' roll star. He later turned it into a screenplay.

Bill Martin – Writer of Cliff's hit song and 1968 Eurovision entry, "Congratulations".

Hank Marvin – The Shadows' lead guitarist.

Chas McDevitt – Skiffle musician who also ran a skiffle club, The Freight Train, in Soho. Cliff played at The Freight Train in 1958.

Tony Meehan (1943–2005) – Drummer with The Drifters and then The Shadows 1959–61,

Aleksander Mezek – Slovenian pop star who has appeared on stage with Cliff as well as recording with and writing for him. He has spent half his time in London since 1972.

George Michael – Singer songwriter who shot to fame as one half of the duo Wham!

Norman Mitham – Met Cliff at junior school in Waltham Cross, became a classmate at Cheshunt County Secondary School and then a founder member of The Drifters. He left in mid-1958 before the group took its engagement at Butlins in Clacton.

Paul Moessl – Keyboard player on *Time* who joined Cliff's band in 1987. Produced the single "Misteltoe and Wine" (1988) co-produced albums *Together with Cliff Richard* (1991), *Cliff Richard: The Album* (1993).

Van Morrison – Singer/songwriter and multi-instrumentalist from Belfast famous for hits such as "Brown Eyed Girl".

Mickie Most (1938–2003) – Appeared on The Kalin Twins' UK tour of 1958 singing with Alex Wharton in a duo known as The Most Brothers. Later became a successful record producer (The Animals, Herman's Hermits, Lulu, Donovan) and owner of RAK Records.

John Muggleton – Documentary filmmaker who accompanied Cliff on a visit to Tearfund projects in Haiti and Kenya.

Mick Mullins – Along with his singing partners, Peter Howarth and Keith Murrell, he has provided backing vocals for Cliff on many tours and recordings since 1987.

Olivia Newton-John (*Left*) – British-born singer raised in Australia. Came to prominence on Cliff's 1970s TV shows. Had a long-term relationship with Bruce Welch. Has been a consistent friend to Cliff for over 30 years. "Suddenly", a duet with Cliff, was a hit in Britain and America in 1980.

Larry Norman – A songwriter and singer whose fusion of rock 'n' roll rhythms and gospel lyrics was dubbed "Jesus rock". Cliff befriended Larry in the 1970s and recorded several of his songs, including "I Wish We'd All Been Ready" and "Why Should the Devil Have All the Good Music?", which were included on the album *Small Corners* (1978).

Jay Norris – Teacher of English at Cheshunt County Secondary School 1952–82. She was Cliff's form teacher in his final year and also ran the school's drama society, which was where Cliff gained his first experience of performing in public. She has remained a close friend.

Father John Oates – A parish priest in Hackney Wick, East London, when he started a ministry to Teddy boys and rockers known as The 59 Club. Cliff became a supporter and frequent visitor.

Stuart Ongley – He ran music-publishing company Patch Music for Cliff, starting in the late 1970s, and with songwriter Chris Eaton and American publisher Val Jannsen was responsible for gathering together the Nashville songwriters who supplied the songs for *Something's Goin' On* (2004).

Caroline Paramor – Daughter of Cliff's first producer, Norrie Paramor, who was asked for her judgement on Cliff's earliest recordings for EMI as a representative teenage female.

Norrie Paramor (1914–79) (*see photo, seated with Cliff*) – Cliff's producer from 1958–72. In his position as recording director of EMI's Columbia Records label, he gave Cliff his first recording contract and oversaw his recording career. He was also a composer, arranger and orchestra conductor.

Brian Parker (1940-2000) – School friend of Cliff's at Cheshunt County Secondary School and talented guitarist. He later joined The Dick Teague Skiffle Group before founding The Hunters. After The Hunters he joined Adam Faith's backing group, The Roulettes, and then had a hit with "Concrete and Clay" (1965) as part of Unit Four + Two.

Larry Parnes (1930–89) – The biggest manager in British rock 'n' roll at the time of Cliff's emergence. He had managed Tommy Steele and was managing Marty Wilde when Cliff came on the scene. He went on to acquire Billy Fury, Vince Eager, Dickie Pride and Johnny Gentle, among others.

David Pawson – Pastoral leader at Guildford Baptist Church (1969–81) at a time when Cliff became a regular worshipping member after his move to Weybridge.

June Pearce – Personnel officer at Thorn Electric when Cliff started work as a credit-control clerk in 1957.

John Perry – Backing vocalist for Cliff 1976–86.

Lauri Peters – American actress who took the role of Barbara Winters in *Summer Holiday* (1963). She married the actor Jon Voight, but they divorced in 1967.

Josie Pollock – Actress, model and friend to Cliff and Cherry Wainer 1958–59.

Craig Pruess – American-born musician, songwriter and producer who worked with Cliff in the 1980s. He produced the album *Now You See Me … Now You Don't* (1982) and co-produced an album with Cliff for Sheila Walsh.

Eddie Purse – Pastor of Hoddesdon Baptist Church in Hertfordshire 1979–92. He invited Cliff as a special guest to a Sunday church service in 1980 and subsequently got to know Cliff's mother, who lived in the area.

Andrew Ray (1939–2003) – Son of the comedian Ted Ray who took the role of Larry Thompson in *Serious Charge* (1959).

Mike Read – Radio One DJ who has written books about Cliff and The Shadows, co-wrote the stage show *Cliff: The Musical* (2003) and is counted among Cliff's closest friends.

Les Reed – Was working as a musician at Butlins, Clacton, when he met Cliff in 1958. He went on to be a renowned composer, songwriter and arranger, writing, among other hits, "Delilah" and "It's Not Unusual" for Tom Jones.

Tim Rice – Celebrated lyric writer behind such stage hits as *Jesus Christ Superstar*, *Evita* and *Chess*. He also wrote the lyrics to the musical *Heathcliff* (1997).

Sylvia Richards – Childhood neighbour in Cheshunt.

Tony Rivers – Backing vocalist 1976–86.

B. A. Roberston – Lyricist on several of Cliff's 1980s songs, including "Carrie," "Hot Shot" and "Wired for Sound".

Henri Rouah – Butlins Redcoat who befriended Cliff at Clacton-on-Sea in 1958.

Ian "Sammy" Samwell (1937–2003) – Joined The Drifters in the summer of 1958, but left after the addition of Hank Marvin, Bruce Welch and Jet Harris. Wrote Cliff's first hit, "Move It", and continued to contribute songs after his departure.

Ernie Shear – The session guitarist who created the celebrated introduction to "Move It" during the recording at Abbey Road on July 24, 1958.

Frances "Frankie" Slade – Classmate of Cliff's at Cheshunt County Secondary School who was dating Terry Smart, drummer in The Dick Teague Skiffle Group. When Teague lost his singer, Terry Harness, she recommended Cliff as a replacement.

Terry Smart – Drummer with The Dick Teague Skiffle Group who broke away with Cliff in January 1958 to form The Drifters with Norman Mitham.

David Soames – Writer of the original script who also wrote and adapted the lyrics for the musical *Time*.

Trevor Spencer – Musician who played with Cliff in the 1970s.

Maggie Stredder – Member of the Vernons Girls, the all-female vocal group that was resident on "Oh Boy!" She went on to form The Ladybirds. The Vernons Girls reunited for "The Event" at Wembley Stadium in 1989.

Una Stubbs – British actress who took the role of Sandy in *Summer Holiday* (1962) and Barbara in *Wonderful Life* (1964). She appeared regularly in Cliff's 1970s TV shows.

Jimmy Tarbuck – Liverpool comedian and entertainer who toured with Cliff in 1959 as an MC.

Alan Tarney – Australian-born musician who played in Cliff's band during the 1970s and went on to become his most successful writer-producer. He produced the albums *I'm No Hero* (1980), *Wired for Sound* (1981), *Always Guaranteed* (1987) and *Stronger* (1989). He wrote a number of Cliff's hit singles, including "We Don't Talk Anymore" (1979).

Dick Teague – Leader of a local amateur skiffle group in Cheshunt that took Cliff on as vocalist in September 1957.

Mick Teague – Brother to Dick Teague and guitarist in the group.

Walter Teague (1902–93) – Father of Dick and Mick Teague and manager of The Dick Teague Skiffle Group.

Rita Thompson – Cliff fan who was injured when a fire hydrant was thrown from the balcony of the Chiswick Empire during a Cliff concert in 1959.

Graham Todd (1943–95) – Keyboard player in Cliff's band from the late 1970s to the mid-1980s.

Mary Tonks (1914–99) – Taught Cliff at Kings Road School in Waltham Cross when he arrived in 1949.

Dave Townsend – Songwriter who composed "Miss You Nights".

Martin Townsend – Editor of *OK!* magazine

at the time when it arranged Cliff's sixtieth birthday cruise in the Mediterranean.

Tulah Tuke – Redcoat at Butlins, Clacton, in 1958 who played an advance copy of "Move It" on the camp radio.

Jan Vane – President of the Cliff Richard Fan Club 1958–70.

John Vince – School friend of Cliff's from Cheshunt County Secondary School who also sang with Cliff in The Quintones.

Cherry Wainer – South African-born keyboard player. A regular performer on "Oh Boy!" who became Cliff's close friend.

Sheila Walsh – Gospel singer and presenter of the TV series "Rock Gospel". Cliff co-produced an album for her and sang a duet with her on the single "Drifting" (1983).

Diana Ward – Member of the chorus for Cliff's 1959 pantomime *Babes in the Woods* whom Cliff dated briefly.

Peter Waterman – Acclaimed songwriter and producer who supplied Cliff with the made-to-measure hit "I Just Don't Have the Heart" (1989).

Dorothy Webb (1920–2007) – Cliff's mother.

Bruce Welch – Rhythm guitarist with The Shadows and producer of Cliff's "comeback" album *I'm Nearly Famous* (1976), *Every Face Tells A Story* (1977) and *Green Light* (1978).

Wally Whyton (1929–97) – His skiffle group, The Vipers, started playing at the 2 I's in 1956. By 1958, the group line-up included Hank Marvin on guitar, Jet Harris on bass and Tony Meehan on drums. They would all soon leave Whyton to join Cliff.

Delia Wicks – A dancer whom Cliff met when performing at the Palladium in 1960. They dated until Cliff broke off the relationship in October 1961.

Marty Wilde – British rock 'n' roll star managed by Larry Parnes, and Cliff's main rival on the "Oh Boy!" show.

June Wilkinson – Actress and dancer who had performed at The Windmill Theatre and went on to be a well-known glamour model

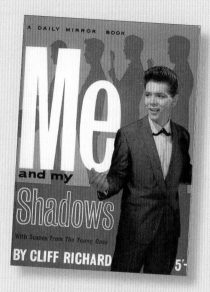

in America. She met Cliff once in 1958 through Lionel Bart.

Dorothy Willis (1921–99) – Cliff's Sunday school teacher at Stanley Park Evangelical Mission, Carshalton, 1948–49.

Jodie Wilson – Singer and actress who played the role of Louise in the musical *Time*.

David Winter – Journalist, broadcaster and radio producer who played an important role in reconciling Cliff's newborn Christian faith with his career in music. He wrote Cliff's biography *New Singer, New Song* (1966).

Peter Wolf – Austrian-born record producer and musician who produced Cliff's album *Real As I Wanna Be* (1998).

Mark Wynter – British pop star managed by Cliff's friend Ray Mackender. He first met Cliff in 1959.

Muriel Young (1918–2001) – TV presenter who first met Cliff when she was working for Associated Rediffusion in the late 1950s. Introduced him to Portugal, where she bought a villa in the early 1960s. She later produced "Rock Gospel" for Granada TV.

Terence Young (1915–94) Director of *Serious Charge* (1959) who went on to direct three James Bond films: *Doctor No* (1962), *From Russia with Love* (1963) and *Thunderball* (1965).

Small Corners (1940–57)

Born in Lucknow in October 1940 and christened Harry Rodger Webb, Cliff Richard spent his first eight years in India. Although his memories of the country are necessarily scanty he was deeply affected by its climate, the luxury of a life with servants and the culture of deference to authority. The England that he first came to in 1948 was drab, cold, and poor in comparison to what he'd experienced as part of the ruling class in India.

His family at first stayed with relatives in Carshalton and Waltham Cross before getting their own council home in Cheshunt, Hertfordshire. It was while at Cheshunt County Secondary School that Cliff developed an appetite for performing as part of the school dramatic society. He also discovered Elvis Presley, and this stirred his ambition to be a singer. His first tentative steps in that direction were made with a local skiffle group but his heart was really set on rock 'n' roll.

Although his parents had always spoken of Britain as "home", neither of them had ever visited the country before arriving at Tilbury Docks as part of the mass exodus of Brits from India. Cliff's mother, Dorothy, had been born in Lahore; his father, Rodger, in Rangoon, Burma. His maternal grandfather, William Edward Dazely, had been a soldier who'd gone missing on the northwest frontier in 1924. His paternal grandfather, Frederick William Webb, had worked on the railways.

Cliff's father's family moved from Burma to India and Rodger Webb attended Allahabad High School before starting work with G. F. Kellner & Co, a European catering company that had lucrative contracts with the Indian railways. Cliff's mother was sent to a boarding school at Sanawar in the Himalayas and her mother remarried a railway inspector, Richard Dickson, and moved to Asansol to start a second family.

While researching my 1993 biography of Cliff, I discovered that William Edward Dazely had not died in the 1920s as reported, but had fled to Karachi and bigamously married a 23-year-old girl. He fathered five sons in India before moving to England in 1948. He died in Balsall Heath, Birmingham, in 1969, unaware that Cliff Richard was his grandson. He had never revealed his previous marriage to his family.

Dorothy Dazely and Rodger Webb met in Asansol in 1936. He was 32 and living in Calcutta. She was 16 and barely out of school. They corresponded for three years and met whenever they could. In April 1939 they married at St Paul's Church, Asansol, and moved to Dehradun, the city that would be Cliff Richard's first home.

Olive Gregory, née Dazely (Cliff's maternal aunt)

My sister and I spent most of our early lives in a military school at Sanawar in the Himalayas above Simla because our father went missing when I was only 18 months old. Our uncle, Vincent (Vincent Bridgewater), was only eight years older than me and he was there at the same time. We thought of him as our brother. It wasn't until I was six years old that I went home for a holiday. Until then we spent our Christmases and our summer breaks at school. Distances were so vast that it wasn't easy to send toddlers home. Eventually our mother got remarried and then she moved to Asansol, so a couple of years before we were due to leave school my sister and I went to Asansol and went to a Catholic school there, the Loretta Convent.

ABOVE
Cliff's paternal grandfather, Frederick William Webb, who moved to India in 1884 to work as an engineer on the railways. He didn't return to Britain until the 1950s, when he came to live in Waltham Cross and Cheshunt

Vincent Bridgewater (Olive and Dorothy's uncle)

I didn't like a couple of the blokes that Dorothy was mixing with in Asansol. I used to warn them off. But when Rodger came he took to her and she took to him. I liked him. He was a good man and a capable man. He was also very smart and he was the only one that I thought would be a good match for her.

Joyce Clarkson, née Webb (Rodger Webb's sister)

I was born in Lucknow, but the rest of my family, including Rodger, were born in Burma. Rodger was working for Kellner's, a company that did a lot of the catering on the railways, and that took him all over India in the 1920s and 1930s.

Olive Gregory

Rodger was very ascetic. I always used to call him a gentleman. He had an aristocratic air about him. He was very slender and had this beautiful way of talking. He had very smooth hair and was very good-looking. I have a photo of him taken at the time and it always used to make me think of the actor Leslie Howard. He had the same sort of bone structure.

Vincent Bridgewater

Rodger's sister, Dorothy Cooke, was living in Asansol, the place where my family was also living. We were in the same block. I naturally got to know her and she taught me shorthand and typing, skills which were very handy to me when I joined the army and was looking after an office as a staff sergeant. At the same time, Dorothy got to know Rodger because he would often come down to talk to us all when he was visiting his sister. He was the sort of man that you could take to.

Olive Gregory

They just fell in love. However, I must admit that at the time I was quite against it. I thought the world of him, but I considered him a little too old for her. After all, he was only two years younger than our mother. Mother didn't want them to marry because she adored Rodger's brother, Tom, and would rather that Dorothy had married him. Tom was the younger brother and he liked playing the guitar and he was the crooner of the family. He was one of those people who worked hard in various jobs, made a lot of money and then blew it all. Rodger was one of these steady people who believed in keeping a job and making sure that there was always something to live on. Tom wasn't the kind of person you could marry and settle down with. He would have given her a miserable life.

ABOVE
Cliff's mother, then Dorothy Dazely, pictured in Asansol during the 1930s, around the time that she met her future husband, Rodger Webb

Joyce Dobra (Cliff's cousin: Rodger Webb's niece)

Tom was the black sheep of the family who would turn up and then vanish. He spent more than he earned. The whole family enjoyed sing-songs together. My mum, Beryl, played the spoons. Rodger could play mandolin and banjo. Their sister Marjorie played the comb with toilet paper.

Olive Gregory

After Dorothy and Rodger got married they were with us in Asansol for a while and then Rodger got transferred to a restaurant up in Dehradun. That was a beautiful place – it really was. They didn't have the number of servants that we had because they couldn't afford it, but they did have a couple. If you worked for the railway or the government they would always supply you with at least two servants: a bearer and a cook. She would have had to pay for the *ayah* to look after the children.

Joyce Clarkson

Cliff was born in Lucknow and christened Harry Rodger Webb. He was named after our oldest brother, Harry, who died during the First World War. We had a sister called Donella, after our mother, and that was the name Rodger later gave to Cliff's sister.

Vincent Bridgewater

Rodger and Dorothy lived in Dehradun. The British and Anglo-Indian communities were very separate from the Indian community in those days. The British community was largely made up of military families, and some of them, of course, married into the Anglo-Indian community. There was quite a comfortable arrangement between the two. If you worked on the railway, as Rodger did, you would have your own institutions and your own dances and get-togethers.

Joyce Dobra

There were great class distinctions in India in those days. I had an education as a civil servant and could get into almost any club, but because my father was born in India, the European-covenanted hands looked down on him. We, in our turn, looked down on the railway people as a lower class. They lived in rented accommodation in massive barracks, as did the post and telegraph workers. There were very strict social codes. You could socialize with rich Indians but they would never be admitted into any of the clubs you belonged to.

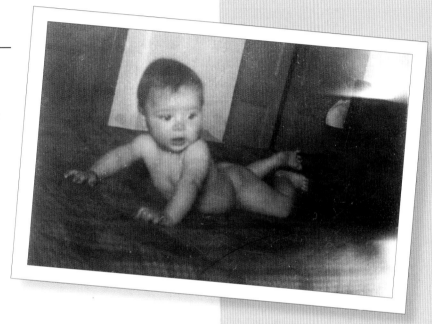

ABOVE
"C'mon pretty baby, let's a-move it and a-groove it!" The baby Harry Rodger Webb in Dehradun, India, 1941

Olive Gregory

Dorothy's second child was a boy called Frederick and he was very weak. Out there in India a child can have 101 complaints and you don't know which one they die of. Some children just don't make the grade, and unfortunately Frederick was one of them.

Joyce Dobra

Frederick was named after Rodger's father, who had been born and educated in England but then came out to India to work on the railways. In the 1950s he came back to England and stayed with his children and that's where he eventually died. By that time he had a long white beard. He wasn't all that tall – I would think about five foot eight – but he held himself very well and that gave him a very commanding manner. He was one of those stiff-necked Englishmen who wouldn't eat Indian food. He always demanded roast beef.

Cliff

In India I wouldn't have been able to identify any particular singers, but my mother
always tells the story that I was always interested in music and records. Apparently,
before I ever went to school or could even read, my party trick was when my parents
had friends over for dinner she would get me to pick a particular record out from
among their collection. All the labels were the same colour. There was a song called
"Chewing a Piece of Straw" and she would send me off to this pile of records and I
would flick through and come back with the right record! I don't understand that
because I couldn't read. My mum is convinced that I had a musical bent even back
then. (2004)

Olive Gregory

From Dehradun they moved to Howrah, close to the railway station in Calcutta.
They lived in a two-storey building. You had to go up some rickety wooden stairs to
get there and they had a little sitting room, a small kitchen, a bathroom and
two bedrooms. I used to spend long weekends and holidays there when I was in the
army up in Burma.

Joyce Clarkson

Because Rodger was working for Kellner's he was provided with accommodation. The place in Howrah was a house, but the lower floor was taken up by a chocolate factory. So Rodger and Dorothy lived on the top floor. Cliff was just a young boy at the time, of course. He was always a very good, lovable boy.

Olive Gregory

When I used to stay, I would sleep in the spare room. I was in the army at the time they moved there and I can remember Cliff in his little grey trousers. He also wore a little waistcoat and a jersey. I used to feel sorry for the little devil because Donna, who was a sickly child, used to deliberately try to get him into trouble. Because he was such a tough little guy he would get walloped by his mother. She just used to belt him but he hadn't done a thing to Donna and I knew it. I would warn Donna that I was having none of this nonsense. If she didn't play properly I wouldn't tell them any more stories. I used to tell them long, serial-type stories in the evenings. I could never be bothered with cooking when I visited them so I would take Cliff and Donna down to Kellner's restaurant and give them a nice high tea. Other times I would take them to the Botanical Gardens or to the cinema to see cartoons or westerns. They were always as good as gold.

Cliff

I enjoyed St Thomas's School. I remember it as being among trees. I used to love having lunch there. There was no canteen there and so the servant used to bring it up to me from the house. His name was Habib. He would always bring it in a napkin. My best friend lived near us but he didn't go to the same school. He was an Indian boy called Lal. I can no longer remember any of the teachers from that school. The only thing I can remember is Donna falling over and cutting her head.

Olive Gregory

The Indians had been told that they could have Home Rule after the war. What the British hadn't bargained for is that in giving them Home Rule, it opened up a split between the country's two main religions, Islam and Hinduism. When the war finally ended and the Japanese surrendered, the troops came back and they were really fired up by the idea of Home Rule. That's when the riots started. I used to worry about Dorothy and Rodger, because being in Howrah they were in one of the hottest spots. They were threatened by people. They knew that one of the first things to go would be the railways and with it, the catering.

ABOVE
A rare picture of Cliff as a child. Most of the Webb family photographs were stolen from Dorothy Webb's bag as they travelled by rail from Calcutta to Bombay on their way to England in August 1948

ABOVE
Cliff and his family witnessed these battles between Moslems and Hindus in the streets of Calcutta during 1946

LEFT
Hindus lining up to buy rail tickets at Howrah railway station to escape the riots of 1946

RIGHT
The Webb family left Bombay on the S. S. Ranchi in August 1948, destined for a new life in England

P. & O. SS. RANCHI, 16,600 TONS GROSS.
India Mail and Passenger Service.

Cliff

We left because of the terrible riots. Things were becoming very unpleasant. I can only remember one violent incident. There was a big park not far from where we lived. We'd gone there for an outing and as we came back there was the terrible sound of gunfire. We had to rush into a friend's house to escape. That's all I can remember about that.

We thought of England as our real home – "Blighty", they called it. I'd never seen any other country than India in my life, but we talked about "going home to Blighty". (1960)

Olive Gregory

I was there in England when Rodger and Dorothy arrived with the children. I was staying in Carshalton with my mother at the time and working in London. They came and stayed with us for a while but it was a bit too crowded so the lady next door, Mrs Luscombe, offer them a room in her place in order to ease the situation. They would come round and eat with us but they were living with the Luscombes.

Cliff

When we arrived in London from India we had £7 between the five of us. If it hadn't been for my grandmother in Surrey we would have had to have roamed the streets. We had a tough life. (1960)

Vincent Dickson (Dorothy Webb's half-brother)

There was a hell of a lot of us in the house in Carshalton in the beginning. We were sleeping all over the place. There was my mum and dad, Jean, Nora, myself, Peggy, Geraldine, Christopher, Cliff's mum and dad, Donna, Jacqui and Cliff. I think Cliff's family had the front bedroom. We had bought the house for £2,500 after leaving India and had hardly had time to settle in. It was a big upheaval.

Cliff

When we lived in India, my father had no need of anything and my mother was surrounded by servants. Together they had a social whirl of a life. Then we came to England because of Home Rule and we were penniless. My father was 44 and couldn't get a job because they thought he was too old, but he scraped around. He was of a generation who had great pride. He had been a clerical worker, the manager of a catering section of the railway, so he had worn a white collar and had travelled around India telling people what to do. The first job he had in England was cleaning up in a hospital in Carshalton. I think it takes a lot of guts to do that. (1977)

Vincent Dickson

Robert van Haeften, who was my sister Edna's husband, worked at the St Helier Hospital. I think he was able to get Rodger the job.

Cliff

When I first came over I must have sounded Anglo-Indian because I had been learning Bengali at school and already spoke Hindi. In fact, when I was in Howrah I can't remember ever speaking to my friend Lal in English. My accent, in conjunction with the fact that my skin was very swarthy, marked me out as someone who was different. I had no Indian blood at all, but Mum said there had been someone Spanish on her side of the family.

Dorothy Willis (Sunday-school teacher)

He was a dusky-skinned boy with a chubby face and he was in my class. He had just come to England from India. He was a quiet child. He wasn't at all boisterous and had no thoughts of singing. I think there was Indian blood in him because the Dicksons looked Indian. The grandmother was very definitely so, and the aunt, Olive. As far as we were concerned they were Indian. They were called Dickson, but that didn't mean anything.

Cliff

I was at school in Surrey for a year then I moved to Waltham Cross in Hertfordshire and I was schooled there until I was 11. (1960)

ABOVE
Cliff (second from right) with fellow Sunday-school students at Stanley Park Evangelical Mission. Carshalton, Surrey, 1949

BELOW
Cliff, (left) with Sunday-school friend Peter Maynard. Carshalton, Surrey, 1949

Vincent Dickson

After Carshalton they moved to the home of Rodger's sister, Dorothy Cooke. They started off living in the box room and then had the back room downstairs. Rodger then got a job with a firm called Eastwood's in the City of London.

Norman Mitham (school friend)

I was a friend of Cliff's before we ever got into music. I met him when I was about nine years old at Kings Road Primary School in Waltham Cross. He hadn't been in England all that long and there wasn't much immigration to Britain at that time, especially to a place like Waltham Cross. There was a certain amount of animosity toward him because the kids knew he had been born in India. They used to call him Sabu (after Sabu Dastagir, star of the 1937 film *Elephant Boy*). There were a couple of times when it ended in skirmishes, but he handled himself very well. On one particular occasion a gang of about five boys hid in some bushes beside a pathway that led from the school to the main road and they attacked him. One of the boys jumped on his back and was really thumping him. In those days he was just a normal person. You wouldn't have picked him out from the crowd. There were a lot of kids at the school who distinguished themselves either in sport or as students but he was just an average kid. If you were to ask his teachers from those days what he was like, I don't think that they'd say that he had something different about him or that he was destined to be a star.

Mary Tonks (teacher)

He was no trouble at all. I can't remember him being notable for anything and if I can't remember, he certainly couldn't have been bad! His behaviour must have been beyond compare! I would have taken him for every subject except music. The school was an old Victorian building and there were 10 classes each with at least 30 children in them and that was quite a big school for the time.

Patricia Henrit (the Cooke family's next-door neighbours)

These houses only had two bedrooms and a box room. I don't know how the Cookes managed to fit all of Cliff's family in. I think they had to live in the downstairs back room. The Cookes had two older boys, both of whom were working by this time. They'd also come back from India. Rodger Cooke was known as "Happy" and his brother Ernie was "Chuckles".

Bob Henrit (neighbour and drummer)

It was very unusual in those days to find a whole family crammed into one room. My mother was very concerned about it and she told a family friend of ours, Rita Bird, who was on the Waltham Cross Council. She knew someone who was involved in the Cheshunt Boys Club and he instigated getting this council house for them in Cheshunt.

Norman Mitham

A huge council estate called Bury Green was built at Cheshunt and I moved there in 1951 and so did Cliff and his family. The house they'd been living in at Waltham Cross belonged to an aunt and uncle and was very overcrowded so they had been put on the council list. Both Cliff and I carried on going to school in Waltham Cross and then in September 1952 we started at Cheshunt County Secondary School.

ABOVE
The mothers and children of Hargreaves Close on the newly built Bury Green Estate, Cheshunt, gathered for a group photograph on Coronation Day, June 2, 1953. Cliff is standing, third from right, centre row. His mother is second from left

Cliff

It was in my final year at Waltham Cross that I failed the Eleven Plus exam. I was shattered. My dad was disappointed. I hated that.

Norman Mitham

None of us were very rich in those days. Looking back I don't think it stuck in my mind that he came from a poor home, although he probably had less than us. There was no furniture to speak of. When they first moved in, you had to sit on packing cases and if they were all taken up you had to squat on the floor. For a time Cliff's grandfather came to stay and that meant that the three girls and Cliff all had to share one bedroom. His dad was quite strict and very much in control of the family but I always liked him. He was very hospitable. He would amuse us for hours with his stories of life in India. He would tell us about tiger hunts that he'd been on and explain to us about kite fighting. Apparently you would go out in the evening and let your kite up and someone down the road would see it and let their kite go as well. You'd stand on the roof of your house and try to get your kite up higher than your opponent's and then you'd swoop down and cut the string. If you did that, you claimed the kite. He gave Cliff some kites and we'd go across the fields and fly them. Cliff was quite skilful at that.

Olive Gregory

In all the old-style families the father was respected. He was the head, he was the master. There was not the same close-knit attachment between the child and the father as there was between the child and the mother. Things drifted between Cliff and his father when they came to England because the children saw less of him. He didn't have the time to take Cliff out because he was either working or too tired. From this you can understand the big bond with his mother. She was a great guiding light for him. It's very much the same with his sisters. He'll do anything for his sisters because it was instilled in him from an early age to respect and look after women. Cliff was brought up at a time when men had to be gentlemen and respect ladies, but he came to a country where there was a lot of looseness and parents took a back seat. The girls were more likely to throw their weight around and ask for this or that without thinking of the feelings of others. Cliff never did that. He thought of other people's feelings before he did anything. He didn't want to hurt anyone in any way. He never wanted to hurt his mother because he'd seen her cry too many times. He always had that soft spot for her, even as a child. He didn't like to see anyone hurt. He couldn't bear to see animals hurt or to see people ill-treated.

Linda Lauezzari, née Holmes (Cheshunt neighbour)

When I was a little girl I was photographed in Hargreaves Close playing hopscotch with Cliff. He was great, really good. I didn't particularly like his father. I used to stay away from him. I don't know what it was about him that made me feel that way. I know he was strict with his children but my dad was strict with me when I was young. He tried to be nice to us but none of us were keen to get too close. His mum, on the other hand, was lovely. I loved his mum. Cliff idolized her. Whatever she said, he would do. As soon as he came back home from anywhere he would go straight to her. There was definitely something there with his mother.

Jay Norris (teacher and friend)

He was acting in plays from his second year onwards. He often played a Chinese person. Janice Berry would be the heroine and Cliff would be the hero and usually both of them died in the end. I had him as the Lord Chancellor in one production and he sprained his ankle badly and had to play it with a stick in his hand and his leg all bound up. If he hadn't have become famous I would still have remembered him as a super kid in drama.

Alan Blows (school friend)

Cliff was a prefect, a position that carried with it an element of bossiness. However, Cliff was generally OK to us younger boys and he was a lively chap to be around.

Brian Cooke (school friend)

He was pretty good at football and rugby when he was at school. Also, a lot of people don't realize that he was undoubtedly the best scrapper in the school. You didn't play around with him. You wouldn't have gone round picking on him. He was very mild-mannered but there was this other side that you wouldn't want to see. I think that he'd had to look after himself when he arrived in England and this had toughened him up. After the first year of secondary school I can't remember anyone taunting him.

John Vince (school friend)

He was a good fighter. When people would wrestle me he would come in and rescue me. He could throw the javelin well and nearly speared me one day. He was also good at throwing the discus.

Pete Bush (school friend)

He was an absolute madman on the rugby pitch. He would go for you and his whole intention was to get you. He was terribly aggressive. He would go in really hard. No one wanted to get tackled by Harry Webb, as we knew him in those days. He certainly didn't mind getting dirty. I can never remember him having days off school for being ill. I think that was the difference with his family. He couldn't get away with things like that, whereas the rest of us could. He always turned up and that helped toughen him up even more. He certainly wasn't taunted at senior school because people there judged on merit rather than colour or creed. If you were good at sport, you stood out.

BELOW
Cliff and friends at the end of their final year at Kings Road School, Waltham Cross. From left to right: Norman Mitham (later to be in The Drifters with Cliff), Bernie Mumford, Percy Kimpton, Roy Linger, Ronnie Skingle, Cliff. July 1952

Jay Norris

Cliff's problem was never in being lazy but in wanting to do too many things. It was hard to get him to sit down and write an essay. He played soccer for the district. He created a school javelin record that was unbroken until about 1972. He was extremely good at sport and had an active social life. There were a lot in his group and they were all very friendly. That didn't leave a lot of time for schoolwork. I'm sure Cliff would agree that he didn't really use his full potential academically. He is bright. He didn't do terribly well at history, but I do think he was capable and he was well-motivated by supportive parents.

Cliff

I had a letter sent to me from someone in Australia who I'd written to as a pen-pal and she sent a copy of a letter I sent her which said, 'Hi. My name is Harry Webb. I am 12-and-a-half years old. I go to this school, I live here and my ambition is to be a famous singer.' That was at 12-and-a-half. I don't remember having those feelings that early on but when I read it I realized that I did write that. (2004)

Frances "Frankie" Slade (school friend)

Even if he hadn't gone on to become what he became I would have remembered him as somebody special. He stood out from the rest, but in a very quiet way. Actually, it was more than that. He was a bit of a peacemaker. We were always getting into the most ridiculous things and he was always able to smooth things over. He had a friend – I think it may have been John Vince – and they would pair up and John would be the funny one and when things went wrong it would always be Harry (I still think of him as Harry because I haven't met him since I left school) who would do the smoothing over. For example, once somebody poked a window pole through the ceiling and Jay Norris noticed it so we pushed Harry forward to do the explaining. Jay always melted in front of him. I think she was very instrumental in getting him motivated. I think he was very shy when he came to school but she spotted something in him. He could read out loud so well. To get a class of idiots like us to sit down and listen to someone reading was quite something. Jay Norris managed to get us all doing it with Shakespeare and the sorts of things you normally have to bludgeon into kids.

Cliff

I was in Waltham Cross with some friends. It was an area known as Four Swans, named after a pub, and there was a gantry across the road with four swans on top of it. There was a car parked by one of the shops there, probably outside the paper shop. The driver must have popped out to get a paper and had left the engine ticking over and the radio on. That's when I heard Elvis for the first time. The guy drove off as the record was still playing so I didn't know immediately who it was but it knocked me out. I thought of it more as a sound than a voice. It was like an instrument. I'd never heard anyone sing like that before. I never saw Elvis as showing me how to rebel. I never saw it as a way of escaping from family life and discovering what real living was all about. Maybe that's the effect it had in America. I never wanted to rip up cinema seats. When I later saw the film *Blackboard Jungle* I just thought, "Wow! What a fantastic film." The way that rock 'n' roll liberated me was that it meant that I didn't have to listen to jazz any more. I liked music, but at that time that was all that got played. Yes, I liked certain Rosemary Clooney and Teresa Brewer songs but none of it inspired me. Thank heavens that rock 'n' roll happened. (1977)

Brian Parker (school friend)

I can remember him coming in with a copy of "Heartbreak Hotel" and saying, "You've got to listen to this." We all sat back as he played. It was really something! If you consider the music that preceded it, this was something utterly different. Why does someone like this come along and sing in such a different way? That's the amazing thing. Nobody had sung like this before and it seemed to fit us exactly. Teenagers like us who were looking for something to latch on to said to ourselves – Boy! This is *our* music. It hit us so hard and Cliff just wanted to do something like it. In those days I didn't think he could do it.

Jay Norris

It was when we were doing *A Christmas Carol* that I first noticed Cliff becoming interested in rock 'n' roll. Elvis was on at that time. We had costumes that involved genuine Victorian drainpipe trousers, which just happened to be in fashion with the kids. Of course, his mother wouldn't let him have drainpipes but there he was wearing drainpipes and singing rock 'n' roll songs.

Brian Cooke

We were doing *A Christmas Carol* and I think "Heartbreak Hotel" was out and we had this tape recorder to play background music on and he would put the record on a Dansette and sing into the microphone of the tape recorder. It started as a sort of joke during rehearsals. We had to wear these tight black trousers for the production and that was the first time I saw girls noticing him as a bit of all right. He was very aware that he was being noticed.

BELOW
Cliff (second from left) in a school production of A Christmas Carol, *directed by Jay Norris, October 1956. He played Bob Cratchit*

Alan Blows

I was in the year below Cliff at school but we were both keen members of the drama group. He played Bob Cratchett in *A Christmas Carol* and I played a Cockney boy. When we were getting ready for the performance Cliff and a couple of his friends from the cast disappeared into a windowless storeroom and began singing rock 'n' roll songs. Mrs Norris had to bang on the door and order them out because it was getting so close to curtains up. She then gave them a talking to and they had to hurriedly get ready and scamper down the corridor to get on stage in time.

Cliff

I started miming to Elvis's records when I was at home. We had a mirror over the fireplace that had a painting on it and I remember imitating Elvis and trying to get my hair right. I used Brylcreem. It was obvious that Elvis gelled his hair up. We all knew how to do it. I always carried a comb and quiffed it over. It was hero worship. I thought Elvis looked great and sang fantastically.

Pete Bush

In our last year at school he became very meticulous about his appearance. He was always combing his hair. It wasn't a fashion show because none of us had a lot of money. It was just that in the latter part he liked to keep looking good.

Norman Mitham

We came to London to see *Jailhouse Rock* and this was quite a thing because it was the first time we'd come to London to see a film. Cliff was absolutely spellbound by it. I think we saw it during the first week of release. After we came out of the cinema all he could talk about was *Jailhouse Rock* and how the soundtrack was slightly different to the LP. We tried to get hold of it but we never could – even though the LP described itself as the "Original Soundtrack".

BELOW
Elvis's third film, Jailhouse Rock, *had its world premier three days after Cliff's 17th birthday. It had a huge impact on Cliff and his friend Norman Mitham*

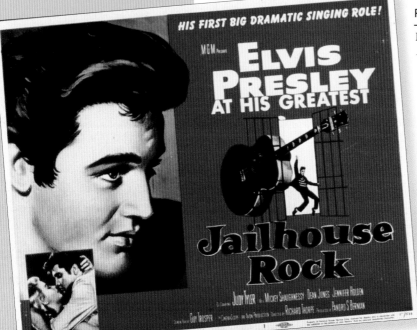

John Vince

The seeds were sown in those early days. It was those drama lessons with Mrs Norris that stimulated everything. Cliff and I would go on long-distance runs from the school and we'd run back to my house in Waltham Cross, listen to a few records and then run back. That was our afternoon jaunt. Cliff and I were also going to Holy Trinity Youth Club during the week to dance. I don't know what gave us the idea, but we thought we'd get a singing group together. There was Cliff, myself, Freda Johnson, Beryl Molineux and Betty Clarke. There was one major song that we could all remember the chords to and that was "Eddie My Love". I think we also did "Over You" by The Hilltoppers and "Sh-Boom" by The Crewcuts.

Betty Clarke (youth club member and school friend)

I used to lark around singing with Freda Johnson, and the youth club had an event coming up and it was decided that we should sing. So a group of us met at someone's house just off Trinity Lane. We got singing and that became our first rehearsal. Of course, Elvis was the rage at the time and "Heartbreak Hotel" was a big hit. Cliff decided that this was what he would sing. Unfortunately I got stage fright and pulled out before the performance. A girl called Eileen Fowler took my place. As far as I can remember there were only two performances. There was the Bastille Day event and then at a 21st party for John Vince's sister, Pamela. We called ourselves The Quintones because there were five of us.

Cliff

We used to sing harmonies and during a little break in our 20-minute set I would do an Elvis impersonation. Most of our gigs were at school. I can remember singing at the end-of-term party.

John Vince

I've got a feeling that The Quintones also played at a few wedding receptions. It was always the same old songs: a few pop songs and a few classics. We had no accompaniment. Cliff wasn't playing guitar then and I was only just learning piano. We would experiment with different harmonies.

Betty Clarke

There was this sweetness between Cliff and me for some time while we were together at school. It was never anything serious, though. It was just a boyfriend-girlfriend relationship. I was going with him while he was at the youth club, but I think possibly it was at that time that I met someone else (the man I'm married to) and we parted good friends. We just went our separate ways.

ABOVE
Cliff's first public performance as a singer, July 14, 1956, at Holy Trinity School, Waltham Cross. That day the Quintones were (left to right): Cliff, Freda Johnson, John Vince, Irene Fowler and Beryl Molineux

Janice Berry (school friend)

Four of us went to the Regal in Edmonton and queued up from early in the morning to buy tickets for Bill Haley and the Comets. We were each allowed to buy two tickets. I think we met outside my house to travel in. We knew that the tickets didn't go on sale until 10 a.m. but we wanted to get the tickets as soon as possible and then go on into school. In fact, it took us so long to get the tickets that we didn't go back to school. That was awful. We were all in disgrace. We lost our prefect badges.

ABOVE
American rock 'n' roll star Bill Haley on his first British tour with The Comets in 1957. Cliff saw them at the Regal, Edmonton, and was thrilled by the antics of bass player Al Rex and saxophonist Rudy Pompilli

John Vince

The next day the headmaster made us all stand in a line and we were being a bit silly and he shouted, "Now, who's being silly?" No one said anything so I said, "It was me, sir." He asked me to step forward and I got a caning across the hand. It wasn't really me who'd been silly.

Jay Norris

Cliff missed school because of that Bill Haley concert and lost his prefect's badge. Actually, I had secretly spoken to the headmaster about not taking it away. He pointed out that he had truanted from school for a day. I said to Cliff, "In 10 years' time you won't even remember Bill Haley's name." He said, "Oh yes, I shall remember him." I said, "Harry, if in 10 years' time you still remember him, I'll personally give you an 11-pound box of chocolates."

Of course ten years from then, in 1967, I was still in touch with Cliff and I bought him a box of Cadbury's Continental Chocolates!

Janice Berry

I remember the concert was absolutely tremendous. People were dancing in the aisles It was just so exciting. Before this music came along we had been listening to people like Ruby Murray and Alma Cogan.

Norman Mitham

The fact that people were standing up during concert was in itself something altogether different for us. Skiffle music had been pretty basic and suddenly there was Bill Haley with what to us was a terrific sound. It was so full and Americanized. We spoke about nothing else for days afterwards.

Frances "Frankie" Slade

I can remember standing up at the concert. I think it was probably quite restrained in comparison to the way rock concerts became, but people were jumping up, shouting, singing along and dancing in the aisles. Stewards had to come along to try to get the audience to sit back down.

Cliff

"Razzle Dazzle" was the first song. I remember thinking that the whole of the circle was going to collapse because we were all thumping and swaying. It was just the most exciting thing. The bass player did all those tricks that we'd seen photographs of: lay on the floor with the bass on top of him, and then threw it in the air. It was fantastic, so exciting! The music was so vibrant! (1995)

Frances "Frankie" Slade

Things were a bit grey in the postwar years in England and I think we all thought that there must be more to life than this. I can remember going into London as a child and it was all bombed out with no splashes of colour. People like Elvis and Bill Haley were the first hints of colour and vibrancy that came into our lives during a period that was otherwise dull and boring.

Terry Smart (drummer)

I knew Cliff because we used to play rugby together at school and we were also in the pantomime. That's how I knew that he could sing. I played drums in The Dick Teague Skiffle Group and the singer, Terry Harness, got his call-up papers to do National Service and so we needed a replacement. I told Dick that I knew someone I'd been at school with who could sing. He asked whether I thought he'd like to be in a skiffle group. So I went round one evening to Cliff's family home, knocked on the door and asked him and he said he would come along to one of our rehearsals and see what he thought. He didn't jump in with both feet.

ABOVE
Drummer Terry Smart, a school friend of Cliff's from Cheshunt, recommended Cliff to Dick Teague's Skiffle Group. This proved to be the break that Cliff needed

Terry Harness (singer)

I was doing most of the singing at the time and Cliff joined the group because I was going in the army. The normal age for call-up was 18, but I'd done an apprenticeship so I was 21. I didn't want to go in the army. It was a shame because we were having fun with our skiffle music. We were together in the group for a short while and then I left for a life on Salisbury Plains! All I can remember about him was that he was Elvis-mad! He used to move around on stage and curl his lip. I can remember Dick saying to me, "I don't like that." In our view, rock 'n' roll was a load of rubbish. We thought he should stick to the good old skiffle.

Cliff

It was a little skiffle band, not particularly good or interesting, but I wanted to sing because of Elvis and there weren't any rock bands in Britain so when there was a band available who wanted a singer I thought, oh well, I'll sing in it even if it is skiffle. (1987)

Dick Teague (group leader)

I played guitar, my brother Mick played guitar and banjo, Ken Simmons played tea-chest bass, Terry Harness was the singer, Terry Smart played drums and Allan Crouch was on washboard. I was mad on traditional jazz and this was a way of getting involved it at a very basic level. I was very much a fan of Ken Colyer, Cy Laurie and people like that. But these guys were professional musicians and we were just a load of bums. There's no question about that. We were just knocking about.

ABOVE
Dick Teague's Skiffle Group, December 1957: the time Cliff was planning to leave. From left to right: Mick Teague, Brian Parker, Terry Smart, Cliff, Dick Teague

Mick Teague (musician)

We asked Cliff to come round and he came and sang a couple of numbers. It was obvious that he had real talent. You could tell immediately. He more or less did all the singing with the group after that. At home he would sing rock 'n' roll, but not in our set. We used to buy songbooks and learn the words and chords. We had one old Ken Colyer song called "This Train" that has a nice chord sequence with a few more chords than we were used to playing so he sang the words to his own tune while we backed him.

Dick Teague

We did "Rock Island Line", a song that all skiffle groups did. There was "Sporting Life", written by Ken Colyer I think. Then we did "Midnight Special" and "Maggie May". We basically learned our set from records by Ken Colyer and Lonnie Donegan. There was a very musical, pleasant quality to Cliff's voice but it wasn't really the rasping, nasty voice that was best for our sort of music. There was no doubt that he was outstanding, but he didn't have the jazzy edge we wanted.

Cliff

It seemed like a professional set-up to me, but after being with Dick Teague for a while, Terry and me both realized that we didn't really like skiffle as much as we liked rock 'n' roll. I hear people say that Lonnie Donegan was the king of rock 'n' roll, but I can't relate to that. Lonnie was good at what he did and we all bought those records because that's all that existed at the time. But the minute that Elvis and Bill Haley came along, that was it. For me, skiffle was as far removed from rock 'n' roll as opera was.

Chas McDevitt (skiffle musician)

There were so many definitions of skiffle, but it was basically good-time music that almost anyone could play. Virtually any tune could be skiffled, but real skiffle was based on American blues and rent-party music. Eventually it came to be known as what Lonnie Donegan played but even that wasn't really skiffle. If you listened to my music, then to The Vipers and then to Lonnie Donegan you'll hear three different styles – but it was all supposed to be skiffle.

Dick Teague

He was probably only with the group for six months. He had never played in public before but any nerves he might have had he lost performing at Flamstead End Youth Club and at the local school dances and St Patrick's Night "hoolies". We used to play at Cheshunt Youth Club, the local hops for the fire brigade and cabaret spots at fêtes. The most regular gig we did was at Flamstead End Hall, where we played the cabaret spot during jazz evenings. What used to happen was that while the jazz band was on, the kids would all flop around looking bored, but as soon as we came on they would go mad dancing. Then when the skiffle stopped they'd all die again.

Walter Teague (Dick and Mick's father and group manager)

On one occasion Cliff's father was chatting to my wife and he said, "If only my son had the confidence that the rest of the boys have, the group would go far. But I'm afraid my son will never do any good because he is so nervous."

June Pearce (Personnel Officer, Thorn Electric)

In those days we used to have mid-morning breaks and his father used to come over to me in the canteen where I was having coffee and a doughnut and say, "Oh, Harry was playing at such-and-such a place last night and they got on very well." He would keep on popping over and telling me about it. We had our own sports club, and Cliff and his father used to play there. In fact, Mr Webb was a badminton coach. He was a qualified coach, I believe, and he would come down and give encouragement.

BELOW
Lonnie Donegan personified the skiffle craze of 1956–57. His exploration of blues, ballads, work songs and spirituals introduced a generation of British teenagers to the roots of American folk music

Dick Teague

There was nothing noticeable at this time in the way that girls responded to him. None of us were scoring left, right and centre and Cliff certainly wasn't. In those days he used to go everywhere with his sister, Donna. They obviously had a great relationship. They were as friendly as anything. He used to take her to dances and would dance with her. They were a great couple and he was a great fellow.

Sylvia Johnson (fan of Dick Teague Skiffle Group)

In those days there was not an awful lot to do. There was only the cinema but that was quite expensive if you were relying on pocket money. Cliff used to play at the Flamstead End Hall on a Friday night. He was a good-looking chap although he did suffer slightly from bad skin – teenage spots. I think he was more into his music than he was into girls. He and Donna were very close. She was gorgeous. Everyone would gather around Donna. I was in her class at school and she was the main attraction.

Terry Smart

Cliff and I started to tire of skiffle because we found rock 'n' roll far more exciting. We had asked a few times when rehearsing if we could try some of the new numbers, but Dick didn't want to; he didn't like the sound. In the end Cliff and I talked together and Cliff knew Norman Mitham, who was learning to play guitar. So we would go round to Cliff's house to practise and sometimes we went to my house or to Norman's. I remember Cliff's father, who could play mandolin, teaching basic chords to Cliff and Norman.

Norman Mitham

Cliff wanted to perform rock 'n' roll while he was with Dick Teague, but Dick said no so he didn't do it. However, he asked me to start learning the guitar and he talked to Terry Smart about forming a rock 'n' roll band. I think he went behind Dick's back insofar as he poached his drummer. Terry said that if Cliff had sufficient material he would gladly join the group. An uncle of mine who was a terrific musician taught me to play guitar. He had played in professional dance bands. Cliff would come over for lessons, too. First of all, Uncle Philip told us what key Cliff sang in and then he'd ask us to find out what chords we needed for a particular song we wanted to learn. We'd play him the record and he'd say, "That's so easy, it's not true." Then he'd teach us the chords, show us where the chord changes came and we took it from there. That's how we built up our basic repertoire. Normal songs went – verse, chorus, verse, chorus, instrumental break and repeat, but we didn't have the ability at that point to play the instrumental breaks so we improvised with a chord sequence.

ABOVE
Cliff's sister Donna assiduously followed his early performances. She also transcribed the lyrics from all the latest American singles so that The Drifters could introduce them into their set

Cliff

Skiffle was a strictly do-it-yourself type of music but it was very limited. You just sang lots of songs that only needed three chords. Although the rock 'n' roll didn't demand much more musically it demanded a lot more vocally. (1962)

Dick Teague

My dad set up a BBC audition for us without me knowing. I came home from work one day and he said, "Don't change. We're going out." This was an audition for Skiffle Club. The rest of the group knew about it but they knew that I was a perfectionist and thought that although there was a lot of individual talent in the group, overall we were crap. They were rushing to places I didn't want to go to yet. When we got there they asked us who the lead guitarist was but we didn't really have one. We were just a bunch of guys thrashing away. They then asked who the lead singer was and we stuck the mic on Cliff. He was able to take the lead and the rest of us just stayed in the background churning out rubbish. The result was a foregone conclusion but the woman auditioning came down from her cubicle and said to Cliff, "You've got a very good voice. You ought to have it trained." That was the only comment made.

BELOW
The original line-up of the Drifters – Cliff, Terry Smart and Norman Mitham – performing for the camera on waste ground behind their homes on the Bury Green Estate, early 1958

Mick Teague

We found out that Cliff was doing something on his own with Terry. We wondered what would happen if the BBC was interested after the audition. We couldn't decide whether an acceptance would be an acceptance of the group or of the singer. In the end we got a letter saying that our tape was not suitable for broadcast.

Dick Teague

Things came to a head when I realized that he wasn't learning the numbers quickly enough. It was obvious that something was happening because he had this amazing ability to learn a song inside out overnight after we'd listened to a record and worked out the chords. When he started to take longer and longer I realized that he wasn't giving his time wholly to the group. A meeting was called at our house where we discussed what was happening to the group. Cliff said he'd like to play more rock 'n' roll and I said, no way, I wasn't into that. The other guys said they liked what we were playing because it was most suited to the instruments we were playing. Rock 'n' roll required far more competence. Then Terry Smart piped up and said he also wanted to play rock 'n' roll. I said that there was no question about it: either they played our sort of music or we'd have to split up. It wasn't unpleasant but it was an agreement that we wanted to do different forms of music. We just packed up that night. I lost contact with both of them completely after that.

I'm Nearly Famous January – July 1958

At the time that Cliff and Terry Smart were considering forming a group, the idea of British musicians creating credible rock 'n' roll seemed unlikely. All of the major stars of the genre were American, and no one from Cheshunt or Waltham Cross had ready access to the musical sources that had been available to the likes of Elvis, Little Richard, Chuck Berry and Jerry Lee Lewis. The Americans had gospel choirs; we had Salvation Army bands. They had country music; we had traditional folk. They had the blues; we had Morris dancing. They had soul: we had music hall.

E ven after five years playing rock 'n' roll, Cliff could say (in 1962), "I don't think anybody here in England has really been an exponent of rock 'n' roll mainly because I believe that to sing real rock 'n' roll you have to be born somewhere like Memphis, sing spirituals, live with coloured people and get that blues feeling. I think Elvis is just about the best white rock 'n' roll singer there is."

For Cliff and his newly formed rock 'n' roll group, the first half of 1958 was full of incredible change. He'd started in the winter as the singer of an unschooled trio that rehearsed in the living room of a Hertfordshire council house and by the summer had changed his name from Harry to Cliff, had been the focus of screaming girl fans and had a recording contract with EMI. By July of 1958, he was able to give up his job and become a professional musician.

His career path was the stuff of Hollywood movies: the manager who walks into a bar and spots star potential; the agent who sees the fan reaction and pulls out a contract; the record-company executive who decides to give the boy a chance, and the television producer who's so knocked out with what he hears that he wants to make the singer the star of his new show.

British music fans loved Elvis but had little chance of ever seeing someone that handsome and authentic in concert. They made do with home-grown stars like Tommy Steele and Terry Dene, who tried hard but never looked anything more than pale imitations. When Jerry Lee Lewis toured England, Cliff and The Drifters turned up to see him at the Kilburn State Theatre and cheekily snuck backstage after the concert for a handshake and a photograph. Lewis was a *bona fide* rock 'n' roll star and they were just kids with jobs and nothing on tape.

Cliff

The Drifters was Terry [Smart] and me at first, and then we realized we couldn't do it on our own and that's when Norman Mitham came along. We realized that with three of us we could make a passable sound. I think there was a bit of a confrontation with Dick Teague because it was becoming obvious that I had my own thing going. I remember wanting to call us "The Planets", and when we looked "planets" up in the dictionary part of the definition read "cosmic drifters", so we thought, "That's it. We'll be The Drifters." My mum can remember me designing a cover for what I thought could be our first record.

Norman Mitham (school friend)

He was breaking away from Dick Teague so he needed a name. We tossed around loads of possibilities and I said "How about The Drifters?" It sounds crazy now, but we then decided on the cover of our first album! We hadn't done anything at all but already we were saying that if we did an LP we could have a snow scene with us tobogganing towards a snow drift. Get it? The Drifters! We had never heard of the American group called The Drifters.

ABOVE
Norman Mitham (right) met Cliff as a nine-year-old and was with him as a member of The Drifters during the first half of 1958

Terry Smart (drummer)

We used to spend evening after evening round at Cliff's. They were a very close family. They didn't seem to mind how many people came in. The house was always full. We used to practise there and the first songs we learned were the hits by Jerry Lee Lewis, Bill Haley and Elvis.

Norman Mitham

There were only three of us in the group, so as soon as Cliff felt we were good enough, that was it. We went out and played. The first public appearance we got paid for was at the badminton club that Cliff belonged to. We asked them if we could do the cabaret at a function they were putting on. We got paid five pounds.

Cliff

It was their annual dinner dance. We only sang songs that were current – Elvis and Ricky Nelson. It felt good. It was all so new. I was elated to think that these people had applauded us, but it was probably a bit faked because they all knew me. I played badminton with them every week. But it felt fantastic – as it still does.

Norman Mitham

The second gig we did was at a pub in Hoddesdon called The Five Horseshoes. That was still just three of us. This was a place where you would go more for the experience of playing because the audience wasn't made up of people who'd paid to sit there and watch you. They were there to drink and play darts. I think the landlord thought that having a group to play might be an added incentive to get people in – it was more appealing than having someone playing a piano. We were put in the public bar. I think there was a stage that was raised maybe two or three inches, and that housed the piano as well. We had no amplifiers. It was just two acoustic guitars and the drums. That's where we met John Foster.

ABOVE
John Foster (right) with Terry Smart (left) and "Sammy" Samwell (centre). Foster was a sewage-farm worker when he spotted The Drifters playing in a pub and volunteered to become their manager

John Foster (first manager of The Drifters)

Even though I was only 17, I'd done about 16 jobs since I left school and I was currently driving a dumper truck at a local sewage farm. This was *not* my life's ambition! I walked into The Five Horseshoes one evening to have a drink at the bar with my mates and The Drifters were playing up against one of the windows. Cliff didn't really have a stage act. He just stood there and moved his legs. He had an acoustic guitar around his neck and when I looked at him I thought of Elvis. I just had a feeling he was going to be huge. So I just walked up to him after he'd finished and asked him if he wanted a manager. I don't know what made me do it. I had no experience. I think I was just lucky in that no-one had asked him that before. I was just judging him by what I knew of Elvis and the fact that British rock 'n' roll stars like Terry Dene and Tommy Steele were making a fortune.

Norman Mitham

We'd just finished playing and John Foster walked up to Cliff. He was quite knocked out by us and asked us whether we'd like to play at the 2 I's in London. That was his opening line. We'd never been to this coffee bar but we'd heard all about it. When we were playing a pub in Hoddeson it seemed a bit of a joke to be approached by a guy we didn't know and asked whether we wanted to play at the 2 I's. Then he asked us if we had a manager and we told him we didn't. We hadn't even thought about management, agents or anything like that. I think that this was on a Monday night and he told us that he would get us on at the 2 I's that Saturday after an afternoon session. He told us that we should get on the 715 bus. It would come through Cheshunt at two o'clock and he'd be waiting for us to get on at the Old Pond bus stop. He said he'd sit at the near side window so we knew which bus to get on. Well, we knew nothing about this guy. I don't think we even knew his surname. We talked about it all week and wondered if we'd all been taken for a ride. But we turned up at the Old Pond on the Saturday and I think it was the second bus that John was on.

Joyce Dobra (cousin)

They didn't even have the bus fare to get to the 2 I's so my husband and I lent them the money. They were then told that it was no good playing there if they didn't have their own amplifier. Rodger said, "That's easy. Get Joyce to lend you the money. It'll cost about £3 and I'll build it." I was the sole wage-earner at that time because my husband was very ill, so we borrowed either from our neighbours or a man who was lodging with us and we let Cliff have the money. They got the parts they needed, took them home and Uncle Rodger blew the lot up as he tried to put it all together. They were naturally all very depressed and wondering what to do next so I think we borrowed even more money and they bought something already assembled and off they went.

ABOVE
The 2 I's coffee bar at 59 Old Compton Street in London's Soho was where the chain of events began that would transform Cliff from an unknown Hertfordshire singer into Britain's first enduring rock 'n' roll star.

Terry Smart

The 2 I's was in Old Compton Street in Soho. The bit where the groups played was in a cellar beneath the coffee bar. There was no ventilation down there. Everyone was smoking and it had a very low ceiling. However, being a cellar meant that the acoustics were quite good.

Cliff

It was an upstairs/downstairs set-up. There was a basement which was fairly narrow. It was a coffee bar and there was no alcohol served. It was the early days of cappuccino and espresso coffee in Britain and you could buy that upstairs, along with orange juice, cakes or whatever. The action took place downstairs at night. It was stinking hot and people just plugged in and played. It was a significant part of British rock 'n' roll. (2004)

John Foster

My only connection with the 2 I's at that time was that I had been there. I had mixed with a couple of the skiffle groups, one of which was Les Hobeaux. They were quite a big group in those days, with a guy called Les Bennett. My big love, though, was for rock 'n' roll.

Chas McDevitt (skiffle musician)

The 2 I's had been named after the Irani brothers who owned the place. They were from Iran and ended up with a nightclub called The Tropicana, which later became The Establishment. Paul Lincoln and Ray Hunter, two wrestlers from Australia, virtually took over the lease. Wally Whyton and his group, The Vipers, became the resident group and then I came in with my group.

Norman Mitham

Paul Lincoln listened to us when we auditioned. We played him one or two numbers and he said, "OK, you're on." We were on that night! It was fantastic to play there. It was absolutely jam packed. They just kept pushing people in until they were lining the stairs as well. To be in the group was such an advantage. You had about two square feet around you, whereas for everyone else it was absolute hell. What was so exciting for us was that the kids just listened. There was no dancing or screaming or anything like that. Afterwards we couldn't stop talking about the fact that people had paid money and had then stood there and listened to us play. We weren't there as an incidental entertainment factor as we had been at the pub or the badminton club. By the time I got home my parents were both asleep, but I woke them to tell them we'd actually played the 2 I's. Not that it meant anything to them! It was the same with Cliff's parents. After that we became fairly regular down there. Whether that was John Foster's influence or whether we were just cheap, I don't know. It was while we were playing down there that Ian "Sammy" Samwell came in and saw us. We were impressed because he'd sat in on a session with Laurie London.

Mrs Foster (John Foster's mother)

Cliff's family didn't have an awful lot of money or a very big house so the boys often used to stay at my house. When they'd been at the 2 I's they would catch the 715 Green Line bus back home from London and I used to wait up for them and get them their supper. I had to put two of them in one bedroom and two of them in another because two of them smoked and two of them didn't.

ABOVE
The only surviving picture of Cliff performing in the basement of the 2 I's coffee bar, probably taken in either May or June of 1958. Left to right: Terry Smart, Cliff, "Sammy" Samwell, Norman Mitham

Paul Lincoln (Manager, the 2 I's)

I used to manage Terry Dene. I put everything into him and he flipped his lid just at the moment when we had him as the biggest thing in Britain. There were others coming up but everyone seemed to think Terry would be the next star now that Tommy Steele was established. The fact that he blew his top almost caused me to have a nervous breakdown. I couldn't cope. Cliff came to me with this guy called Johnny Foster. Johnny kept asking me if I would manage Cliff but I told him I didn't want to know because I'd finished with this business.

Ian "Sammy" Samwell (musician and songwriter)

Cliff was playing at the 2 I's with Terry and Norman and I think they had played there maybe twice by that time. I was playing with a skiffle group out in Kent. We'd done fairly well locally and had broadcast on the BBC but the other guys weren't really interested in going into rock 'n' roll. So, I was wandering around the West End not particularly looking for a rock 'n' roll band because there weren't any but I saw Cliff at the 2 I's and I thought, "That's exactly what I want. That's exactly what I *need* to do." I just walked up to him afterwards and said, "You don't happen to need a guitarist, do you?" He said, "Well, we're playing here again on Saturday. Why don't you come down in the afternoon?" So I auditioned for them and that became my first rehearsal, too. I played at the gig that night.

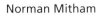

ABOVE

After becoming a Drifter, "Sammy" Samwell became one of Cliff's significant songwriters. He later compared their relationship to the one between Ritchie Cunningham and The Fonz in the 1970s' TV series "Happy Days"

Norman Mitham

Soho was such a different environment to Cheshunt. Next to the 2 I's was a coffee bar called the Heaven and Hell and we'd go in there because it was a bit more exciting. Upstairs was Heaven and it was very bright. Downstairs was Hell and that was very dark and gloomy. I remember one of us noticing the girls walking the streets and mentioning that they were prostitutes. We'd never had anything to do with prostitutes and here they were and we were right in the middle of it.

Chas McDevitt

In the mid-1950s there was a coffee-bar society in the West End of London. The Gaggia coffee-making machine had come into the country and coffee bars were springing up everywhere. When skiffle came in, a lot of these places became skiffle venues. There was the Bread Basket, just behind the Middlesex Hospital; the Gyre

and Gimble in Villiers Street; the Cat's Whiskers in Kingly Street, and the Skiffle Cellar in Gerrard Street. Then others came in like The Macabre that had tables made of coffin lids, which really just cashed in on the trend.

ABOVE
Skiffle musician Chas McDevitt with Nancy Whiskey. He ran The Freight Train in Soho, where Cliff performed with The Drifters

BELOW
Terry Dene performing with The Dene Aces. Dene met Cliff at the 2 I's during 1958

Norman Mitham

One Saturday we were rehearsing in the cellar of the 2 I's and we heard a commotion upstairs and found out that Tommy Steele had come in. It was a big thing for us to meet someone as well-known as Tommy Steele. Then we saw Terry Dene down there and Terry spoke to us. Over the next few days we bought every Terry Dene record we could find because we had met him. Reading about him or seeing him on TV we hadn't liked him, but meeting him turned us into fans.

Terry Dene (1950s' rock 'n' roll star)

Johnny Foster came to me and asked if I'd listen to this guy sing. I said, "Sure." Cliff was there and he came up and shook my hand. I'd already been going for a while and Cliff was obviously keen to hear what I had to say because he respected what I'd done. So he sang for me in the basement of the 2 I's and I told him I thought he was great and then I turned to John and told him that I thought he'd make it.

Jan Vane (fan and later fan club president)

I remember exactly when I first saw Cliff. It was on my 16th birthday, April 1, 1958, and a male friend took me to the 2 I's as a treat. I'd never been there before. It was just somewhere you heard about when you were that age. I just wanted to go somewhere different. I can still see him performing that night. The place was so full we ended up sitting on a Coca Cola fridge. I can't even remember what he was singing but he was unusual. Afterwards I went up and asked for his autograph. I don't think I even knew his name at that point. He was young and exciting and I had never been to a place like that before.

Norman Mitham

Sammy was in the RAF but he was able to get a fair amount of leave. We had a rehearsal with him. He fitted in quite well so we bought him a jumper and he was in the group! He hadn't been with us all that long when a guy called Harry Greatorex came down. He ran a ballroom in Ripley, near Derby, and he'd come to London specifically to find a group that he could promote locally as being "Direct from the 2 I's Coffee Bar in London." He saw us and booked us on the spot.

Ian "Sammy" Samwell

Harry Greatorex wanted to bill us as a singer with a name and his group, not just as The Drifters. Harry Webb and the Drifters obviously didn't sound right so we retired to the Swiss Pub on Old Compton Street to come up with something. See, all the Americans had such cool names: Chuck, Rick, Gene and things like that. The best thing about Hank Marvin when he joined was his name! He was known as Hank and he looked like Buddy Holly! We came up with Cliff Richards. I suggested knocking the final letter "s" off.

John Foster

Sammy said we should knock the final "s" off the surname so that when people asked it was two Christian names: Cliff and Richard. He said that would get us well known. It sounded like a great idea.

Norman Mitham

We had thought of changing his name at different times, but this was the day it finally happened. He was completely open to suggestions. Someone suggested Russ because of Russ Hamilton. Then someone said Clifford. So Russ Clifford was tossed around. Then it was Cliff Russard. He liked the ring of that. It was getting closer to what he wanted.

BELOW
It was for this show at the Regal Ballroom in Ripley, near Derby, that Harry Webb changed his name to Cliff Richard. It was thought to be a more American-sounding name

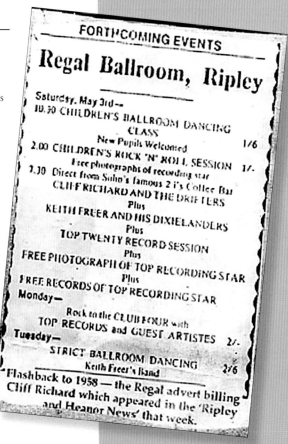

ABOVE
Larry Parnes, who managed Tommy Steele (seated), was the biggest pop manager in Britain when Cliff turned professional. He would later make an offer for Cliff, but it was turned down

John Foster

Larry Parnes came up with names for all his acts: Tommy Steele, Marty Wilde, Duffy Power, Billy Fury. In those days it just didn't seem to be right to use your own name – it was too normal. We went back to Harry Greatorex and said, "It's Cliff Richard and The Drifters." That became the first time he was billed as Cliff Richard.

Larry Parnes (manager of Marty Wilde and Billy Fury)

There was always an image I wanted to project. Marty Wilde was tall and looked quite tough, so I wanted a friendly first name that didn't worry anybody. There was a film out at the time called *Marty,* about a friendly character, so I chose Marty as the first name. But in order to get his sex appeal across I added "wild" but with an "e" on the end out of superstition. Billy Fury's real name was Ronald Wytcherley. He was very sensitive-looking, so needed a friendly, boy-next-door first name but with a touch of sensitivity... so, "Billy". Then I picked the surname "Fury" because I wanted to project this sex appeal and mystique – so it became "Billy Fury".

Cliff

From the day I came home and said, "I'm going to change my name to Cliff", my family have always called me Cliff. My youngest sister Joan sometimes goes "Harr..." and then she says, "Oh! What have I said?" as though she's said something wrong. My old school friends still call me Harry. My old English teacher (Jay Norris) is very stubborn. She refuses to call me Cliff. It can be very embarrassing! (1960)

Norman Mitham

The thought that we were going to travel all the way to Derbyshire for a booking was fantastic. We really thought that we'd made it. It was the Regal Ballroom in Ripley and because we were promoted as the latest thing to come out of the 2 I's, the place was packed. As we travelled on a bus from the station in Derby to the gig, we were excited to see posters that said "Cliff Richard and The Drifters". We were excited. I can remember us wondering if they were expecting too much. We weren't even sure if our equipment was powerful enough to cope with playing in a big hall.

Ian "Sammy" Samwell

There was a stage with curtains, which was quite something after having played at the 2 I's. The curtains parted, we were all set up there and we really rocked that night. Then we had to sleep on some hard benches, which were very uncomfortable, before catching the train back home the next morning.

Cliff

It felt very exciting because we felt the big time was coming for us. Suddenly I was fronting a band. We had to play throughout the evening in 15-minute slots. It was a Saturday night hop. It was too late to get back home by train and so we had to sleep on these benches that were around the hall.

Janice Berry (school friend and first serious girlfriend)

I must have started going out with Cliff in about February 1958, over six months after we'd left school. We had fun together. We were always laughing and were really good friends. The Drifters used to rehearse at my house because his neighbours couldn't stand too much noise and our house was a lot older and I suppose the walls were thicker. In fact, they wore a hole in my mum's carpet! I can remember that because they always had to rehearse in the same place because the drums had to be set up in the bay window and Cliff would be in front of that. I can remember this distinct bald patch appearing in the place where they worked.

Cliff

Being a male singer, my fans like to see themselves as perhaps having a chance of dating me. Or they look on me as being the boy they'd like to have next door. I have to stay this way as long as I possibly can. (1960)

Janice Berry

He obviously wanted to succeed, and the fact that everyone was starting to applaud him reinforced the idea that he was going to succeed. I think the idea of "this is what I want to be" started when he was about 16. He never said, "I want to be Elvis", but it just sort of happened. I remember him saying that he wasn't going to be able to see me much, but it didn't really need to be said.

ABOVE
Cliff meets Jerry Lee Lewis (centre). He and his manager John Foster (left), guitarist "Sammy Samwell" (right) and drummer Terry Smart (second from right) managed to get backstage at the Kilburn State Theatre on May 25, 1958

BELOW
Even in the early days, Cliff was conscious of his boy-next-door image. He gave the impression of being every girl's ideal boyfriend

Chas McDevitt

I remember in the early days saying to Paul Lincoln, "Look, you've got this young bloke with a crucifix hanging round his neck singing down at your club. The girls are going wild about him and yet he's only got this young lad managing him. Why don't we take him over? With my show-business connections and your money we could really do something with him." Paul uttered these immortal words to me: "Chas, we've had Tommy Steele and then Terry Dene. Rock 'n' roll is finished."

Norman Mitham

One night we were at the 2 I's and this guy came up to us and told us he thought we were very good. It turned out to be the songwriter Lionel Bart. So the next day Johnny Foster arranged for us to visit Lionel at home. He lived in a mews house and to us boys from council homes in Cheshunt this guy's home was really something. We thought this was how it must be after you make it because Bart had written some successful songs for Tommy Steele at the time. I remember that he had a loo roll that played music as you pulled it. We talked to Bart about writing songs and then he later visited us in Cheshunt to listen to our songs. He said he'd write something for us, but at the time we never heard back from him. Of course later, when Cliff was big, he wrote "Living Doll".

BELOW
Lionel Bart was best known as a songwriter for Tommy Steele when he first met Cliff in Soho. He went on to write "Living Doll" for Cliff and created the classic musical Oliver!

John Foster

Lionel Bart was Mr Success at that time. He had a toilet that played Handel's *Water Music* as you flushed it. He phoned Larry Parnes to come over and we sat and talked about how big Cliff was going to be. It was only later that I learned that Lionel had actually phoned Larry and said, "Come on over. I want you to meet my new boyfriend." Both Lionel and Larry were gay. Billy Fury told me of a time that Larry invited him to stay the night. There was only one bed. Billy got into the bed and Larry said, "Wow. Isn't it cold? Let's cuddle up." Billy grabbed hold of the bedside lamp and smashed it over Larry's head! Larry later offered me £60,000 for Cliff. That was an absolute fortune in those days. That was after I had stopped being Cliff's business manager and had become his personal manager. I turned him down.

Janice Berry

I was there when Lionel Bart came up to Cheshunt. It was an evening when the group was going to rehearse at my house and Cliff came early to tell me that there'd been a change of plan. We didn't have phones in those days. He said that Lionel Bart was coming to see them at Terry's house. Cliff came back to collect me and then walked round to Terry's, where Lionel Bart had already arrived with this glamorous actress called June Wilkinson, who was dressed in a tight-fitting, light-green dress. She had a huge bosom, a tiny waist and a mass of auburn hair. She stunned everybody. To us she was like someone straight from the pages of a magazine. She sat glamorously in a chair while the boys played and we all listened and watched.

Lionel Bart (composer and songwriter)

June Wilkinson was 17 going on 18. She had a 43-inch bust and was the first British centrefold in *Playboy*. She used to share a flat in Great Newport Street with Tommy Steele's wife, Annie. I had introduced Annie to Tommy and was best man at their wedding. June and I used to run around together.

June Wilkinson (actress and model)

Lionel drove me there. He was interested to know what I thought of him. I don't know if Cliff knew who I was, but he may have done because I was getting a lot of press at the time. I think I was doing cabaret at The Embassy Club and before that I'd been a Windmill girl. Cliff's mum and dad were there and Cliff sang for us and I thought, "Boy! That's a hard thing to do." It's really tough environment to perform in but Cliff was excellent. Lionel asked me what I thought of him and said, "I think he's terrific. The kid has real talent."

Terry Smart

We didn't think of rock 'n' roll as a rebellion against our parents at all. It was just a sound, and we enjoyed it. It was something different to what we'd been used to hearing. We wanted to be a part of it. Most teenagers in those days didn't go around wrecking things; they were in awe of their parents. Cliff was naturally very pleasant and clean-cut. It wasn't something he had to work at – that's the way he was.

ABOVE
June Wilkinson met Cliff when he was an unrecorded and unknown musician living in Cheshunt. After moving to America, she became one of the most recognized pin-up models of the late 1950s and '60s

Cliff

Rock 'n' roll has been used by people who want to do things that aren't so good. They use rock 'n' roll as an excuse. Kids tear up cinema seats, but that's not real teenagers. That's just plain hooliganism and it's just ridiculous. (1960)

Norman Mitham

We played The Gaumont Theatre in Shepherd's Bush one Saturday morning. That audience was a lot younger than the ones we had been used to. The stage felt a lot bigger than anything we'd ever been on before. This was the first time that we saw Cliff reacted to as a sex symbol. At the 2 I's and also at Ripley you felt that people were excited by the music alone. At Ripley, for example, people danced. At other places they might clap. But at The Gaumont everyone was seated and they were screaming at Cliff. There was no doubt about that.

John Foster

We invested in new shirts for that gig. Cliff had a white one with gold beading. Terry had a red one and I went on to do some backing vocals wearing a blue one. The girls were screaming their heads off and I could feel Cliff's reputation building.

Ian "Sammy" Samwell

At that time our set was mostly composed of songs recorded by Elvis, Jerry Lee Lewis, Eddie Cochran and Little Richard. We used to buy singles every week and because we didn't have that much money we would discuss among ourselves what we were going to buy so that we didn't duplicate. I think Johnny Foster had access to an American air base and was able to get used records from the jukebox. In that way we were able to get our hands on stuff that hadn't been released over here. That's how we came across Chuck Willis's "Hang Up My Rock 'n' Roll Shoes" and "Get A Job" by The Silhouettes.

Cliff

I think it was the last Saturday of every month that they had a talent competition at The Gaumont. We decided to go, but told the manager that we didn't want to participate in the talent competition. We said we'd top the bill but we'd do it for nothing. He accepted the deal so we went in, set up our equipment, played a set and I got screamed at! I was chased down the street to a loo and had to wait there until they got me a taxi. I had my shirt pulled off. I loved it! It was fantastic! (2004)

John Foster

We made a demo record. I think we did it at the HMV record shop in Oxford Street. I'm sure "Breathless", the Jerry Lee Lewis song, was one of the tracks. The result was that I now had a reel-to-reel tape. I started blagging my way into places to try to get people interested in Cliff. I got an appointment with Ian Bevan, who had Tommy Steele. I played him the tape and he said, "I like rock 'n' roll. I manage Tommy Steele. But I suggest you tell your boy not to give up his day job." I saw him a few years later and he said, "I remember you. You brought a singer to me, didn't you?" I said, "Yes. His name was Cliff Richard." The blood drained from his face. He'd missed out.

Ray Mackender (adviser and friend)

I still have the original acetate that Cliff cut at HMV. It was Little Richard's "Good Golly Miss Molly" and Jerry Lee Lewis's "Breathless". It has Cliff's writing on the label. It's a double-sided 10-inch acetate. A lot of people said he recorded a tape, but he didn't. It was definitely a £5 acetate from HMV.

Ian "Sammy" Samwell

We got invited back to the Gaumont as 'special guests' and as we'd gone down so well there I thought it would be the ideal place to get an agent to see us. I just looked through a copy of *The Stage*, saw the listings of agents and picked one of them out. It was a guy called George Ganjou, who I knew nothing about. He agreed to come and see us. I took the news back to Cheshunt. Everybody agreed that Johnny Foster should go and see him.

George Ganjou (agent)

John Foster and Ian Samwell came to see me at my Albermarle Street office on the Friday. The next day I had a choice of either playing golf or doing business. I decided to do business and went to see the singer who turned out to be Cliff Richard. I was impressed with his performance. I was especially impressed with the reaction of the audience. I was never a big fan of rock 'n' roll, but I had a sense about what would be commercial and what would entertain. I saw great possibilities in that young man. He struck me as being not only very good-looking but also full of humility and charm.

John Foster

George Ganjou was really a circus agent. He was a lovely man but he didn't know what had hit him when we turned up. He'd been in one of the greatest *adagio* acts in the business – The Ganjou Brothers and Juanita – who had done royal command performances. He saw Cliff play at The Gaumont, and although he didn't know anything about rock 'n' roll, he saw the effect that Cliff was having on the girls and decided to take him on.

Terry Smart

Without wishing to sound big-headed, after having heard and seen all the other acts on at The Gaumont that day, I thought that we were the best. We got a great reception. There was more screaming and we really thought that we'd made it. George Ganjou came to see us in the dressing room after the show. He was a friend of Norrie Paramor, who ran the Columbia label at EMI, and so he made an appointment for us to take our demo and play it to Norrie.

Cliff

George was the person we gave our first-ever demo record to. He took it to Norrie Paramor at EMI.

ABOVE
Norrie Paramor pictured in 1956 with his Big Ben Banjo Band, a group made up of prominent session musicians. He was label manager and producer for EMI's Columbia label when George Ganjou introduced him to Cliff

Ian "Sammy" Samwell

I had written bits and pieces of poetry before, but I'd never [written] anything to music. I was on the 715 Green Line bus from London Colney to Cheshunt and I started writing my first song, which was called "Move It". I was sitting upstairs in the back seat and I had my guitar with me. I'd been inspired by an article in *Melody Maker* that was saying that rock 'n' roll's days were numbered. The words came out in a rush. When you write on a moving bus you don't have time to think. It was basic 12-bar blues with four bars stuck on the front, which makes it odd in the sense that is a 16-bar blues but also in the sense that it only has one verse which comes around twice and is linked by a solo. By the time I got to Cliff's place, it was complete. I just played it to them. I had to write the lyric out again because my original was full of bits and pieces and Cliff needed to be able to read it. I used to put every "ah" and "oh" in because I knew that if they weren't there, he wouldn't sing them. You have to put every nuance in.

John Foster

The first thing Norrie did was he put us in the studio at Abbey Road to do a test recording. I think we again recorded "Breathless". Norrie went on holiday and we heard nothing back from him. Then we heard from him that, yes, he'd like to record us. That put us over the moon!

George Ganjou

After listening to Cliff's tape, Norrie said, "Now, George, I'm going on holiday. Come back in two weeks and then we'll see what we can do." I left it in abeyance until Norrie came back. He then told me, "Can you bring Cliff Richard, or whatever he calls himself, into my office?" That's how I brought Cliff to see him.

Terry Smart

We all took the Green Line bus into London and met up with Norrie. He said, "You need a bass player to hold you together." Then he said, "I've got a record here that you might like to cover. Go away and learn it and I'll arrange a recording session where I'll have a couple of good session men to play for you." The record was "Schoolboy Crush" by Bobby Helms.

Norrie Paramor (Recording Director, Columbia Records)

I asked Cliff and the boys if they could try it. So, after practising for a few minutes, they launched into it and I knew then and there that I was going to record them. (1959)

John Foster

It was an American song because, in those days, anything good had to come out of America. It was a song very much in the style of the Terry Dene hit "White Sports Coat", which itself was a cover of an American hit by Marty Robbins. Then Norrie asked if we had another song to put on the B-side. That's when Cliff suggested "Move It", the song that Sammy had just written. The boys played it to Norrie and he was happy for it to be recorded at the session. This was probably because B-sides didn't matter in those days.

ABOVE
American singer Bobby Helms, whose June 1958 single "Schoolboy Crush" was offered to Cliff by Norrie Paramor as a record to cover for the British market. Cliff duly recorded it for his debut single. Helms, who only enjoyed US chart success in 1957, died in 1997

Ian "Sammy" Samwell

Two session guys were brought to Abbey Road to augment what we were doing. Ernie Shear played the lead guitar and Frank Clarke played double bass. I had invented the introduction and showed it to Ernie. He played that now-famous opening and put in some Bill Haley-type fills which I wasn't happy with. Anyway, it was only going to be the B-side so I couldn't do anything about it.

Norrie Paramor

I added a couple of professional musicians to enhance the sound but the vocal group we were planning to use didn't arrive. It transpired that due to a mix-up they hadn't been booked, so we had to start phoning around to find someone else. While this was going on we decided to press ahead and record "Move It" without the vocal backing. So the arrangement was adapted on the spot and Cliff waxed it without the originally intended vocal support. The hastily summoned group arrived at last and they were used on the other song, "Schoolboy Crush". (1959)

Malcolm Addey (engineer)

I had started working at Abbey Road on March 3 of that year and I was 10 years younger than the two other pop engineers and so able to relate a little easier to the younger artists who were starting to come to EMI. The other engineers, Stuart Eltham and Peter Bown, had great faith in me and helped me a lot in the early days. They had no problem recommending me for this session even though I was still an "apprentice". It became my session right from the beginning. I chose the positioning of the microphones and the layout of the studio. Although Norrie later spoke as though we recorded "Move It" first, we most certainly didn't. The bulk of the session was spent on "Schoolboy Crush" because that was intended as the A-side. It was normal not to want to waste musicians' overtime fees on a B-side. So we completed "Schoolboy Crush" in two or three takes and the Mike Sammes Singers were dismissed and then started on "Move It", a song that Norrie thought was rubbish. Sammy Samwell couldn't hack the guitar playing on that, so Norrie had hired a great session guitarist, Ernie Shear.

Ernie Shear (session guitarist)

For me, it was just a busking session. I could read music but this was one of those times where we just talked about what was wanted and let it develop. It was just another day's work. What made it worse was that it was a night session, which meant we were all a bit tired. I'd played on a lot of rock 'n' roll records. I used to play a Hoffner acoustic that had an American DeArmand pick-up. To get the sound I wanted, I used to push it near the bridge. I wanted the toppiest sound I could get, and in those days there were no Telecasters or Stratocasters around.

Malcolm Addey

Ernie played an absolutely wonderful introduction. He was one of those guys who could play whatever was required without getting uptight. He just turned up his EQ and let rip. It came out sounding really great and that really held everyone's attention. For his part, Cliff liked to play while he was singing, so Norrie allowed him to hold on to his guitar.

Frank Clarke (session musician)

He had his band with him but they wouldn't risk using them on the record. I remember the session very well. Cliff's mum came and she sat downstairs with us. Cliff was quite confident, but not cocky. They'd been knocking around Cheshunt and Soho and knew what they were doing. I remember that guitar lead of Ernie's. It became a rock 'n' roll classic and Ernie got nothing but a straight session fee. We were around for quite a few of Cliff's records. We were invited along by Norrie just in case things went wrong.

Terry Smart

Norrie played piano and he took us through the songs before we did a take. As far as I can remember we did a few takes of "Schoolboy Crush" and then did "Move It" in the same way. We weren't there for long at all. It was great to hear it played back in the control room. The reproduction was marvellous. Norrie originally wanted "Schoolboy Crush" as the A-side.

Cliff

When I first started singing there seemed to be no way that any of us would ever get into a studio. We only knew of Decca and EMI. The rest of the record companies came from America. Decca and EMI, we knew, were somewhere in the metropolis, somewhere in London. We had no idea how to get into a studio. Nowadays almost anyone can make a brilliant recording at home. We never had that, so when I finally got into a studio with Norrie Paramor the excitement I got was of something brand new. This was a whole way of life that, up that point, had only been a dream. I'd constantly been thinking, "If only I could be like Elvis or Ricky Nelson or Jerry Lee Lewis or Little Richard..." then, suddenly, the opportunity was there. Suddenly I was in a studio making a rock 'n' roll record.

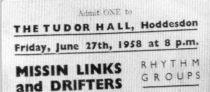

ABOVE
Ticket for a local Hertfordshire dance that took place after the addition of "Sammy" Samwell but before the recording of "Move It". The Tudor Hall, in Conduit Lane, was a regular stomping ground for Cliff in his pre-fame days

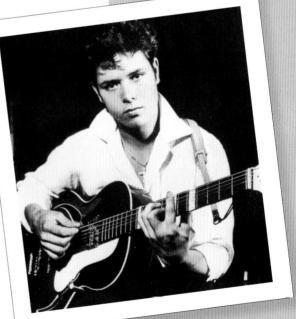

ABOVE
Cliff in his first publicity picture, taken by Ritchie Howells in the corner of one of the studios at Abbey Road, during the recording session for "Move It", July 1958

Caroline Paramor (daughter of Norrie Paramor)

I liked "Move It" because you could jive to it. We had an old-fashioned radiator at home that was quite high and had a big knob on the top. I used it as my dancing partner! I can remember playing "Move It" a lot, and my dad showing me a photograph of Cliff. I thought he looked absolutely lovely. He was something different and I knew that he would appeal to my age group.

Franklyn Boyd (music publisher)

I was managing director of Aberbach Music on Savile Row and Cliff had recorded "Schoolboy Crush", which was one of the songs I published. When the white label was ready I took it around to get airplay. I went to Dennis Mayne Wilson, producer of BBC TV's "6–5 Special", and he said he'd like to use Cliff but couldn't do so for six weeks. I needed something more immediate, so I rang Jack Good, producer of "Oh Boy!", and arranged for him to meet Cliff at an audition room near Cambridge Circus in London's West End. He played a couple of numbers and Jack loved him, but Jack's wife, a German girl, didn't like him at all.

BELOW
A rare copy of a test pressing of "Move It", Cliff's debut single, sent out to record reviewers, disc jockeys and TV producers

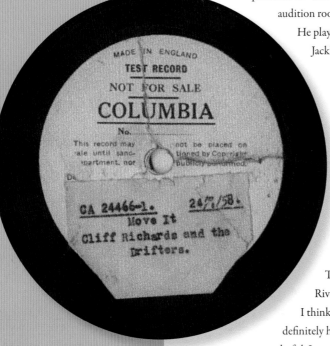

Jack Good (Producer, "Oh Boy!")

I suppose my tastes were diametrically opposed to those of "6–5 Special". They would have listened to "Schoolboy Crush" and loved it. I played both songs – even though Franklyn Boyd was interested in pushing "Schoolboy Crush" – and I loved "Move It". I couldn't believe it! I couldn't wait to see him. I remember thinking, "He can't also look good. That would be too much to ask." We met at Max Rivers' Rehearsal Studios and he was with his band. I think he sang "A Whole Lotta Shakin'" and I would definitely have got him to sing "Move It". I thought he was wonderful. In my mind I immediately erased the guitar he had round his neck. I think he was casually dressed in a striped shirt and jeans. I remember that immediately afterwards I walked with him to Leicester Square tube station. I don't think I was leaving, but he was. I suppose I needed to talk to him privately. I had to tell him things about what he should do but didn't want to do it front of the others. I told him that I didn't like his sideburns and I didn't want the guitar. I don't think he was too pleased to hear that. Unfortunately, at that time he was in no position to argue. I seem to remember he gave me one of those looks that said, "Do me a favour. You must be kidding!"

John Foster

Jack basically told Cliff if that if he wanted to be on his show, he had to shave the sideburns off. Until then Cliff had always tried to be like Elvis, but it was Jack who started changing his image and making a new image called Cliff Richard. Up to that point we were doing all the Elvis numbers and the Elvis movements.

Jack Good

Even then, sideburns were a little bit Teddy boy. Not a lot of people had them. Even his short sideburns were enough of a statement to make it known that he wanted to be like Elvis, and although we were keen to have someone who could make the same impact, we didn't want someone giving an Elvis impersonation or even appearing to give one. Also, he clearly couldn't play the guitar very well. Neither could Elvis, as it happens, but it was very limiting for the kind of camera shots I would want to get if the guy couldn't play. I wanted to do a dramatic performance because it was my theory that rock 'n' roll could be like drama and all the shots had to be planned. We had to know what all the looks were going to be and, even though it was all prepared beforehand, it had to look spontaneous.

Cliff

That was the look Jack created for me and it took me away from being just a simple carbon copy of Elvis. He was trying to wean me off the Elvis look. I was against it but, in a way, I guess it ensured my longevity. (1987)

Franklyn Boyd

Jack rang me a couple of days later and said, OK, I'm going to use him but he's not going to be doing "Schoolboy Crush". I said, "Why not? It's the A-side." He said, "No. He's going to sing the B-side." So I saw Norrie Paramor and he said, "But Frank – all the publicity has gone out and all the flyers have gone up saying 'Schoolboy Crush', not 'Move It'." I said, "Well, I understand that, but I'm not going to lose this spot. They'll see him on television whatever he sings." To cut a long story short, he did "Move It" on that show.

John Foster

Janice was Cliff's steady girlfriend at the time. All I can remember is that when we started looking to go on the road, Cliff was very down. He talked to her and told her that he wasn't going to be around very much and that kind of finished it.

Janice Berry

Cliff knew that it wasn't a good idea from the point of view of his girl fans to be known as having a girlfriend. It obviously looked better if he was on his own as an available single fellow. All these things meant that, from both our points of view, it was better that we separated. He was going away, I didn't really like going to the concerts where he was mobbed by fans and he knew that it was better for his career if he was single. We decided that it was better if we stopped being boyfriend and girlfriend but remained as friends. It seemed inevitable. I wasn't the type to tag along – I'm not like that. He wouldn't have wanted me to. It was far better it happened the way it did. The actual end was upsetting for me in the same way that it is when any relationship finishes but it may not have been upsetting for him. I don't know how he felt about it.

Cliff

I did have a girlfriend before I came into show business. Yes – you could say she was my steady, although we were only going out for six months. Then I had to leave. It was a mutual decision. (1960)

Jan Vane (fan-club president 1958–70)

It was on the night I first met Cliff in 1958 that I asked him if he had a fan club. I knew that rock 'n' roll stars had fan clubs and that this was a way of keeping in touch with what they were doing. When he said he didn't have one, I offered to start one. They had no way of getting back that night, so my friend offered to drive Cliff and Johnny Foster back to Cheshunt in his Morris Minor. When we got there, Cliff and I exchanged addresses and we started corresponding. I ended up spending a lot of time with him and his family just as friends. I would go to his home for a weekend, or my family would come over and we'd all go out for a picnic. They were what I would have described as a nice, ordinary family and we all got on well together.

George Ganjou

Since 1957 I had been the booking agent for the Butlins holiday camps, and so I booked Cliff into their camp in Clacton with his two boys called The Drifters. I booked him to give him some polish, which he lacked at the time. I was the sole booking agent for all the Butlins camps in Britain.

Norman Mitham

George Ganjou found us work at Butlins in Clacton. The idea was that we would all give up our jobs, but I wasn't adding anything to the group as such. I was wasted money. I wasn't singing and I was playing the same chords as Cliff. So you had two guitars playing where one could suffice. So that was it as far I was concerned. When I left the group I felt as though I had to start my life again. This wasn't easy because the only circle of friends I had at that time was Johnny, Terry, Ian and Cliff.

Cliff

It was always an executive decision when someone had to leave. I wasn't the boss. I think Norman became a much more competent guitarist afterwards. John Foster would have been the one to tell him our decision.

John Foster

Cliff gave up his job at Atlas Lighting when the Clacton gig came up. We went down by train and stayed there for a month. I shared a chalet with Sammy while Cliff and Terry were in the chalet next door. We were basically employed as Redcoats, although as entertainers, we didn't have to wear the uniform. When we got there we were introduced to the entertainment manager who arranged for us to play in what they called the "Rock 'n' Roll Ballroom". But then he came back and said, "You're not right for the ballroom. We'll put you in the pub." The next night the same thing happened. He said he was moving us to the Hawaiian Bar. On the first day he admitted he'd been wrong and put us back in the ballroom. So we went to the Rock 'n' Roll Ballroom where there was a rock 'n' roll band headed up by Vic Flick, later to become guitarist in The John Barry Seven and to play on the original James Bond theme tune, with Les Reed (later to write "Delilah" for Tom Jones) on piano. We had a ball. We had finally found our niche and were playing to people who wanted to hear rock 'n' roll.

Vic Flick (guitarist)

I had formed a band with my brother which we called The Vic Alan Quintet and we were auditioned by Eric Winstone, who was in charge of all the music for Billy Butlin. We were hired and put on in the Rock and Calypso Ballroom at Clacton which was above the South Seas Coffee Bar. We were like a five-piece rock 'n' roll band, and when we were playing I would notice a couple of kids who would come up to the side of the stand and stare at me. I then found out that they were Cliff and Sammy Samwell who were playing beneath us in the South Seas Coffee Bar.

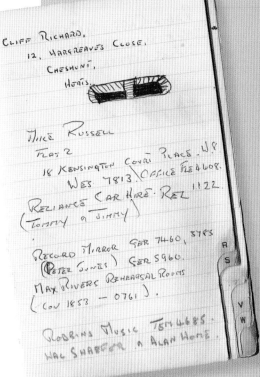

ABOVE
The address book of manager John Foster, showing his entry for Cliff and also for Max Rivers' Rehearsal Rooms in Covent Garden, the location of Cliff's audition for Jack Good

RIGHT
Cliff with fellow Butlins entertainer Henri Rouah, an acrobat and sportsman who helped out at the swimming pool at Clacton

Les Reed (pianist)

They were great guys, but in those days Cliff was rather shy and he didn't socialize a lot. But, always the gentleman, he was good to the young fans who came to holiday at Butlins and who clearly adored him.

Ian "Sammy" Samwell

The gigs were fun to do, and I personally would have liked to have done more. We did something each lunchtime and then again in the evening. The evening show would be in the ballroom or as one of many acts at the theatre. It was while we were there that Stan Edwards, one of the Redcoats, made a recording of us in concert.

Stan Edwards (Butlins Redcoat)

Cliff was easy to get to know in those days. He was a very nice, level-headed guy. I was a Redcoat entertainer and I was doing a Danny Kaye-type routine in a cabaret situation. In the middle of week we did one main show called "The Redcoat Show" in which all the entertainers from around the camp did a little bit. So Cliff was in that and that was how I got to know him. During the peak season you had to repeat every show three times because the entertainment was all built around the meal sittings. It was no problem in the theatre settings, but it was difficult in the bars and that's where they put Cliff in the first place.

Henri Rouah (Butlins Redcoat)

I was in charge of the swimming pool at Clacton and I also did an acrobatic act as part of my Redcoat show. Cliff was so enthusiastic. It was unbelievable. I took to him straight away. The were one or two people who were trying to put him down behind his back, and someone said he should come and talk to me. I told him, "Cliff, you've got no worries. You've got a great group and you'll go a long way." I could see it immediately.

Tulah Tuke (Butlins Redcoat)

I played an acetate copy of "Move It" over the camp's radio. There were between 50 and 70 speakers around the camp and we did programmes sponsored by the various major record companies. This would have been on the programme sponsored by Columbia and I would have said something like, "This is a new record on the Columbia label and it's by someone you can go and see in person playing with his group."

John Foster

We were sent a pre-release copy of "Move It" and we asked Radio Butlin to play it. They did and it became well-known around the camp. The first plug ever was on Radio Luxembourg, on a late show, and it was the first time that they'd heard themselves on radio. It was unbelievable. They may have played "Schoolboy Crush" as well but I definitely remember "Move It".

BELOW
Cliff during an afternoon rehearsal at Butlins Holiday Camp, Clacton, August 1958. Helping him out on backing vocals are (left to right) John Foster, unknown, "Sammy" Samwell and Henri Rouah

Joan Bosse (fan from Butlins)

There were four of us girls, two from Birmingham and two from Coventry, and we used to hang around with Cliff and his crowd. We'd go to the café in the morning, watch them rehearse in the afternoons and then see them play in the evenings. I remember he was wearing a chain around his wrist and he broke it so he gave each of us a link and told us if we ever wanted to visit him backstage all we would have to do is show this link. Well, I've still got the link but I've never used it.

BELOW
Cliff at Butlins wearing his Redcoat entertainer's uniform. This photo was taken by a young female fan from the Midlands, Joan Bosse

Stan Edwards

Cliff only seemed to know about 10 songs when he was at Clacton. The Vic Alan Quintet could play anything you asked them to but Cliff was very limited in those days.

Vic Flick

Cliff was considered "too loud" for the South Seas Coffee Bar, which was where a lot of the older holidaymakers went to relax, so they put him in the Pig and Whistle, a huge pub that was full of waitresses running everywhere with drinks on trays. I used to see Cliff in the indoor swimming-pool area where he'd get his guitar out and practise. He used to like it because of the echo. The girls used to come in and swoon over him.

Jan Vane

I managed to take a week off to go down to Butlins. We had a lot of fun that week. Cliff was still very boyish at this time. He was just a local lad and until this time he had always been at home with his mum. I suppose he wasn't really sure how to handle things. He wasn't quite sure why these girls were following him. There were times when he'd come by the chalet I was sharing with my sister and he would say, "Quick! Can I come in? There are girls after me."

Henri Rouah

Me and some friends did backing vocals for him when he took part in "The Redcoat Show" and it brought the house down! This show was the highlight because all the campers would get to know the Redcoats throughout the week and then they'd see them performing on stage.

Derek Johnson (*New Musical Express* journalist)

I did a bit of management work for the band leader Eric Winstone and he had the resident dance band at Butlins at the time. He took me down to Clacton and said that there was this guy there with a rock 'n' roll group who was in need of a manager. He wanted me to take a look at him. I saw him play but at the time there were so many other rock 'n' rollers coming up that I dismissed him as just another one of the crowd. That puts me in much the same category as Dick Rowe, the A&R man from Decca who turned down The Beatles.

Mrs Foster

When they went to Butlins they didn't have a penny, so John's dad used to go down every weekend and take them out for a good meal.

Les Reed

Within a few weeks, Cliff's contract with Butlins was terminated and The Drifters were replaced for the rest of the season by two very soft guitar players. There were a lot of red faces at Butlins when "Move It" became such a big hit. I think they were reflecting on what could have been if Cliff and The Drifters hadn't been deemed too loud.

BELOW
"Sammy" Samwell, Cliff and Terry Smart outside one of the chalets at Butlins, Clacton. It was the first time Cliff had ever slept away from home for longer than one night

John Foster

We came back to Cheshunt from Clacton, and the first thing that happened was that I got a message to contact the promoter Arthur Howes. I rang back and spoke to a guy at the office who offered us a spot on an upcoming tour topped by The Kalin Twins who had just had a hit with "When".

Established 1958 1958–60

In 1958 British television viewers only had access to two channels, both of which were in black-and-white. There was the licence-funded BBC and the commercially funded ITV. The high interest in the relatively new medium and the lack of choice meant that television shows had an incredibly powerful impact. A single appearance could introduce an act to a sizeable proportion of the population.

It was Cliff's appearances on Jack Good's "Oh Boy!" that made him a star. The prime-time exposure on the innovative rock 'n' roll show pushed "Move It", his first single, into the charts. Good was also responsible for creating his early image, tutoring him in the art of the moody look and giving him advice on clothing and hairstyles.

Cliff's first UK tour in 1958 was as a support act to The Kalin Twins, an act that had recently had a chart hit with the single "When", but it soon became obvious that the fans wanted to see the teenager from Cheshunt rather than the older (and chubbier) Americans. Hank Marvin and Bruce Welch had been recruited to The Drifters to beef up the sound, and while on the tour they were joined by bass player Jet Harris. The next year, drummer Terry Smart was replaced by Tony Meehan and the group name was changed to The Shadows to avoid confusion with the American group, The Drifters.

In 1959, Cliff acted in two films – *Serious Charge* and *Expresso Bongo* – and it was a song written by Lionel Bart for *Serious Charge* that cemented his success. His three singles after "Move It" were hits, but the impact was lessening. It was a re-recorded version of "Living Doll" that showed that he could do more than rock 'n' roll. It became his first number one and sold almost two million copies.

Cliff believed that the secret of longevity was to appeal not just to the young but to their parents, and he developed a sound and look that had just enough rock 'n' roll to excite the youngsters and just enough easy listening to win over the middle-aged. He would do "Oh Boy!", but he would also do pantomime; he would sing R&B-influenced material, but also record ballads; he would wear pink jackets but also don tuxedos. Before the arrival of The Beatles there was no reason to believe that anyone could make a career out of rock 'n' roll alone.

Jack Good (Producer, "Oh Boy!")

Cliff's first-ever TV appearance was on "Oh Boy!", September 13, 1958, where he sang "Move It" and "Don't Bug Me, Baby". Because it was a live show, everything had to be very carefully rehearsed. It was the most difficult thing I'd ever had to do because I had to take the songs apart and go over them bit by bit to discover what we could make them mean. Then, having got the details, I had to put them back together again. I knew what I wasn't going to do and then I had to think about what Cliff was going to mean to the public. There was a good deal of pacing around afterwards and thinking, "I can do something wonderful with this kid." We must have started work at least two weeks before the show in a room attached to a pub in Islington. It was very hard for Cliff because it was like nothing that he had ever experienced before but he was very receptive. He didn't laugh the whole thing off or mess around. He was very shy, of course, and I remember that we never rehearsed with anyone else present because if anyone else was around he would just clam up. There were some rooms downstairs where it was possible for us to be alone. That's where I would work with Cliff. Upstairs was a bit noisy. The trouble was, Cliff soon became terribly popular and there was very little time for rehearsals.

Cliff

In the very early days, my image was of someone who never smiled and who was a bit moody. The girls screamed, so I went for that. I loved it. What no one at the time knew was that the only reason I didn't smile was that I had one tooth that was smaller than all the others. It looked like a tiny fang. Under strong lighting it looked like a gap, so I didn't smile to save the tooth from showing. When I filmed *The Young Ones*, I had it capped.

Maggie Stredder (Vernons Girls)

When we first saw Cliff at the rehearsals for "Oh Boy!" we just thought, "Look at this poor little boy!" We thought he was lovely. He was just so thrilled to be there. The Vernons Girls stayed at a hotel in Maida Vale called The Colonnade and we christened it "Heartbreak Hotel" because so many of the girls were falling in love. Jean fell in love with Jerry Keller. Joyce fell in love with Marty Wilde. Cliff always kept himself to himself on those days.

BELOW
Cliff's irregular teeth are noticeable in this 1958 photograph. Because of them, he avoided smiling too much, and this led to him being described as "moody" in early press reports

BELOW
*Cliff with "Oh Boy!" regular Cherry Wainer,
who lived in an apartment near Marble Arch,
had her own car and took Cliff under her wing
as he entered show business*

Marty Wilde (rock 'n' roll star)

Jack Good played me an acetate copy of "Move It" in his room at the rehearsal studios. He asked me what I thought of it, without telling me who it was. I told him that I thought it was brilliant. I said it must be an American record but he told me it was British. I knew that he would be competition for me but the good thing about it was that we got on pretty well, so in the end it didn't matter. I was a different character and my appeal was slightly different. I think I appealed across the board – to both boys and girls – whereas Cliff's appeal was to girls. The only time I became really envious of him was when he came with his band. I had a band but I wasn't able to use them and that was ridiculously frustrating. Our mothers got on very well with each other as well. The only animosity came later on between my manager and Cliff's manager.

Rita Gillespie (Director, "Oh Boy!")

Cliff was a good kid. He was very amenable, he listened and he was easy to get along with. He was only 17 when he first came on the show and very inexperienced, so he wanted to be told what to do. I don't think he had any idea what a sex symbol he was becoming. He was too young to know what a sex symbol was. I got the impression that he wasn't aware of what was going on even though he could hear the kids screaming. The reaction puzzled him. I loved shooting him, though. He had the perfect face for television. You couldn't go wrong with close-ups of Cliff.

Muriel Young (TV presenter)

When Cliff started we weren't allowed to use him in our kids' programmes because he was doing the shaking hips bit. This was when I was doing a programme called "Tuesday Rendezvous" and he was doing "Oh Boy!". Our lady lawyer at Rediffusion said, "That boy is too suggestive. You can't use him on your programme."

Terry Smart (drummer)

The regulars on "Oh Boy!" became Cliff, Marty Wilde, Cherry
Wainer and Lord Rockingham's XI. I don't think Adam Faith
ever did "Oh Boy!". I can remember going along to the rehearsal
rooms and Cherry Wainer and the rest of the regulars were all
there. Jack sent us all off to get kitted out.

Jack Good

I must have seen a picture of Elvis or Ricky Nelson or one of
those American artists wearing a pink jacket and a black shirt
and I thought this would be good for Cliff. I think he got his
clothes from Cecil Gee's shop on Charing Cross Road, almost
opposite Foyles bookshop. All Lord Rockingham's XI had
their suits made-to-measure there.

Cliff

I decided I was going to be a bit outrageous and I bought
myself a pink jacket, black shirt, pink tie, luminous pink
socks and grey suede shoes. Why grey? Because Elvis had
sung about blue suede I didn't want to follow. So, I was
one of the original bad-taste dressers.

ABOVE
*Cliff's early stage uniform was a pink jacket and
tie, black shirt, black trousers, luminous socks
and shoes that were either two-tone leather or
grey suede*

Stan Edwards (Butlins Redcoat)

If we had been able to see "Oh Boy!" in colour it would have been great because
everyone in the studio was wearing really glaring clothes. Lord Rockingham's XI
would have pink band jackets and fluorescent colours. Great!

Jess Conrad (pop star and actor)

You have to remember that men couldn't even buy yellow socks in those days; there
were only black and grey ones. You couldn't buy anything outrageous. You couldn't
wear jewellery. We started the revolution here and we were American look-alikes.
We would look at the early films and copy the fashions. We wore our fathers' jackets
which were so big they looked like drapes on us. When you went to Manchester with
a suit made in London, the people up there had never seen anything like it. Going
up north was like visiting another planet. In those days, the West End of London
was a year ahead of Manchester, two years ahead of Newcastle and five years ahead
of Scotland. London was the Mecca, and London looked to America and the Left
Bank in Paris.

ABOVE
Cliff's chief competitor on "Oh Boy!" was Marty Wilde (right), managed by Larry Parnes. When, in a fit of pique, Parnes pulled Wilde out of the show, Cliff became its unchallenged star

Jack Good

With "Oh Boy!", I wanted to create a tremendous tension and excitement. I justified it in my mind by saying this was a form of catharsis as described by the Greeks, that the kids would let off steam in the theatre and then be all passive and peaceful on the streets. Absolute rubbish! It worked quite the other way. I should never have been let loose. I wasn't into pop music as such at the time. I fell in love with rock 'n' roll because it had this effect. It's a drug really, although I didn't realize it at the time. Everything had much more impact in those days because mine was the only programme on television doing it. People now just don't notice it. They don't feel any more. It would be impossible to produce the same feeling in someone today, unless they came from Mars.

Stan Edwards

I was amazed at the difference in the response of the girls at "Oh Boy!" compared to the response he had been getting in Butlins. I went to the Hackney Empire only a couple of months after Clacton and they were all screaming at him. I spoke to the caretaker and he was saying, "I hate these bloody things. I hate them." I said, "Why? Do they leave a lot of rubbish behind?" He said, "No. But there are a lot of wet seats." The girls used to wet themselves.

Cherry Wainer (musician)

Before Cliff came on the show, Bernice Redding was set to be the star but her manager, who was married to Winifred Attwell, didn't want her to do it because he had something which he thought was better. He pulled her out at the last minute. When Cliff came on the show he didn't even have his own transport, so I drove him everywhere. I was like a mother figure to him.

Josie Pollock (actress and model)

I shared a flat with Cherry Wainer in 1958. Cliff didn't have a telephone or a TV and so he used to come over to our place a lot. He was wonderful. He was just the sweetest person you could ever want to meet. He wasn't leery in any sort of way.

Franklyn Boyd (music publisher)

To cut a long story short, Cliff went on "Oh Boy!" and did "Move It". Two weeks later, the single came out with "Schoolboy Crush" as the A-side. The reaction was tremendous. All the girls were going into the record shops asking for "Move It". This then became the A-side. We flipped it over. The biggest thing that happened to his career at this point was indirect. Jack wanted Cliff to come back the next week and sing "Schoolboy Crush". Larry Parnes, who was Marty Wilde's manager, didn't think this was fair. He thought that Cliff was getting more attention than Marty, who was the compere of the show and its main star. Larry told Jack Good that if this went on he'd pull Marty out of the show. Jack told him to go ahead if that's what he wanted. This spat went on the front page of the *Daily Mirror* and it created an immediate star out of Cliff. Eventually Larry and Jack made up and Marty came back, but the damage was done. Cliff had got publicity in the national press that even having a number-one single wouldn't have got him.

Jack Good

I think the Cliff v. Marty thing was an important factor in his rise to fame. Cliff suddenly had the show to himself for several weeks. The other thing was that he had the publicity that went with it.

Marty Wilde

Larry was jealous. I think he thought that Cliff was getting too much time on the show. He wanted things his own way because he was looking after my interests. He took me off the show for a while. I think it was partially to do with Cliff and partly to do with internal politics. I think he basically wanted more of the artists he managed to be appearing on the show.

BELOW
The stars of "Oh Boy!" including The Dallas Boys (left), Cherry Wainer (front, in shorts), Billy Fury (back, third from right) and Cliff. Jack Good peers in at the top right

Cliff

"Oh Boy!" encapsulated the whole feel of the music. Anyone who dreamed of being a rock 'n' roll singer was able look at the "Oh Boy!" show and see what they could become. It had the fashion, the style and the music. It was really what rock 'n' roll was about. (1977)

ABOVE
Cliff with Vince Taylor, another performer from the 2 I's. Taylor's guitarist, Tony Sheridan, later to record with The Beatles in Hamburg, was originally targeted to join The Drifters

ABOVE
Hank Marvin. When Tony Sheridan missed an audition for The Drifters, the guitarist position was offered to Newcastle-born Hank

Mark Forster (promoter)

Arthur Howes was a big promoter, but he was living in Peterborough. I wouldn't say that he didn't know what was going on, but when he was offered a big American act to tour he would ask me who I thought would be good to put on with them. As I was based in London and quite involved with the 2 I's, I had my finger much more on the pulse. I was handling Vince Taylor and The Playboys, Rory Blackwell and Larry Page. Through Larry Parnes I'd handled Marty Wilde. So Arthur was offered The Kalin Twins and I told him about this new guy, Cliff Richard.

Hal Kalin (one-half of pop duo The Kalin Twins)

This was the first tour we'd been offered outside of America. We couldn't bring our 15-piece band with us because in those days the exchange of musicians between Britain and America was difficult. Our musical arrangements were sent over but they didn't arrive, so on the opening night we hadn't even rehearsed and so, deservedly, we got horrible reviews. In those days American entertainers felt that the British press was slightly against them anyway. Two or three days into the run we got the arrangements right and so we asked the press to come back but they didn't. For the tour of one-night appearances we were backed by Eddie Calvert and a trio called The Londonaires who were semi-jazz musicians. The problem was that our material was a little more rocking than this band could play.

John Foster

Mark Forster offered us The Kalin Twins tour for £200 a week which seemed like a fortune at that time. The Kalin Twins had had a number-one single with "When" and Eddie Calvert was to be the special guest star on the tour. The Most Brothers – Mickie Most and Alex Murray – would also be on. While we were at Butlins we'd used an extra guitarist, Ken Pavey, but when this tour offer came he didn't want to stay. He'd been offered a residency in a pub in Wood Green and said that he didn't want to lose out on what seemed like a secure job! With the tour a matter of weeks away, I went down the 2 I's to find this guitarist called Tony Sheridan who I'd been impressed by. As I waited for him, Hank Marvin walked in and someone told him that I was Cliff Richard's manager and looking for a guitarist. So Hank played me a few riffs. By late afternoon Sheridan still hadn't turned up, so I asked Hank if he'd like to come on tour. He told me that he was already on the tour playing for The Most Brothers, so I suggested that he double up. He said, "OK. But can I bring my mate? He plays rhythm guitar." His mate was Bruce Welch and so they both came down to Cheshunt a few days later and did a rehearsal with Sammy, Terry and Cliff.

Hank Marvin (guitarist)

Neither Bruce nor I were great shakes on musical theory. We picked everything up from records and tried to emulate things, but Bruce had a great sense of rhythm. He has a nice feel: a very dancing, rhythmic style.

Bruce Welch (guitarist and producer)

Nothing fazes Hank. His image is what he is. The only thing the public didn't see is that he's always later than he should be and has been driving everyone mad for 50 years.

Wally Whyton (musician)

I had a group called The Vipers and we played a lot at the 2 I's. Jet Harris was in the group, Hank Marvin was on guitar and Tony Meehan played drums. Bruce Welch wasn't in it. I split Bruce and Hank up because I didn't have room for the two of them. Cliff virtually took over what had been my band. I'd had enough of it by then. I'd had The Vipers as a skiffle group and then we'd gone electric and had a disastrous tour because our amplifiers blew up. At this point I thought I'd had enough of electric music so I went off to the South of France to busk. That's when the lads asked me if it was OK if they went out on tour with Cliff. He was going to be on the road for three weeks. I said, "Do exactly what you want."

BELOW
By the time The Drifters became The Shadows, they were, left to right, Hank Marvin (lead guitar), Bruce Welch (rhythm guitar), Tony Meehan (drums) and Terence "Jet" Harris (bass)

John Foster

Jet Harris was on the tour playing bass with The Most Brothers and he would keep bending my ear saying that he'd love to play with Cliff. So The Most Brothers had half of what would eventually become The Shadows and they did a really bad act in which they tried to sound like The Everly Brothers.

Mickie Most (one-half of the pop duo The Most Brothers)

In retrospect, I would admit that we were not very good, but on stage we were crowd-pleasers. We did very well in concert and on tour. We were like The Everly Brothers with bad harmonies. It was a case of good current popular songs, a good backing band and a lot of activity upfront by Alex Murray and me. It did alright; otherwise we wouldn't have worked more than once whereas we were together for a year-and-a-half.

Ritchie Howells (photographer)

I did all the initial photographs of Cliff, all his publicity shots. I caught him at Bedford on his first tour. He certainly had a magic touch, although he hadn't yet developed his mannerisms. He was swinging his hips a bit but not really letting himself go. His background had been quite rigid. His mother, in particular, watched everything that he did and I believe that created inhibitions.

Cliff

John Foster gave me the cross that I wore in the early days. He was wearing it when I first met him. I commented on it and he said he'd give it to me as soon as I was a star and he did. It had no religious significance for me whatever. It was on a short chain so it hung over whatever I was wearing. It was on the first publicity photographs I had taken. Eventually a fan pulled it off me. I didn't mind. It was quite a thrill really that people suddenly wanted bits of me.

Jet Harris (bass player)

Cliff came to me on that tour and said, "Excuse me. Are you Jet Harris?" I said, "Yes." He said, "Would you like to play bass for me?" Up until that point I had never seen anyone with a pink jacket and pink socks. I'd been around a lot longer than Cliff, Hank and Bruce. I'd spent half my time playing modern jazz in Soho. I played double bass with both Ronnie Scott and Tubby Hayes. I was touring with Tony Crombie and Wee Willie Harris while Cliff was still at school.

ABOVE
Although not a practising Christian at the time, Cliff always wore a crucifix around his neck. This one was given to him by John Foster, who promised it to him as soon as he became a star

Mickie Most

As "Move It" went up the charts, Cliff began to get more and more screams. I remember him being very nervous about the fans that would be waiting outside the theatre doors. He seemed to be someone who had spent his life hidden away. I imagined him as the sort of person who had spent his time locked in his bedroom listening to Elvis records and miming in the mirror.

Cliff

The mobbing started and I just loved it all, I must admit. It was wonderful being screamed at and torn at and the girls tearing their hair and bursting into tears. It was great because I was still so young. The chaps hated me but they all came to see Hank – the guy who looked like Buddy Holly and played like James Burton – so we had it both ways. (1987)

Ron King (bus driver)

In those days the stars, whenever possible, travelled with the rest of the show. The Kalins would have had their hotel found for them, but everyone else would have had to have found their own digs and pay for it. They would always take the cheapest place they could find or even sleep on the bus. The theatres used to keep lists of people who were prepared to offer bed and breakfast.

BELOW
The Kalin Twins (Herb left, Hal right), whose single "When" earned them a British tour on which Cliff was invited as a support act. By the time the tour ended, Cliff was the star

Hal Kalin

Cliff was such a hit he would tear the house down and the audience would have to go from that to "And now, ladies and gentlemen: The Kalin Twins!" and you'd hear a five-piece jazz band trying to outdo what The Drifters had just done. Our volume was only half what theirs had been. It was a constant battle. If my memory serves me right there was a shift during the last four or five dates where it was arranged to put Cliff on last because it wasn't working out with us. Our music was just not keeping up with the rock 'n' roll that preceded it. It was a nightmare for us. It didn't affect us on a personal level because we'd always got on well with Cliff, but we realized that we were getting a raw deal. We'd been brought over for very little money, were being used, couldn't bring over our own band and could in no way compete with an up-and-coming 17-year-old.

Ian "Sammy" Samwell (guitarist and songwriter)

I don't think we ever closed the show on that tour but we did change our slot because when the tour started The Kalin Twins had a number-one hit, but by the time we were halfway through, "Move It" was rising, although it never got to number one. Connie Francis hogged the number one spot with "Stupid Cupid".

Hal Kalin

For the first few concerts I thought Cliff was an Elvis impersonator and didn't have a hell of a lot of talent, because The Most Brothers were that type of act. They didn't have much musical ability, but they were exciting. I assumed Cliff must be one of those types. Then I realized that he could more than just sing. I had worked with Fabian in America, and Fabian couldn't sing a note but he was good-looking and young. He couldn't follow the beat. I soon realized that Cliff was not another Fabian. He knew how to sing and he had presence.

BELOW
Eddie Calvert, another EMI artist produced by Norrie Paramor, known as "The Man with the Golden Trumpet". He joined The Kalin Twins tour

Cliff

When the tour was booked I was still an unknown. "Move It" hadn't become a hit and I was given the slot right before The Kalin Twins came on. Then, at the start of the tour my record went to number two and The Kalins' hit started dropping. All of a sudden I was a star and The Kalin Twins couldn't follow me. They nagged me to change positions on the bill and, it's the most vicious thing I ever did, but I refused. It was a cruel thing to do, but it was too good for me to change because I was stealing the show. Night after night the girls screamed "We want Cliff! We want Cliff!" through The Kalin Twins' set. It must have been a nightmare for them but it was fantastic for me. (1985)

John Foster

It was when we came off that tour that Sammy left and we brought Jet in on bass. Then I think it was on the following tour that Terry Smart left and Tony Meehan joined on drums. I think Tony was playing with The Vipers at the time. Terry just realized that he wasn't competent enough.

Ian "Sammy" Samwell

It might well have been John Foster who had to break the news to me that Jet was taking my place. The tour was over and there was nothing in particular going on. I assume what happened was that they got Jet in for rehearsals that I wasn't a part of. I didn't come back for a few weeks – when I had another song written, I guess. Then it transpired that Jet was in the group. He really knew how to dress. He was moody. He dyed his hair blonde. He always had a cigarette in the corner of his mouth and it looked just right. It didn't look phoney.

Cliff

Sammy was our lead guitarist but obviously not very good. On our first tour he played bass, which was not his first instrument. When Jet sat in with us it made such a difference that we had to make a decision and say, well, it was OK using Sammy on this tour, but from now on it has to be all systems go. It's a hard decision to make.

Ian "Sammy" Samwell

Cliff was The Fonz and I was Ritchie Cunningham. He looked the part. I was the one who should never have been in it.

Hank Marvin

Jet was the first bass guitarist we'd ever come across. He could really play loud and strong. He had a concept of advanced chord sequences and how to play against them. He saw himself as a moody James Dean character and he liked to adopt this stance in his photos, and yet he was a bit of a mixture. He could be mean and moody and yet could also be a lot of fun. He could be quite nervy. He could face up to five or six lads who were twice as big as him.

BELOW

Jet Harris was playing bass for The Most Brothers on The Kalin Twins tour and gradually became part of The Drifters. His cool image added a "dangerous" edge to the group

Bruce Welch

Jet looked the part. He wore a suede suit, would sometimes have a monkey on his shoulder and played bass really well.

Ron King

Jet and Bruce were always at each other. Bruce couldn't stand Jet drinking like he did. Sam Curtis was the road manager of The Shadows, but he looked after Jet more than anyone else because the others didn't need looking after. Tony was the intellectual. Hank was very easygoing.

Terry Smart

After the tour with The Kalin Twins we had a few more bookings but I didn't think it would last. I had wanted to join the Merchant Navy when I left school but I wasn't old enough. I finally joined up in April 1959. I can't remember if I left Cliff before or after Christmas 1958. I recorded five numbers with Cliff and The Drifters, but I know that at least one of them was re-recorded with Tony Meehan on drums.

Tony Meehan (drummer)

I first saw Cliff play at the Metropolitan on Edgware Road. It was his first variety tour. I went along because I knew Hank, Bruce and Jet. They were complaining about how lousy their drummer was and they felt they couldn't handle it any longer. They were putting out feelers to see if I'd be interested. So I went to see them and I was impressed with what I saw. I thought Cliff was terrific. He really was hot at that time and I was stimulated. Terry Smart was a really nice guy, a sweetheart, but not a great player by any stretch of the imagination. It was a big wrench for Cliff when he left, but Cliff could be quite ruthless about getting on. He was very determined. He never put friendship before business.

ABOVE

Tony Meehan was a teenager when he replaced Terry Smart in The Drifters. From a large north London Catholic family, he studied theories of psychology when not beating the drums

Bruce Welch

Tony was a great drummer. He was a very precocious teenager. He was lazy inasmuch as he would miss calls, miss trains and not get out of bed. We would turn up at Tony's flat to drive to a gig in Newcastle and he'd still be in bed. He'd then get up and make himself a breakfast of fried eggs and bacon. For one so young, he was very deep.

Hank Marvin

Tony was the youngest in the group. He was a good drummer, played with a lot of feeling and was very composed and mature. I think he was trying to create the aura of someone older, but underneath he was a teenager trying to grow up. He was very eloquent and seemed well educated and yet by the age of 15 he was already playing drums professionally.

Franklyn Boyd

Jack Good was a stickler for making sure Cliff rehearsed every day. This meant that Sunday was the only time we could get him to do concerts, but Cliff was terrible on stage in those early days. The public liked him but he didn't really have an act. He didn't know how to take a bow. He didn't know how to make an entrance and exit. By this time Norrie Paramor had asked me to manage Cliff and Cliff had agreed.

However, I made it clear that I was a music publisher and wasn't going to give up my job to be a rock 'n' roll manager. I said that I was happy to advise him, travel with him and look after him. I'd do everything I could, but at the same time I would keep my day job.

John Foster

I had always told Cliff that I didn't want a contract between us because I trusted him. We were going to be together forever. When he became successful his parents quite rightly said that I didn't know anything about business. They approached Norrie, who spoke to Franklyn Boyd and asked him to run the business side of Cliff's career. So Franklyn became Cliff's business manager and I was hired as his personal manager for £12 a week. By that time we had moved to London and we were living in a three-bedroom flat in Marylebone High Street. None of us could drive. Franklyn booked Cliff in for two weeks at the Finsbury Park Empire but at the same time contracted him to act in the movie *Serious Charge*. The workload was really too much.

Cliff

I got my first movie within three months of the start of my career. They wanted an up-and-coming rock 'n' roll singer so I got the job because "Move It" was a hit and "Living Doll" was on the soundtrack, although not the version that became a hit single. (1995)

Andrew Ray (actor)

Serious Charge was originally a play, but it didn't have the character in it that Cliff eventually played in the film. That was written in. They may even have written the part in just for Cliff. I think all of us on the film were uncertain as to whether Cliff was just going to be a shooting star or whether he was really going to last. The director, Terence Young, was looking for someone who would act as a selling point. There were established actors in the film but I think they knew they needed a couple of good songs and a face that the teenagers could relate to. Cliff was a lovely fellow but on set he was very nervous about acting. He seemed to just want to get on with the songs. Because the subject of homosexuality was tackled in the film it was quite controversial at the time. The idea of a vicar being framed for molesting a teenager was hot stuff. It meant that the film was X-rated. I think it went out with the names of Anthony Quayle, Sarah Churchill and me above the titles and then beneath it said, "Introducing Cliff Richard as Curly".

ABOVE
Cliff's rise to fame was so quick that he was invited to write his first autobiography before he was even out of his teens

Terence Young (director)

It was a music publishing company that put Cliff's name forward. We need someone in *Serious Charge* who would appeal to a teenage audience. I went to a concert at the Chiswick Empire and was sold on him right away. The film took about 10 weeks to make and I think Cliff was on it for about three weeks. The picture looked a hell of a lot better than it cost. Then we needed a song and Lionel Bart was brought in to write something. He showed us about 10 songs.

Lionel Bart (songwriter and composer)

I wrote three songs that were used in the film – "Mad about You", "No Turning Back" and "Living Doll". When I was a boy there was a song around by The Mills Brothers that I always liked called "Paper Doll" – "I want to buy a paper doll that I can call my own/A doll that other fellows cannot steal/And all those flirty, flirty guys/With their flirty, flirty eyes/Will have to flirt with dollies that are real…" "Living Doll" had a similar sort of message.

Tony Meehan

We did the music for *Serious Charge*, but then we rearranged it for a Cliff EP. It was pretty ghastly in the film. "Living Doll" was frantic. We said, "Cliff. This is junk – it's rubbish," and he said, "I know, but I've got to record it." We hated it all so much that we completely changed it and out of that came "Living Doll", the hit single. It was my decision to slow it down and turn it into a country-and-western type of thing.

Bruce Welch

That record changed his whole career. It made him accessible to a much wider audience. I sort of arranged it because it had been a big band number.

Jack Good

That was awful, awful. It is still my least favourite song in the world. It was so twee, especially the lyric. No, actually the whole thing was twee. The tune was trite and the lyrics about

locking the girl up in a trunk so that she couldn't be stolen by "no big hunk" – what a sell out! I had the same feelings about "Living Doll" that I did about Elvis when he went into the army and appeared on TV with Frank Sinatra singing a Sinatra song. In those days rock 'n' roll was a religion for me, and these people were abandoning the faith.

Father John Oates (priest)

I was a young curate in Hackney Wick where there were about 2,500 young people between the ages of 14 and 21 out 25,000 inhabitants. What worried me was that we had a youth club of only 12 people. Cliff was on "Oh Boy!" at the time and I managed to get his phone number. I called him up and told him I was going to open a youth club called the 59 Club but that if I opened it alone, no one would pay attention but that if he came, everyone would notice. He came and it was a tremendous night. The place was packed and the next Thursday 450 teenagers turned up. It was chaos. It got the club underway and Cliff came back a number of times. Cliff at that time was terribly polite but he wasn't interested in religion.

Mark Wynter (singer and actor)

Some Fridays several of us would go to the 59 Club. Father Oates rode a Harley Davidson, was quite a character and was known to us as "Hip Vic", short for "hip vicar". The club was always packed out and aspiring pop singers such as myself and Vince Taylor would go along and perform a couple of songs each. Cliff occasionally sang there as well and as he was already an established star because of his appearances on "Oh Boy!", this was a very big deal. It was a time of great discovery and Cliff was without doubt the spearhead for the rest of us hopefuls. His confidence was formidable and without realizing it he was enormously encouraging to me as a boy of only 16. In the terminology of today, Cliff was "awesome", and we were certainly all in awe of him.

Franklyn Boyd

Everybody at the time thought I was overworking Cliff, and in a way I was, but I thought to myself that if he was as big as

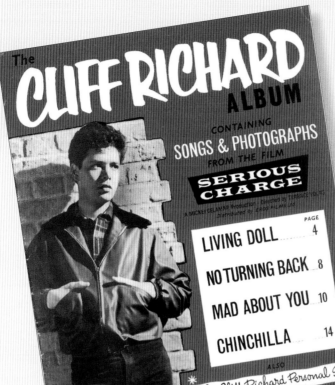

he was, he had to learn very quickly how to work on stage. He had been an overnight success and if you don't know how to carry yourself you can be gone in no time. That's why I got him the three-week stint at the Finsbury Park Empire. At night I could tell Cliff how to walk on stage, what to do after each number, and after a few nights we had the lighting correct and everything was moving. He used to do things with his hand behind his ear and wiggling his hips but by the third or fourth number no one was applauding any more because it no longer meant anything. So we had to tell him not to do it in this number but to do it in that number. We told him where to slow things down. We built up his act so that all the best numbers were at the end and the show had some form to it. Before that, there was no form.

ABOVE
Cliff riding a Lambretta in Chelsea with adviser Ray Mackender (centre) and friend Ron Ernstone

Ray Mackender (adviser and friend)

In January 1959, Cliff's dad was distressed at the way that Franklyn Boyd was handling Cliff. He hadn't minded the agent George Ganjou, but then Ganjou was ineffective and out of his depth. Franklyn Boyd was very actively involved in Cliff's career. It all came to a head when Cliff was filming *Serious Charge* at the same time as he was playing the Finsbury Park Empire. His health suffered. I was an underwriting member of Lloyds of London during the day and at night I was a rock 'n' roll DJ at Battersea Town Hall. I'd met Cliff in October 1958 at a party thrown by Cherry Wainer and the magician Channing Pollock. When Cliff's dad met me, I seemed like a godsend. Everything was happening too quickly for them and he confided in me that he was looking to get rid of Franklyn Boyd. His sole interest was in preserving Cliff's health, but he also imagined that he would be quite good himself at managing Cliff's career and he asked me to help him do so. I said that I would help, but impressed on him that it was a much bigger job than a part-time manager could handle. Eventually we had these meetings with Cliff's accountants in Fleet Street and it was decided that we really needed to bring someone full time in. That's when Tito Burns came into the picture.

Franklyn Boyd

I started to get problems from his father saying I was working him too hard, and eventually I got a letter from him saying that he no longer wanted me to manage him. I never had any quarrel with Cliff or his mother. It was his father who was a pain in the neck. I knew that Cliff was struggling a bit but I think he learned more in those three weeks at the Finsbury Park Empire than he would have learned in a year of weekend appearances. Everyone has to go through this phase. The old man was still working for Atlas Lighting but various managers were wining and dining him. I knew that Tito Burns was sending limousines to Cheshunt to bring Cliff's mother to the London shows. In other words, everyone was wooing the parents because they could see the dollar signs in Cliff. I made hardly any money out of Cliff. My main interest was in getting the songs out.

Cherry Wainer

I didn't tell Cliff to go with Tito but I did arrange a meeting between them at the Lotus House restaurant in Edgware Road. Cliff came with his mum and dad. They knew nothing about show business, bless their hearts. Cliff had become so big so soon and people were trying to get at him all the time. Everyone wanted him. I think he was grateful that it was happening but at the same time he was bothered. I was basically trying to take care of Cliff so that nobody did him any harm.

Tito Burns (manager)

Franklyn Boyd was dismissed because he was a publisher and paid to be a publisher. He didn't have time to manage Cliff. George Ganjou assumed I was taking over as agent and reported me to the Agency Association which we both belonged to for taking a member's client away. I had to tell them that I was not his agent, I was his manager. George kissed me and told me that he'd got the wrong end of the stick. I made sure George got his 10 per cent agency fee, but from then on he did nothing and was happy to do nothing. He just sat there and drew his 10 per cent. I did all the business because I knew the direction I wanted Cliff to go in, which was to establish him as a personality, a stayer, someone who meant something. I didn't want him to be known only as a rock 'n' roller with a couple of hits. I left the rock 'n' roll to Cliff and concentrated on the things that would consolidate him – things like television and the London Palladium.

Cliff

Unfortunately, I have to leave my teen audience but I hope they'll grow up with me. I will be 20 soon and the people who follow me are usually aged between 10 and 18. That is my audience at the moment. But as I grow, I'm hoping they will grow. If they change, well, I shall have to try and change with them, to sing the kind of music they like. Tito Burns once told me, "You can never try to make an audience like what you do. You must do what they like." You can't tell the audience that this is the right kind of stuff for them to like. (1960)

ABOVE
Driftin' with Cliff Richard *was ostensibly a memoir by Jet Harris, but was written by teenage poet and pop culture pundit Royston Ellis*

Ray Mackender

Cliff played for a week at the Chiswick Empire. On the Saturday evening someone in the circle threw a fire extinguisher into the stalls. Injuries resulted. Cliff was naturally very upset but he had to go after the show down to Croydon to play at a midnight charity event. We drove down together and picked up Alma Cogan on the way from her home in High Street Kensington.

Rita Thompson (injured fan)

I was living in Hammersmith at the time. This was when Teddy Boys were all over the place and they often rioted at concerts. The fire extinguisher they threw hit me on the head and I needed seven stitches in it. The incident was reported in the *Daily Mirror*.

Jan Vane (fan-club president)

I ran the fan club from my parents' home. We actually had to move to a larger house to accommodate the office. We moved into Romford where we had a large room, plus an extension. I married and had two children and was still working from home. We had to hire staff as it grew bigger. There were up to five or six of us. We had over 40,000 members and all letters got replied to. Can you imagine how long it took to type 40,000 names and addresses on sticky labels? There was no other way back then. When we first started we even had our own Gestetner printing machine and we used to type stencils and print our own. I think the membership fee was five shillings, and when they joined they got a badge, a membership card, a signed photo and a monthly newsletter.

Royston Ellis (journalist and poet)

Ray Mackender was gay but I don't think anyone knew what that was all about. He first got involved with Cliff's mother and she trusted him so a lot of fan mail that came for Cliff would be shunted off to Ray. I wrote a letter to Cliff saying that I wanted to meet him and so Ray wrote back and that's how I got to meet him.

Ray Mackender

In those days I had a flat at 6 Danvers Street in Chelsea and it became known as "The Shrine on the Second Floor" after the song of Cliff's. I have a visitors' book which I kept in those days and in February 1959, for instance, I had a party that was attended by Cliff, Vince Eager, Jess Conrad, Ian "Sammy" Samwell, Gerry Dorsey (later to become Englebert Humperdinck), Hank Marvin, Bruce Welch, Tony Meehan and the poet Royston Ellis. Royston was quite a character.

Jess Conrad

Ray Mackender ended up managing Mark Wynter. We would have morning coffee with Ray and take pictures along the Embankment. There was also this priest in the East End who used to invite us over on Friday nights and we'd have Coca Cola. We were these well-known people and yet we all did these innocent things. The fact of getting together was the main thing. None of us drank. We just liked meeting and playing records. That was the thing to do because our parents didn't like us to play records so we had to go somewhere where a group of us could play records together, talk and have coffee.

Mark Wynter

Every Sunday morning Ray would have these coffee mornings. The milkman used to leave about 22 pints of milk and Ray would invite all these up-and-coming people, including Cliff. People would just get up and sing with their guitars. It was all totally innocent – no drugs, no booze, very clean. That would go on from about 10 a.m. until 2 p.m. and then we'd all go our separate ways. Ray was a real personality. Everyone knew him. He managed my career up until 1967.

Ray Mackender

Norman Parkinson, the royal photographer, had a two hour session with Cliff at my flat. This was for an article in *Vogue* or *Queen*. It was quite a breakthrough.

Val Guest (director)

We searched for a long time to find someone for *Expresso Bongo*. Marty Wilde was our original choice. Then one day Tom Littlewood called me and asked me to come and see Cliff at the 2 I's. I saw him with The Drifters and was very taken by him. I asked to see him and he came with his mother. He was too young to sign a contract on his own. I told him what the picture was about. I remember him asking if his mates could be in it and that's how The Shadows got roles. Cliff was an absolute newcomer as far as film was concerned. He'd done *Serious Charge*, but that hadn't involved much acting. He used to ask me if he could come on the set just to watch on the days he wasn't working! He was friendly with everyone on the set, but I think he felt slightly out of his depth. It was all very strange and new to him. After all, he was playing the title role and it scared him a little in the beginning. He handled himself very well though. I never had any problems.

BELOW
Cliff with Mark Wynter, one of Ray Mackender's protégés, who later had a big hit with "Venus in Blue Jeans"

Wolf Mankowitz (screenwriter)

Expresso Bongo was initially written for the stage and was based on the impact of Tommy Steele on the pop market. This market was just becoming influential through the buying power of 14–15-year-old kids. The story was softened a bit for the film. The stage version was a lot sharper. I didn't have any particular singer in mind when I worked on the screenplay. We were making a film of a show that had already run for 18 months and we were late in getting it onto the screen. The question really was of finding a pop singer who could take a stab at it and who was cheap. The fact is that pop stardom is constructed on an absolutely simple archetype. I'm not saying that Cliff is simple but the archetype that he has assumed is simple. It's mother-loving, Jesus-loving and harmless. It's a very nice little package of a rather old fashioned type. Cliff had a mother who came to negotiate with us and did all the talking and that was it. I don't think he ever liked *Expresso Bongo* and he didn't like the part. Basically, it was too satirical and satire is not Cliff, is it?

Yolande Donlan (actress)

I saw Cliff on "Oh Boy!" when Val Guest was weighing up all these boys for the film role and he stood out as a super-sexy, super-young star. There was no comparison between him and the others who were under consideration. He was lovely to act with. He was completely inexperienced but so willing to learn. He was very sincere and hard-working.

Ray Mackender

When *Expresso Bongo* was being filmed at Shepperton, *Suddenly Last Summer* was being shot on the adjoining stage with Elizabeth Taylor, Montgomery Clift and Katherine Hepburn. I was extremely impressed to be in such company in the lunch commissary. Naturally Laurence Harvey, Yolande Donlan, Sylvia Sims and Cliff were there, too. Most days it was a choice of toad in the hole or the more inferior shepherd's pie. Not good!

Yolande Dolan

He knew exactly what to do when he kissed me in the film. It was a very gentle kiss. It wasn't one of those hot, throbbing kisses that they're doing now under the covers with bare bottoms.

Cliff

Expresso Bongo was all very tongue-in-cheek. It was a send-up of someone cynically using things like love of mother and religion to wring emotions from a crowd, when, in his personal life, he didn't get on with his mother at all.

BELOW
Expresso Bongo *was loosely based on the rise to fame of Tommy Steele and his image-moulding manager, Larry Parnes. Cliff played pop star Bongo Herbert*

"*Expresso Bongo*"

Souvenir Programme

Bruce Welch

We called ourselves The Shadows because we were always in the background. In 1958 and 1959 when you went to a theatre there was a spotlight and only one person could have it. So we were, literally, in the shadows. Jet, bless him, came up with the name. He and Hank had gone for a Lambretta ride to Ruislip and came back with it.

Hank Marvin

Tito Burns never managed The Shadows. He managed Cliff and Cliff employed the Shadows. As far as Tito was concerned, I think we were just a bunch of young scumbags. He probably hated the music anyway and would much rather have seen Cliff with a group of professional musicians. I don't think he really understood what we did or what was happening. That created a slightly difficult situation. There was certainly a period when we got more than an impression that he was trying to drive a wedge between us and Cliff. I think he wanted us out of the way. Fortunately we had a good relationship with Cliff. It wasn't like Cliff and four musicians; it was more like a five-piece band. We hung together. We were like five mates.

Tony Meehan

Tito tried to turn Cliff against us and turn him into his idea of an all-round entertainer. None of those people like Tito, and including Norrie Paramor, thought that rock 'n' roll was going to last and they wanted to get their last pound of flesh out of us and it really caused a lot of problems. Firstly, we weren't paid what we were worth. Cliff was getting £1,000 a week and we were getting £25. Secondly, the records were selling in the millions and we were just getting session fees. So there was a lot of stress that could have been avoided. What we were getting was good by the standards of most musicians, but I think we were worth a bit more.

Ray Mackender

I insured the musical equipment for Cliff and The Shadows at Lloyds through a firm called E. J. Walton. This was the start of what would go on to be a very large, lucrative form of insurance at Lloyds.

Cliff

I know it's a hackneyed phrase but I'd love to be an all-rounder. I don't think I could be an absolute all-rounder because then I'd need to be able to dance fantastically, sing like Bing Crosby and all that. But I would like to have a little dabble at everything if I can. That way I can find out what I'm best at and find out what the people would like me to be best at and then stick to it. (1962)

ABOVE
Photos of a bare-chested Cliff in bed were considered quite risqué at the time. Most men wore pyjamas – and didn't allow cameras into the bedroom!

ABOVE
Cliff was the first British pop star to invite fans to observe his intimate moments. Here, he takes an early morning wash

Ronnie Ernstone (friend)

I think what maintained my friendship with Cliff was our mutual interest in cars. I gave him driving lessons and then organized the purchase of his first car, a Sunbeam Alpine. I ordered one for me in "Calypso Red" but Cliff had his in grey. He was always very conservative like that. I was probably friendlier with Tony Meehan than Cliff and used to go out with The Shadows when they were on tour. The Shadows used to party pretty hard whereas Cliff was a bit removed. He did come to some parties but would never partake. At the time he had great power but he chose not to use it. I don't think it was a case of him choosing not to use it. He just didn't want it.

Tito Burns

From the moment I first knew Cliff women were of no interest to him.
I'm not saying that he was gay. I just don't think sex meant anything to him. He grew up surrounded by sisters and the mother was the dominant figure in his family. His father, I think, he feared. He showed respect towards him but I don't think he had respect for him. His mother was a sweet person. The father still thought of himself as lord of the manor.

Cliff

I've never felt like exploiting my position to go out with as many girls as I can. In fact, I've only ever dated one fan. Just once. I found out that the reaction from the other fans wasn't good so I just gave up altogether. (1960)

Franklyn Boyd

Cliff never had a rapport with women. His mother had always instilled into him what I think Elvis's mother had instilled it into Elvis, which was that if you get too involved with girls, your career is over. In other words, if you stay away from them you can have a long career. He thought the world of his mother but I don't think he liked his father at all. I know there was no love lost between Cliff and his father. When his father died he had the same sort of relationship with his mother that Elvis had: deep and strange.

Jimmy Tarbuck (comedian and entertainer)

I did all the sound checks on the tour after the one with The Kalin Twins and Cliff was very much a sex symbol. It was a wonderful way to pull birds – to tell them that they could come and meet Cliff. We all used to do that. Of course, Cliff was already gone by then! It was just Hank, Bruce, Jet, Tony and me!

Ronnie Ernstone

In 1959, Cliff and I went on holiday to Italy with a girl named Pam, who I met in a coffee shop in Kensington, and Tony Meehan. We drove there non-stop and it took us 36 hours. When we got there we mostly sunbathed, swam, listened to music and went out for meals.

Tony Meehan

Pam made a play for Cliff but he kept her at arm's length. It was back-off time! He was in the back of the car sitting next to her while I was navigating in the front and Ronnie was driving. She tried to snuggle up to him and that's when I really saw that he wasn't interested. He'd play with it. He'd flirt a little bit and pretend. It was a bit like those ghastly films they were making at the time with Bobby Darin and Sandra Dee. I remember thinking that he didn't have the same kind of masculine appetite for women that you normally have at that age.

Cliff

We were sitting out one evening and I was thirsty. Tony and Ronnie were drinking wine and they offered me some. At first I refused but then they told me how thirst-quenching it was. I believed them and took a glass. Whatever anyone tells you about wine quenching your thirst, don't you believe them. The more you drink, the more you want. Before I knew what happened I was tight. And was I ill! (1960)

Ronnie Ernstone

We drove there non-stop in 36 hours and on our way back I said to Tony, "Wouldn't it be good if we could find out where Elvis lives and perhaps get a meeting?" When we got to his home in Bad Nauheim we were all too frightened to knock on his door but in the end we voted that Cliff, who, after all, was the star, should do it. He walked up, knocked on the door and there was no reply. Then I think he made an enquiry at the house next door and they said he had left to travel about 30 minutes before. I think it would have been a memorable occasion if they'd met. We were all pretty hyped up at the thought of meeting Elvis Presley. Cliff was very disappointed.

Cliff

We located the street in Bad Nauheim pretty easily because everyone seemed to

BELOW
Cliff sports a striped, American-style sweater. Rock 'n' roll was seen as a pointer to a more exciting and hopeful future in postwar Britain

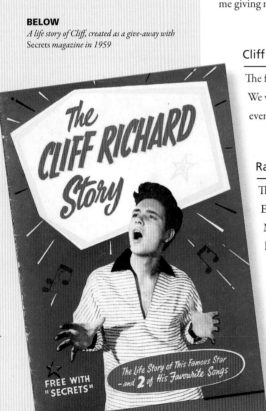

know where he lived. I remember there was graffiti on the wall outside. I think that when I knocked someone answered and told me that he wasn't there. I think he said he was on his way to Paris. I didn't leave a message because what was there to tell him? He wouldn't have known who I was.

John Foster

When I left Cliff it was actually quite nasty. Cliff, his dad and me were sitting in the flat one night. It must have been in late 1959. We seemed quite happy. We'd come off one tour and were set to go on another. Cliff's father asked Cliff if he was hungry and Cliff said he hadn't eaten so the father had a go at me saying that I should have made sure Cliff was well fed. I said I was happy to go and buy food for him but I wasn't going to put a bib on him and stick the food down his throat because he was a big boy now. This started a big row between the father and me and we said a lot of nasty things to each other, some of which were true and some of which weren't. Cliff walked out. We went off on tour and when I came back there was a letter waiting for me giving me two weeks' notice.

Cliff

The first pantomime we did was *Babes in the Wood* at The Globe in Stockton. We were just there as the musical interlude. We were written into it. I don't even remember having a proper role.

Ray Mackender

That Christmas Mark Wynter was appearing in *Aladdin* at the Glasgow Empire. Cliff's mum, my sister Rita and I decided to spend Christmas with Mark, and Cliff drove up from Stockton to join us. We stayed in a guest house near Paisley. On Christmas morning we all went to church and then to the matinee of *Aladdin*. We also managed to fit in a tour of the Trossachs. Cliff went back to Stockton early on Boxing Day.

Diana Ward (dancer)

I went to a party with Hank after one of the pantomime performances and Cliff was there. All the girls wanted to dance with him and Cliff would say, "No. I'm queer." He actually said that! But wherever I went with Hank, Cliff would be there. Whenever we moved, he moved.

When I said I'd like to go home he jumped up and said, "Did you hear that? She's ready to go home now." So we had to go in Cliff's car. I knew he liked me. I said, "I suppose I'll have to sit on your knee, will I?" Secretly I was pleased. The next night he was following me even more and then started asking if he could take me out. I was being cautious because I'd recently been hurt by another big star. On the last night he came to the dressing room where I was scantily clad. I was as embarrassed as he was and as I walked off he said, "You're not going to walk off without saying goodbye, are you?" I said, "No," and he said, "Promise you'll come and see me if you're ever in the same town as me?" That was it. I didn't hear from him at all while he was in America.

Tito Burns

Irving Feld promoted the first US tour that Cliff was on. It was a bill with Frankie Avalon, Freddie Cannon, Clyde McPhatter, The Isley Brothers, The Crests, The Clovers, Sammy Turner and Johnny and the Hurricanes. It was either Frankie Avalon or Bobby Rydell who headlined. Cliff was billed at "England's Number 1 Singing Sensation". I think he did four numbers halfway through the evening. I went for the first couple of weeks and then came back in order to take his parents out.

Ian "Sammy" Samwell

I went out as an unofficial manager for The Shadows. A tour like that couldn't happen today. A lot of the acts only did three or four numbers and on some dates there were three shows. After the last show had ended we'd get back onto a bus, travel through the night and then stay in a hotel. The number of shows that were played and the distances between them meant that there wasn't an awful lot of spare time. My most lasting impression of America came when we flew into New York. There were two limousines at the kerb to pick us up: one white and one black. There was a police motorcycle escort. They roared alongside us up the ramp and on the freeway and left us. This was at night and out of the fog there was a distant red glow which came closer and then resolved into three letters which told me more about America than I'd known before. It said "EAT".

Tony Meehan

I got close to Frankie Avalon. We became great friends

BELOW
Cliff and Ian "Sammy" Samwell (top) with Freddie Cannon (kneeling) who was one of the headliners on Cliff's first American tour in 1960

and I used to hang out with him. I don't remember Cliff being particularly friendly with any of the American artists. It was quite an overwhelming position to be in because he was at the bottom of the bill and yet he was a huge star in Britain. All credit is due to him, though, that he wouldn't go without having The Shadows with him. I don't know how he swung that because Tito was always trying to get him to work on his own.

Hank Marvin

We felt incredible to be in America. We expected to see musicians on every corner playing the blues! We were going to this place we had seen in the movies where people drive huge cars and lived in houses on the beach. Of course, it was a bit of an eye-opener when we realized that not every American lived in a beach house!

Cliff

Everything we knew and related to was American, so that was why it was so exciting for us to go out there and tour. We stopped the show every single night. Every night Bobby Rydell, Clyde McPhatter and me and The Shadows would stop the show. It happened right from the first show. We went sightseeing and saw the Alamo when we were in San Antonio, Texas. When we were in Lubbock we saw Buddy Holly's family. They were all in tears because Hank looked so much like Buddy on stage and Buddy had been killed while on a tour the year before for the same promoter.

Hank Marvin

We met a couple of guys who had apparently done backing vocals on Buddy's records. Then Buddy Holly's father came in on the afternoon when we were doing the sound check and chatted with me for a few minutes. I think he was a bit taken aback because I had got my glasses for that tour and although my Stratocaster was red it looked fairly similar to Buddy's when I was standing on stage and I think it was a little bit spooky for those who'd known him.

Jet Harris

Elvis was in the army by now and so Cliff went on stage in a white suit, looked a bit Elvis-ish and stole the show.

Freddy Cannon (US pop star)

I can't remember anything about him. If I had something to say, either good or bad, I'd say it. But I've nothing. I know who Cliff Richard is but I just don't remember seeing him or meeting him. He didn't make an impression. I did so many of those tours. I was doing them with Eddie Cochran, Gene Vincent – everybody.

Bruce Welch

The tour was an eye-opener for us to be on a tour with top American acts who were playing 10,000-seater arenas. This was the country where rock 'n' roll music came from. We didn't get much time off, although we did get to see Bo Diddley and James Brown when we were in the South. We rushed out and saw them and rushed back. It was a different world in those days. Just flying on a plane was so unusual that it became a mind-boggling experience.

Ian "Sammy" Samwell

In New York I stayed at the Forest Hotel on 42nd Street close to the offices of the music publisher Hill and Range. It was there that I met the songwriters Doc Pomus and Mort Schuman and I was surprised that they were so much older than us. Then I met Sid Tepper and Roy Bennett who had written "Travellin' Light" for Cliff. I was surprised how many of these "old" guys were writing rock 'n' roll. I spent a lot of time in Jack Dempsey's restaurant on Broadway near Times Square.

Cliff

I got homesick for England. Perhaps I'm staid and old-fashioned – if you can be old fashioned at 20! We were in New York for three days doing nothing and I just rehearsed for a TV show. Then we started the touring. I just didn't seem to go with their way of life. I had to come back. I could never leave here and go and live somewhere else. It would be ridiculous. (1960)

Tito Burns

There wasn't much money for Cliff out of the American tour. He didn't lose. He was covered. The point of the exercise wasn't to make money but to try and establish him over there. We got him on "The Pat Boone Show". We did a TV show in Toronto. The thing was, there were too many singers like Cliff in America already. They didn't need another one.

BELOW
Cliff and his mother with his sisters Joan (left) and Jacqui. He never liked being away from home for long periods and played an almost fatherly role in the girls' lives

Cliff at the Movies 1960–64

It had always been Cliff's dream to make films because it was the career path established by Bing Crosby, Frank Sinatra and Elvis. His first two films he'd fallen into almost by accident, but by 1960 he was a major music star who filmmakers realized would get teenagers into the cinemas if he found the right vehicle.

With *The Young Ones* (1961), *Summer Holiday* (1963) and *Wonderful Life* (1964), a formula was found that allowed Cliff to be a purveyor of harmless good fun. The films captured a sense of youthfulness and adventure without ever verging on the rebellious or controversial. Overall they were a huge commercial success.

However, at the same time that Cliff was being filmed saving a youth club, touring Europe in a double-decker bus and frolicking in the sand dunes of the Canary Islands, new bands were emerging who would challenge Cliff's supremacy. For acts like The Beatles and The Rolling Stones, Cliff's music was too sweet and his image too nice. They favoured music that was more dirty and dangerous.

Cliff seemed unruffled by the revolution in the music industry, but he was bothered by unanswered questions in his own life. By the age of 24 he had achieved so many of his dreams. He was financially secure, had been able to buy his family a house and was at the top of his profession, and yet he sensed a void inside. He began to ask whether this was all there was to existence.

Tito Burns (manager)

I battled for a month to get him on at the Palladium. We had blood on the floor before we got it the way we wanted. Van Parnell controlled the Palladium. He was the governor of the Moss Empires. Leslie Grade had the booking for a six-month period, and the way it worked was that agents like Grade would make a deal with the theatre to put on a show and guarantee three number-one stars or whatever. My job was to make sure that Cliff got the correct percentage of what was on the table. Grade wanted to buy

Cliff for two years but I only wanted to go deal by deal. If I knew that the Palladium would get £1,000 a week I would be happy for Grade to give us £800, because I wanted the Palladium for Cliff. I wanted the Palladium more than I wanted Grade. I was trying to push Cliff to get the middle-of-the-road customers. Cliff knew it made sense. I told Norrie that he should do an album of standards with him. He eventually did this on television.

Cliff

Quite a lot of the older people will not like rock 'n' roll because it started off on the wrong foot. It was called "sexy" and the kids screamed and caused riots. But I got a letter recently from a woman who said, "You must understand that us older folk can't allow our emotions to let us shout and scream. We have to sit down and clap and smile and look and go, 'Tut, tut!' to the girl who's screaming in the next seat." But she went on to say that if she was younger she would probably scream as well. I felt very pleased because I like to know how I stand with the people who are older. They mean as much to me as the teenagers do. (1960)

Mike Conlin (tour manager)

By the time Cliff did the Palladium he had his own house in Winchmore Hill, which is in Enfield, northeast London, and I would stay there. We'd get up late every day, sunbathe in the garden and didn't have to leave home until late afternoon. We then used to drive into the West End of London, park at the Lex Garage and walk down Oxford Street. As long as we got to the theatre before the kids expected us to arrive, we'd be OK. Russ Conway was in the show along with Joan Regan, Des O'Connor, Billy Dainty, Edmund Hockridge and David Kossoff. The whole show was called *Stars in Your Eyes* and ran for six months.

Bruce Welch (guitarist and producer)

We played for 15 minutes. Cliff dressed up as Little Lord Fauntleroy, David Kossoff told his stories and Edmund Hockridge sang.

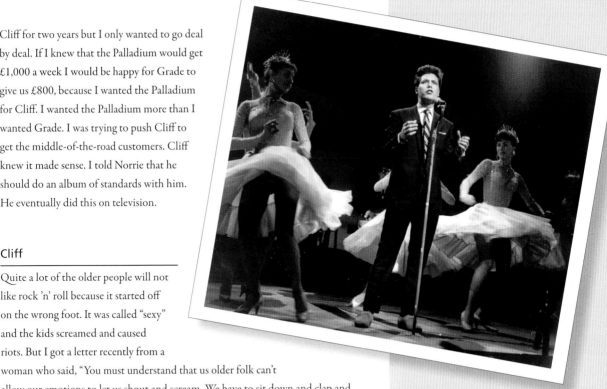

ABOVE
Cliff surrounded by dancers at the London Palladium in 1960. This residency confirmed his transition from overnight sensation to established star

BELOW
Stars in Your Eyes *allowed Cliff to perform rock 'n' roll, but also to sing ballads and take part in sketches to appeal to an older audience*

The famous **LONDON PALLADIUM**
"Stars in Your Eyes"
6.15 — 8.45
Opens FRIDAY, JUNE 3rd at 7.30 p.m
SUBSEQUENTLY
TWICE NIGHTLY
MATINEE SATURDAYS AT 2.40
(NO MATINEE SATURDAY, JUNE 4th)
Book Now for this "Show of Shows!"

David Kossoff (actor)

The show overran to such an extent that the director, Robert Nesbit, decided to cut the sketches that had been specifically written for me and just do 12 minutes at the end with Cliff. The audience thought the show was over, and then I'd turn up as Alf Larkin, the character I was playing in a hugely popular television comedy series called "The Larkins". This beer-drinking cockney would appear in the royal box, screaming abuse at Cliff and interfering with his finale. After that we sang a number together and did a soft-shoe routine.

Mike Conlin

It was while we were at the Palladium that The Shadows released "Apache", their first single, and Tito wouldn't allow the show to be changed to give them a spot on their own. It was bloody stupid because they had the number-one hit in the country and they couldn't play it.

Bruce Welch

Our success was all fluke. There was no master plan. We didn't have enough money for a master plan. What Hank created with his guitar style meant that every lead guitarist suddenly had glasses, even if they didn't need them. Although we'd been with Cliff since 1958, it wasn't until the summer of 1960 that we cracked it. From then on we became the first group where people knew the names of the individual members. Everyone knew that The Shadows were Hank, Bruce, Tony and Jet.

ABOVE
Cliff in his dressing room at the London Palladium with his tour manager, Mike Conlin, responsible for getting him to the show on time and ensuring all costumes were on hand

Hank Marvin (guitarist)

I wasn't aware that we were creating something different. Our aspiration had been to play music, and we admired people like Eddie Cochran, Buddy Holly and Gene Vincent, which was very un-British and un-European. Because we failed to emulate these people, a style developed that was slightly British. And people called it the "Shads" sound'.

Delia Wicks (dancer)

I was chosen by Robert Nesbit, the director of *Stars in Your Eyes*, to do this thing with Cliff. I remember all we dancers were lined up and he said, "I'll have that little girl on the end", which was me! I didn't know at this time that I was going to do this solo. I had to come on during this night sequence and kiss him and I think I was the only one who had ever kissed him like that and the girls would go absolutely berserk, especially during the Saturday matinees. They were all crazy for him.

Mike Conlin

Soho in those days was like a little village and the stories that spread in those days were that Cliff was having it off with Tony Meehan because Tony was so young and fresh-looking. Then they discovered that Tony was married to an incredible woman who was half Swedish and half black, so the idea of Tony being queer went out the door. Then it was Hank, but Hank was married so that went down. Then they thought it must be Jet, because Jet dyed his hair blonde, but Jet was known as one of the biggest ravers in town, so they decided it had to be Bruce. Then Bruce got married. Cliff certainly became a target for gays. He was recognized as being probably the biggest British sex symbol of the time and as there weren't any stories of him having it off with birds, the assumption was that he was gay. So gay men came along and tried to wheedle their way in to see if they could score. There were several closet queens in the press in those days, but Cliff didn't want them let in. Tom Driberg, the Labour MP for Barking, was well known to be a philandering homosexual and he used to come to the Palladium stage door on Saturday nights. Poor old George, the doorman, couldn't keep him out because he was a Member of Parliament. Driberg would come in half-drunk and try to get into the number-one dressing room to see Cliff. I used to meet him outside and say, "I'm sorry. Mr Richard is unavailable for interviews." If a reporter known to be gay came along to do an interview, Cliff would tip me the wink and I would stay in the room.

ABOVE
Cliff's rise to fame saw him pursued by the powerful and famous. Lord Boothby (centre), a Conservative politician, caused a scandal in the mid-sixties by partying with the gangster Ronnie Kray

Cliff

I got the shock of my life when I discovered that the painter David Hockney had made a picture about me. It was called *Boy Doll*. He did it in his student days. Apparently he was besotted with me and did this picture although I've never met him. It was just this image of a guy and instead of calling it "Living Doll", he called it *Boy Doll*. I find that really strange – really weird. None of us can control how other people feel.

Carol Costa (wife of Jet Harris)

I took my younger sister, Julie, who was 13, to see Cliff at the Chiswick Empire. I'd hardly heard of him. I was a staunch Tommy Steele fan at the time. We went with a friend of mine, a boy, and we sent Julie in to see the show while we had a drink at the bar. I was interested in the show. While we were there a chap asked me if I was going to watch. I thought he said his name was Jack Harris and that he worked there. He asked why I didn't come back the next night. I said that one night was enough. He invited me to come backstage and ask for him. It's only when I later stood in one of the doorways and saw Cliff on stage and saw Cliff with The Shadows that I realized the fellow I'd been talking to was in the group. The next night I took my sister along to meet him. That was the start of my relationship with Jet. The next year we got married. I was 17 years old.

ABOVE
Cliff (second left) talking to Jet Harris and his wife, Carol, formerly Carol Costa. Cliff began a short-lived affair with Costa in 1960 that remained secret for many years

Tony Meehan (drummer)

Carol dragged Cliff into it. She dominated him totally. Jet was starting to drink by then and he was a very weak man.

Carol Costa

Cliff was striking. Jet was lovely and Cliff was even lovelier. We used to go over to Cliff's house and Cliff used to be very friendly to me. It didn't make a lot of difference to me at the time because Jet and I were together, but then it became more obvious. It was just a crush. He had a crush on me and I had a crush on him. I think Jet was quite chuffed at the time that Cliff was paying me so much attention. Bruce used to get jealous because Cliff didn't take as much notice his wife, Ann. It was a high for Jet. I became pregnant six weeks after I got married and when I was seven months pregnant I was in a car crash. While I was in hospital with a fractured skull and broken ribs Jet started an affair with a dancer. After my son was born I found that he was seeing someone called Pauline from Sheffield and I called up and told him I was leaving. He tried to stop me and he and Cliff came over. I spoke to Jet alone in the lounge. I said, "How could you do this to me with a new baby?" He smacked me in the mouth. Cliff was in the kitchen so he didn't see it but he saw the blood afterwards. He took me and my son, Ricky, back to my mum's house. I got myself a job in a garage to keep myself.

Cliff

Some people can drink really well but Jet can't. His problems domestically and artistically were to do with drink. His problems with Carol were down to the fact that he was drunk most of the time. It bothered me that they weren't happy together.

Carol Costa

I was sharing a flat in Ealing with an actress called Vicky Marshall. One night we were both in our beds with rollers in our hair when there was a sound of stones being thrown at the window. Vicky looked out and said, "It's Cliff." She opened the door and he came in and bounded up the stairs. He'd spent the night at the flat before but we had never done anything sexual. This night we did. From then on we started writing passionate letters to each other saying how wonderful everything was and it was one of these letters that got opened by his mother.

BELOW
Cliff at a party in Hounslow with The Shadows and other friends. Carol Costa is to the left of Jet Harris at the back

Bruce Welch

Carol was like Brigitte Bardot in image: slim waist, large breasts and pouting lips. She was a 1959 darling. If she wanted somebody she got them, and she got Cliff. The fact that he was her husband's boss made no difference. You have to remember that Cliff was the most desirable person in pop music at the time. He was like Elvis.

Tony Meehan

I think Cliff felt quite guilty on the one hand, but on the other hand there was sexiness to it. The question now was, what are you going to do about it? Cliff asked me to call her. It was making a lot of demands on his [time] and the whole set-up. It came to the point of deciding between her and his career and he chose his career – quite wisely, I think. It had to be broken. There was no way it could be allowed to drift on.

Carol Costa

Tony called up and Vicky was absolutely disgusted because he said I couldn't talk to Cliff. It was awful. I was devastated. I said, "How can you be making love one day and breaking up the next?" He said the reason for not seeing me was because the whole thing could have killed his father.

Mike Conlin

It was all made much worse because his dad had been getting very ill. He was always a very quiet, thoughtful sort of man, but he'd become much more subdued. It was a long, hot summer that year and Cliff and I went through a phase of shooting at targets in the garden with air pistols and Cliff's dad would come out to watch us. He'd sit there in the hot sun and he'd joke and laugh with us but he wasn't really full of energy. At first I thought it was just the effect of the heat, but it was obviously more serious than that.

Cliff

My relationship with my father actually got better when he became ill, because he became helpless and I had to do everything for him. I had never done anything before. I suddenly became the head of the house. Not only was I the breadwinner but I had to mend the plugs. I had always been fearful of my father. He was a very dominant man.

Tito Burns

I had a dispute with the old man. He was getting ill and becoming quite edgy. The way he got out of the contract annoyed me. I had a clause written in that he could terminate in three months, although it also stipulated that there had to be specific reasons. He had no reasons. It was all engineered by Leslie Grade, who wanted control of him but felt I was in the way. Grade wanted him to make films and I said that was great but he already had a deal with Michael Delamore with an option that had to be taken up within two months. In the middle of these negotiations the old man came in smoking a big cigar and the only person who could have given him a big cigar was Leslie Grade. I think Grade was paying him money to make my severance pay. When the offer came to within what I would have got if I'd have stayed the full three years, I said, "OK."

Mike Conlin

When Peter Gormley showed up, everybody was impressed with how honest and straightforward he was and how hard he'd fought to get Frank Ifield off the ground.

Ray Mackender (adviser and friend)

Once Cliff's dad didn't like Tito, he gave him a very difficult time. He didn't think Tito was devoting enough time to him. Peter Gormley, of course, was the best manager any artist could ever have had and that was another lucky stroke for Cliff.

ABOVE
Cliff leaning on a radiogram with a couple of small bears sent to him by fans. His image, although sexy, was never as predatory as that of American stars such as Elvis or Jerry Lee Lewis

Mike Conlin

Cliff's dad was suddenly taken into hospital again and
it was downhill from then on. When he died, Cliff was
upset, but not disastrously so. I would say he was as upset
as anybody would be at losing a relative that was that
close. But his father was an old-fashioned man – very
much so. He was much older than Cliff's mother
and she was much more in tune with our generation.
She had a much broader interest in pop music, fan
letters and things like that. Her opinions were worth
listening to. His father was more of a Victorian
type. He was more like something out of Dickens
than someone on the ball in the sixties.

Cliff

I wasn't with my dad when he died. He'd been ill for some time and the local
doctor gave him tablets but didn't have him taken into hospital. We got really
worried one night. He could hardly get his breath and I called Leslie Grade and
said, "We need a specialist." He got his doctor to come down and within an hour,
my father was in an oxygen tent in an emergency ward. He survived that night, but
died shortly afterwards.

ABOVE
*A fan of the Everly Brothers, Cliff met them in
1960 when they passed through London. Years
later he performed with Phil Everly (right) and
recorded a duet with him*

BELOW
*Yet another publication devoted to Cliff. This
one, in 1960, was authored by Jack Sutter*

Mike Conlin

When he started, he was essentially a kid who had heard rock 'n' roll and had
been profoundly affected by it. When I first met him it was rock 'n' roll 24
hours a day. After his dad died, he began to think a bit more about life, both
the meaning of life and the direction his career should take. Rather than just
living for the day, he began to think that there must be more.

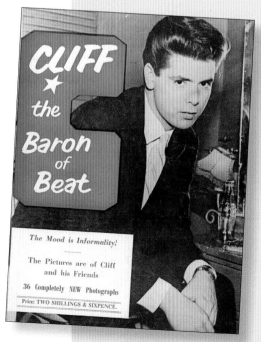

Jerry Lordan (musician and songwriter)

He didn't smoke and drink, he wasn't into girls and as a consequence
he led a bit of an unnatural life. What do you talk about to a guy like
that? He wasn't a very vivid person. It was difficult to get beneath the
surface. I remember one time when we were on tour together – I was in
a band backing everyone but Cliff – we were in Cannock and he was so
surrounded by fans that he had to be taken out through the skylight,
across the cinema roof to the next building, down through that building
and out through the back door. Imagine Cliff trying to get into a boozer
for a drink or to play a game of darts! He's never known that life.

Kenneth Harper (film producer)

I joined Leslie Grade in 1960 with a view to producing films. I saw Cliff in concert and thought we could make a musical with him. Jimmy Wallis at ABC looked into the whole thing and realized that Cliff was filling cinemas as a performer. I found a director called Sid Furie who had made a good short film I had been impressed with. Peter Myers I had enormous respect for. So I put a team together and then decided that the only thing we had to have was a tip-top American choreographer because I didn't think we had any great choreographers in the UK. I had seen the work of a fellow called Herb Ross and got him on board.

Ron Cass (screenwriter)

Peter Myers and I wrote the entire screenplay, the original story and the score for *The Young Ones*. We wrote all the production numbers. We weren't given a chance to write any of the pop numbers, though. They were brought in from New York. The inspiration for us was the great Hollywood musicals.

BELOW
Carole Gray, real name Diane Todd, was an unknown dancer from Rhodesia when she was invited to co-star with Cliff in The Young Ones

Kenneth Harper

We watched every old MGM film that Mickey Rooney had ever made. I don't see anything wrong in pinching from things that have already been as huge success. Most people have forgotten them anyway. Eventually we developed a not very original idea of a youth club.

Ron Cass

For *The Young Ones* we needed to manufacture some conflict in the story and came up with the conflict between father and son based on the alleged fact that young and old don't get on together. The film was meant to appeal to young people at the same time as appealing to a wider audience. It was a romantic story in the sense that in the end everybody loves everyone else – the youth club was going to be there and Hamilton Black was going to be alright.

Cliff

I made a vow never to make a movie because I thought they were so difficult to make and so easy to have a flop with. I didn't want to go down the Elvis route of making a couple of great movies followed by a whole string of duff ones. So, when I started *The Young Ones* it was almost under duress. Then, a couple of weeks into filming, I started to see the rushes and an excitement built up.

Kenneth Harper

Cliff wasn't and never pretended to be a great actor. He's not Olivier and therefore you had to disguise two things. One was the fact that he wasn't an actor and the other was that he wasn't a dancer. Therefore you had to surround him with people who could act and who could dance.

Cliff

I'm trying to break into films. With my first two films I literally just played myself; the second time because I wanted to. They had me play Cliff Richard under the name Bongo Herbert. But in *Serious Charge*, I didn't know how to act. I want to do it because only two years ago, when I was one of Elvis's staunchest fans and heard that he was doing a new film, I wanted him to be as good as he could be so that I could be proud of him. I'd now like to be able to do this for my fans. (1960)

ABOVE
The Young Ones *was Cliff's first film in colour and the first to be devised with him specifically in mind*

Delia Wicks

The year after the season at the Palladium, Cliff came to see me at my parents' home. He was performing at the Odeon, Leeds, and he called me to say he was coming over. I told my mother, "Cliff Richard's coming", and she didn't believe me. That's when it all started. I know he became very fond of me. He phoned me from Paris and brought me some perfume back. He just seemed to like to be with me. Then, in August 1961, while he was in Australia, he wrote to me and said that he'd had time to think things over and that I should find someone to marry. He said I deserved someone better. So that was it. I knew I just had to get on with my career. I'd been offered this job in Italy and I was going to tell Cliff about it but I never got the chance. I went into mourning for about two weeks and didn't speak to anyone. I wanted to tell the whole world that I had this letter but I realized that there was no point. He has never asked if I got the letter. He's never mentioned it since. I always felt that sending a letter was the coward's way. He was not really facing up to it. He obviously wanted to get involved but then got frightened and that was it.

ABOVE
Delia Wicks was a young dancer Cliff met while performing at the Palladium. They dated during 1961, when this photograph at Cliff's home in Winchmore Hill, London was taken

Tony Meehan

He's always belonged to his mother and, all things considered, she has been quite a forbidding creature. That must have set up a terrific barrier for him which I don't think he has ever grown out of. This is the classic diagnosis of male sexual dysfunction: either men who hate their mothers or men who love their mothers too much.

ABOVE
Cliff's relationship with his mother is seen by most as the key to his ambition – as well as to his enduring bachelorhood

BELOW
In Blackpool, summer, 1961. This was the period Cliff met dancer Jackie Irving: his first public date as a pop star

Delia Wicks

Cliff was saying that everything had become confused since his father died. I never really got to the bottom of it. When I last saw him I wanted to ask him, "Cliff, what happened? Did you ever find happiness?" It's so sad, really. He's had all this wonderful success but there's something lacking. He must go to bed at night and think, "Maybe I did the wrong thing. Maybe I should have got married."

Tony Meehan

I left The Shadows because we had a row. I was under a lot of stress and pressure one way or another. I got tired of the whole showbiz thing. I wanted to do something with my music and they were getting into what became the whole *Summer Holiday* trip. I didn't like that direction. Jet was thrown out around the same time. Drink was his downfall. He just screwed up. It was a difficult situation. When we first teamed up I was quite reluctant to work with him again. In fact, on the first single, "Diamonds", he played on it, but it took him two days to lay the track down.

Brian Bennett (drummer)

It wasn't the culmination of my career when I was asked to replace Tony Meehan in The Shadows. I'd already played with people like Eddie Cochran, Tommy Steele, Marty Wilde and Gene Vincent. I just treated it like a load of fun.

Brian "Licorice" Locking (bass player)

I took over after Jet left. My first gig really was flying out to Athens to be on the set of *Summer Holiday*. I came straight into the film.

Melvyn Hayes (actor)

The Young Ones was the biggest smash-hit British musical film ever and one of the reasons it was this successful was that it used a top American choreographer: Herb Ross. When we did *Summer Holiday* he was even stronger, and this time it used the director Peter Yates who went on to make *Bullit*.

Kenneth Harper

For the next film I thought we had to go much further afield and hit a higher target. That's when I thought of the idea of basing a screenplay on a summer holiday.

Ron Cass

Peter Myers and I thought that it would be wonderful to do a film on the Continent because we loved travelling, but we had to justify the idea of *The Young Ones* going abroad. I was sitting on a London bus one day and I thought how fantastic it would be to take one and convert it so that it had living quarters. That was it! It was born out of the necessity for Peter and me to have a bloody good summer holiday. Everything else grew from that.

Kenneth Harper

There was a boom in foreign travel at this time and that's why I suggested going to Greece. We got some cooperation from the Greeks, but not a lot because the country was going through a tricky time politically. We bought the buses very cheaply from London Transport and had a lot of help from them because their main depot for training and maintenance was near the studios in Elstree. That's where we did the opening number.

Lauri Peters (leading lady in *Summer Holiday*)

I had been in *The Sound of Music* on Broadway for two years and then signed a seven-year contract with Twentieth Century Fox and did *Mr Hobbes Takes a Vacation* when I was offered *Summer Holiday* by Herb Ross, who I'd worked with in the theatre. Fox let me out of the contract to do it, but things were complicated by the fact that I had just met and married the actor Jon Voight, and so there was a lot of soul searching before I decided to take off to Greece.

Mike Conlin

I think Lauri had been in a film with James Stewart and they thought she would be a name that would help open up the American market. I was never impressed with any of his leading ladies.

Cliff

They wanted a leading lady who could look boyish because the girl in the story is someone who is disguised as a boy.

BELOW
A part of a series of pop specials that would later feature an issue devoted to The Beatles

ABOVE
The idea of filming Cliff in exotic locations was inspired by the boom in foreign travel in the early sixties

BELOW
Actress Una Stubbs, personally chosen by Cliff to appear with him in Summer Holiday, *went on to become a close personal friend*

Una Stubbs (actress)

Lauri was newly married and very much in love. I hardly got to know her on the film. Like most people who've just fallen in love, she was wrapped up in that one person. She was nipping back and forwards from America to see him, and then he came over to see her and they just kept themselves to themselves. I think that when he'd gone and she was filming she was dreadfully homesick. She couldn't wait for it to finish.

Cliff

I was there when they auditioned for the girls' parts on *Summer Holiday*, and when Una Stubbs came to do her bit I looked at the director and made a sign in the shape of her haircut because I thought she was fantastic.

Una Stubbs

It was a wonderful film to do. I had spent years in the chorus, and although I'd done featured dancing on television it was so special to be able to make a film. I couldn't believe it really. To be working with someone like Cliff! He's such an exceptional person. It was also fun to be abroad because you didn't get abroad in those days unless you were wealthy. I had only ever been to Paris, and that was only for a weekend.

Kenneth Harper

We had tremendous problems with the Yugoslavs. In the film, the bus is held up at the frontier and the Yugoslav guards talk. They were actually Greeks, but we got some Yugoslavs into the dubbing theatre to make it authentic. God knows what they said, but when it came out the Yugoslav Embassy wanted it banned. They said, "This is an insult to Yugoslavia. Our guards would never say this." They objected to the shotgun wedding as well. They said, "We would never do this sort of thing." I explained that it was only a bit of fun. All of the actual filming was done in Athens. We never went beyond 15 miles outside the city.

Melvyn Hayes

They got me to dye my hair blonde because they said that in American films the sidekick is always blonde. It took five hours to do it and had to be done every 10 days. When we finished on *Summer Holiday* and all the rushes were cleared I went out immediately and had it all cut off and the rest of it coloured to take it back to my natural colour. Then I had a phone call saying, "We're putting a new song in. It's called 'Bachelor Boy'." There was no "Bachelor Boy" in the film as we'd shot it. They put us in a studio in front of another bus. There were The Shadows, Cliff and I dancing around this bus and I've got a blonde wig! There's a line in it where you see my lips move and say, "Bachelor Boy?" This was re-voiced because the actual line was "Talk about American dollies!" When the film came out, they had an enormous picture of me outside wearing this wig.

Kenneth Harper

Summer Holiday was a huge success. I said to Leslie Grade, "It's all about the summer. You must get it ready for the winter and let's pray for snow!" We were lucky. It snowed. Everybody was frozen and they went into the cinema and it was like having a summer holiday.

Lauri Peters

Cliff was very nice, decent and amusing. There was a wonderful atmosphere on the set.

Una Stubbs

He was just as natural as he always has been. He was sweet. He had no airs or graces.

ABOVE
Although Summer Holiday *was the story of a bus journey across Europe, it was all filmed in and around Athens*

Melvyn Hayes

When reporters asked me what Cliff was really like I would say, "He's a lovely guy. He's a hard worker and he's always willing to learn." One day I said to Cliff, "I'm always telling people you're a great guy. Why don't you ever tell people that I'm wonderful?" He said, "Because you're not." I said, "Right. Next time a journalist asks me that question, I'm really going to have a go." He said, "I know you will." One day this journalist calls me up to say she is collecting comments on Cliff. I said, "Right. Cliff Richard is the biggest bastard I've ever worked with. He upstages you constantly. He wants to be the star all the time. He's one big pain." There was a long pause. I said, "Surely that's what everyone else has said?" She said, "No. They've all been saying what a great guy he is." I said, "I just wanted to say the opposite one time."

Mike Conlin

The music-paper polls used to have Cliff as top British male vocalist and Elvis as top international male vocalist, with Cliff at number two. He never thought of The Beatles or The Rolling Stones as competition to what he was doing. His repertoire had expanded so much since 1958. He had learned from doing television, films and stage shows. He had learned to overcome that raw nervousness. He was no longer tied to rock 'n' roll.

Cliff

I liked The Beatles. I wasn't mad about The Rolling Stones. I always thought they were a slight rip-off of Chuck Berry and some of the old blues people and they never seemed to change. If people compare me to Mick Jagger and The Stones I'll always be the one to be put down, but I've been far more progressive musically than any of them.

ABOVE
Cliff was consistently voted Britain's top male vocalist by readers of New Musical Express. *Bruce Forsyth, whose career proved similarly enduring, handed him his award in 1960*

Hank Marvin

John Lennon told us that Brian Epstein took The Beatles to see us at the Liverpool Empire to see how a band should perform on stage compared to working in a Hamburg club. Then, when we first saw The Beatles in concert with Tommy Roe and Chris Montez, they were all wearing suits, the Vox amps were set up just like ours, with the drum kit at the back and the three guitarists in a line at the front, and when they finished, they all bowed together as we tried to do.

Jet Harris

Paul McCartney used to practise my stuff in front of the mirror. When I met Linda she said, "Oh, my God! I've heard all about you." Then Paul told me that he had learned how to do things by listening to my stuff. I took that as quite a compliment.

Mike Conlin

The night of the party they told us that when we played the Liverpool Empire John and Paul would be there greedily eyeing the two Gretsch guitars that the boys had on stands as spares. In the act they would play Fenders, but they had these Gretsch guitars for acoustics and The Beatles were so envious that they had such a choice.

Bruce Welch

We went to Paul McCartney's 21st birthday party. We were playing up in Blackpool and Paul met us in the doorway of the Liverpool Empire. That was the arranged meeting point. He was with Jane Asher. Then The Beatles came over to my place in Harrow after they'd played a concert in Lewisham in 1963. We were a big group and we had stranglehold on the group situation in Britain. George had written a tune in emulation of our style of music when he was in Hamburg and called it "Cry for a Shadow". John was more like me – cynical and not afraid to call a spade a spade. He could be very snide about Cliff because our whole image at the time was very establishment. It was tuxedos, *Summer Holiday*, "Bachelor Boy". John was very gritty.

BELOW
Cliff and Hank Marvin in front of a mixing desk at Abbey Road. Behind them are producer Norrie Paramor (left) and engineer Malcolm Addey (right)

Cliff

It was a party that Bruce had thrown and The Beatles were there. This was the first time that we had any inkling that we were in trouble, that these guys were really on the ball when it came to commercial hits. John picked up one of Bruce's guitars and played "From Me to You" in the kitchen. We all just looked at each other. We all knew. In our estimation it could not fail. Of course, we never met them again because they became so huge.

John Lennon (The Beatles)

We always hated [Cliff]. He was everything we hated in pop. But when we met him, we didn't mind him at all. He was very nice. Now when people ask us if he's a bit soft, we say no. We still hate his records but he's really nice. (1963)

Cliff

Apparently one of the reasons The Beatles went to play in Germany was because me and The Shadows had the UK market sewn up. It was hard for a band without an obvious lead singer to make an impact. So they went away and did their own thing and it was the best thing they could have done because they found something different. Something happened to them between 1961 and 1963 that turned them around. I guess it was the writing, really, because they wrote the most brilliant songs, played them in the way they played and just took off in such a way that none of us could think of catching up. The world's media kind of disregarded the rest of us after that. I must admit we felt left out for quite a while.

BELOW
Programme for Cliff's 16-week season in 1963, the first show at Blackpool's new ABC Theatre

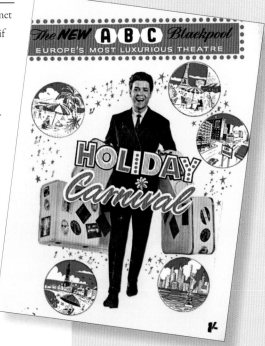

Brian Bennett

Cliff did his second tour of America late in 1962, right in the middle of the Cuban missile crisis. Sometimes the houses were half-full, sometimes less. When we hit Miami we played at a hotel on the beach and there must have only been 300 people there. There were fortifications on the beach and every other advert on television was for a fallout shelter. We were doing what they called in America at that time "cine-Variety". They would show a film – in our case *The Young Ones*, retitled *It's Wonderful to be Young* – and then the stars of the film would perform something from the film.

Mike Conlin

A lot of the religious interest started because of Licorice Locking, who was a Jehovah's Witness. Licorice was a bit of a nut. I'll never forget when we were flying to Spain; Franco was still the country's dictator and I discovered on the plane that Licorice had a case full of Jehovah's Witness literature, which I made him give to one of the air hostesses. He was a fanatic and he would go on about things. I'm sure he got Cliff thinking about there being more to life than rock 'n' roll. He got him to start questioning, to thinking that there is a deeper meaning to life than Coca Cola. I could see him evolving.

Brian "Licorice" Locking

It all started when we were doing *Summer Holiday* in Athens. That was my first gig, really. It was flying back from Athens that I sat next to Hank and he started asking me questions and it all took off from there. Every now and then in a dressing room he would bring out another little point, but I never pushed it at all. I just kept cool. Cliff was more distant. He was the boss.

Hank Marvin

Licorice was a great character with a sense of humour and we knew that he studied the Bible. We were all impressed with him because we felt that he actually practised what he preached. When we were all out roaring and raging, he wouldn't come. I remember people commenting, "That makes a nice change." At least he wasn't a hypocrite. We used to ask him questions and it sowed a new seed in my mind.

Brian "Licorice" Locking

I got the impression that Cliff was interested. He was searching for something to be committed to. It's difficult to work out what his motivation was. I never got that close to him. He was just a normal guy. Admittedly he was at the top in show business but he handled himself very well.

Vincent Bridgewater (Cliff's great-uncle)

My wife and I were approached by the Jehovah's Witnesses in around 1952, when we first moved to England. We later told our niece Dorothy about it and sent her books and magazines. Cliff later became interested, but then he got involved in a standard group that had the sort of teachings that go on in the rest of the church. It was talking about the Christian religion but it was a religion mixed up with a lot of other ideas and therefore it didn't stand for the true way.

Cliff

I thought this was it. I thought I had found the answer to all life's problems.

Hank Marvin

You don't have to be poor or sick or to have been a criminal to want to change your life and become a Christian. Often people think that is the case. But Jesus said a very interesting thing in Matthew chapter 5. He said, "Happy are those who are conscious of their spiritual need." In other words, a person who recognizes their spiritual hunger and who wants that hunger satisfied. Obviously Cliff realized that he had spiritual hunger. It came to me also. We filled the need in different ways.

BELOW
At the peak of his early career, Cliff experienced a sense of inner emptiness, which led him into an exploration of religion

Brian "Licorice" Locking

I don't think Cliff was totally convinced by what the Jehovah's Witnesses believed. He was in mid-air. I think he came to some JW meeting in Salisbury, Rhodesia, when we were out on tour. We did a show in there. Jackie Irving and Carole Gray from *The Young Ones* came out to do a dance routine in the show and I think Jackie came to one of the meetings.

Cliff

Of course I like women, and of course I've known what it's like to be in love. I've had a couple of false alarms. The first time was with Jackie Irving, later to marry Adam Faith. That lasted three years. (1977)

Tony Meehan

Jackie Irving was a real beauty. We met her in Blackpool when she was dancing in the show. It must have slowly started there, but I left The Shadows shortly afterwards. I think she was the first of many decorations for Cliff. I felt that Jackie was keener than he was but that she performed a certain function.

Brian Bennett

Jackie was lovely. She was attractive from the inside out. She wasn't just flashy. She wasn't arrogant in any way. There was a great warmth that flowed from her. I understood that she and Cliff were friends for some time. It wasn't like a passionate romance that started on a certain date and ended on a certain date. All his girlfriends have been just friends. As far as other people could see there has never been any great passion involved.

ABOVE
Cliff with Jackie Irving, his "steady date" for three years. A dancer from Blackpool, she married singer Adam Faith. This photograph was taken in South Africa in January 1963

Mike Conlin

The relationship with Jackie took off reasonably quickly. She was the apple of his eye. However, it never progressed beyond the holding-hands stage and this didn't exactly please Jackie. I would say that she got frustrated.

Olive Gregory (Cliff's maternal aunt)

I met Jackie at Winchmore Hill. She introduced herself to me and then I went in to speak to Dorothy and Dorothy said, "That girl you were talking to is fond of Cliff." I said, "Well, she's a nice-looking girl." She didn't tell me then that she wasn't keen. I only found out from other people. In fact, it was our mother who told me. I said to mother, "That's not very nice. Surely Cliff isn't going to be a mummy's boy and let her run his life." I don't believe in allowing sons to become mummy's boys.

Jackie Irving (dancer)

He is a wonderful person to be with – just like any ordinary boy. Sometimes we manage two or three dates a week, but usually it's only one. He's so busy. When we are out Cliff likes to eat steak and we just talk when we're together, mainly about serious subjects. He's very intelligent. Other times he takes me to parties after a show. We always dance together – twisting and jiving. Afterwards he takes me home and says goodnight on the doorstep. It's usually pretty late and he has to get back to his hotel. (1963)

Jet Harris

I went out with a dancer called Patsy who was a friend of Jackie's, and after Cliff had been going out with Jackie for about a year, she wrote to Patsy and said, "I don't know what to do. I've been going out with him all this time and he hasn't laid a finger on me."

Ray Mackender

That relationship was played up to seem to be much more than it was. It was hyped. There was a woman on the *Daily Express* and she pushed that story.

Cliff

I don't like to run around with more than one girl at a time. Jackie is the only one I am seeing now. But we are not planning marriage. We both know that all this talk about us getting engaged or married can harm me as far as my fans are concerned. (1963)

Tony Meehan

Cliff was timid with women. To be even-handed about it, Cliff had a romantic notion of sex and romance. It was like a schoolboy's view. As soon as he was confronted by the reality – *i.e.* a woman who menstruated and had to wash under her arms – the sexual side disappeared. As soon as he had to deliver anything, the forbidding was too strong. So, he was never able to make the leap from schoolboy to man.

Bruce Welch

With Cliff, it was never a case of trying to present a clean image. He *was* clean. There were no hidden women he went back home to at night or anything like that. There were no sex parties. There was no shit to find, basically.

ABOVE
John Rostill (far right) replaced "Licorice" Locking in The Shadows when Locking left to devote more of his time to his religion

RIGHT
Wonderful Life *was filmed on location in the Canary Islands, but bad weather affected continuity as the colour of the sand changed on a daily basis*

BELOW
A ticket for the world premiere of Wonderful Life *held at the Empire, Leicester Square, in July 1964*

ABOVE
Cliff was originally to have played a guardsman taken hostage in Mexico by bandits, but the script changed to fit the location and Cliff became a pop star making a movie in the Canary Islands

ROYAL WORLD
PREMIERE
in the presence of
HER ROYAL HIGHNESS
PRINCESS ALEXANDRA

in aid of the NATIONAL ASSOCIATION
OF YOUTH CLUBS Expansion Fund.

at the
EMPIRE LEICESTER SQUARE
Thursday July 2nd. at 8.15 p.m
DOORS OPEN 7.15 p.m.

ELSTREE DISTRIBUTORS Present AN IVY PRODUCTION

CLIFF RICHARD
WALTER SLEZAK
SUSAN HAMPSHIRE
THE SHADOWS IN.

Wonderful Life

Produced by KENNETH HARPER Directed by SIDNEY J. FURIE
TECHNICOLOR® TECHNISCOPE ● Released through WARNER-PATHE

TWO GNS.

TICKET HOLDERS ARE REQUESTED
TO TAKE THEIR SEATS BY 8 p.m.

STALLS   N   III

Cliff

It was all quite innocent. On the road, it was all just work, really. I used to hate beer and I had a very sweet tooth so wine and spirits were out of the question. As for drugs – well, I'm convinced that the reason I never got involved with drugs was that I never smoked cigarettes. I really didn't like smoking. I had an aversion to it when I was a child. If my father asked me to pass the ashtray I would get my sister to do it. I couldn't bear the smell of it and if I touched an ashtray I had to scrub my hands immediately. So, because I didn't smoke, I never got offered pot. (1987)

Mike Conlin

Wonderful Life was a disaster to film. We were stuck in the Canary Islands for six weeks because all the action was supposed to take place in a desert, but we couldn't get any continuity because it rained every second day and all the sand turned a different colour.

Kenneth Harper

Originally it was going to be set in Mexico, but the expense was prohibitive. So we went looking at various islands and went where the weather was good and finally ended up in the Canaries. We then changed the whole story.

Ron Cass

I didn't think it was that successful. There were a lot of reasons for that. One was that we broke the sequence. We didn't do it at the right time. We had made the others at a particular time of the year in order to get a Christmas release but Cliff went and did a summer season in Blackpool and it broke the rhythm. I didn't think the story-line was good, either. Originally it was going to be set in Mexico and Cliff was going to be a guardsman kidnapped by bandits. It was a very funny story. However, when we shifted the location we realized that we couldn't have Mexican bandits among the sand dunes of the Canaries, and so a completely different story had to be created.

Royston Ellis (poet and author)

I was asked to write a book about *Wonderful Life* being made. There was a scandal on set because the actor Dennis Price was totally drunk and incapable of filming, so he had to be flown back to England. I was eventually banned from the set because they got the impression that I'd been a bad influence on him. Cliff kept a bit of a distance from me. By this time I had become notorious because I had a TV programme called "Living for Kicks", where we would talk about teenagers having sex before marriage and that wasn't in keeping with Cliff's image. The book was never published.

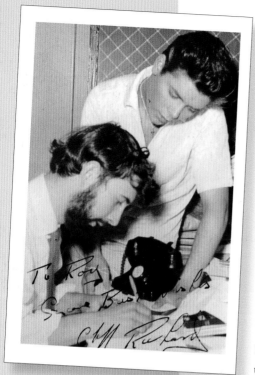

Mike Conlin

We started taking breaks in Portugal. Peter Gormley had a place down there and so did Norrie Paramor, Hank, Bruce and Cliff. That's when Albufeira was a tiny fishing village. He loved fishing at night, lying in the sun, listening to records and strumming his guitar. Cliff began to get to know the local people. There was a guy who was Portugal's water-skiing champion and his father owned a big boat. We went sailing on that a few times. There was a fellow from Mozambique and his girlfriend that we would hang out with.

Bruce Welch

I had a villa. So did Peter Gormley, Frank Ifield, Cliff and Leslie Grade. There were six houses in a strip. At the time Cliff was enormous. He was like Elvis. He couldn't walk down the street unrecognized. Muriel Young the DJ had a villa down there and she said if he was to get a place there he could walk around without ever being bothered. There was no airport at Faro in those days. You had to fly to Lisbon and then it was a five-hour drive. It seemed as though it was the other end of the earth. None of the Portuguese knew who we were. They didn't speak English. They'd never heard of Cliff.

Muriel Young (TV presenter)

When we built our house we were only the third English couple to be on the Algarve. A friend of mine was renting an old coast-guard house. The next English house was in Luz Bay, where a famous society photographer called Roy Narbutt had gone to live. The coast was utterly unspoiled and untouched by modern buildings.

Ray Mackender

Winchmore Hill was a modest house but much nicer than the house they'd had in Cheshunt. After Cliff's success in films he bought Rookswood, which was in Nazeing, Essex. I think that was bought in late 1963. I can remember being down there with Cliff, his mother and his Aunt Olive the day that Kennedy was assassinated. We were all devastated.

LEFT
*Cliff didn't headline in America until 1962.
The fans were eager on his arrival, but the
Cuban Missile Crisis kept them at home
once the tour hit the road*

Brian "Licorice" Locking

I left The Shadows because it was clashing with my desire to go into full-time
ministry. I loved both of them, but the music business requires dedication and I can't
be dedicated to two things. I had to make a decision. Another person in my position
might make another decision. Being a minister for the Jehovah Witnesses is not a
full-time position so I've done a lot of other jobs. I've been a window cleaner and a
cleaner in a mental hospital.

Cliff

After two or three years of success, I realized that having all these things did not
mean that I had the answers to life. I didn't have the answer to being happy, satisfied
and purpose-filled. This led ultimately to my Christian conversion. I started to look
into spiritual things. I found it very confusing that the one thing I'd always wanted
was actually not working for me.

Good News 1965–67

The religious quest that had started possibly as early as 1963 culminated in a conversion to Christianity and a very public admission of his faith at a Billy Graham meeting in London, during an event at Earl's Court Arena in 1966. At a time when pop culture was embracing drugs, sex and eastern religion, Cliff was standing up for the Ten Commandments and the Nicene Creed.

Not surprisingly, he became a figure of fun. Although never a tearaway and always polite, courteous and law-abiding, this new direction was obviously more profound and life-changing to Cliff than simply wanting to be a "decent bloke". It had, he said, given him stability and hope. It had reorganized his priorities.

For a while it seemed that he might even abandon his career. He felt that show business encouraged vanity and took people's attention away from the state of their souls. Briefly he considered becoming a schoolteacher until some Christian friends pointed out to him that his God-given gift was the ability to entertain rather than instruct.

As a result, Cliff continued his career but also recorded gospel songs, made appearances at church events and fundraised for Christian charities. He rapidly became Britain's best-known Christian layperson and was invited to share his thoughts on faith in books as well as on TV and radio. He was also recruited to endorse such moral campaigns as the enquiry into pornography headed by Mary Whitehouse and Lord Longford and the Nationwide Festival of Light.

In his corduroy jackets and black-rimmed spectacles, he now looked more like a theology student or a slightly cool curate than a hip-shaking rock 'n' roll star likely to make girls go weak at the knees. His new friends were from the worlds of education, accountancy, medicine, charity and the church, and he adopted a modest lifestyle. On behalf of the relief agency Tearfund he began to visit some of the poorer parts of the world.

Brian "Licorice" Locking (bass player)

What I didn't know at the time was that he had some other friends in the evangelical area. He obviously made his own mind up.

Ray Mackender (friend and adviser)

Bill Latham had a great influence in helping Cliff achieve faith.

Jay Norris (teacher)

I introduced Bill Latham to Cliff. I made them into friends because I thought it would be good for both of them. I thought they were two very nice chaps who had a lot to offer each other in terms of ideas, religious commitment and all sorts of things. I was specifically concerned at how involved Cliff was becoming with the Jehovah Witnesses, but when I put them together at a local car rally I just thought that they'd like each other as people. I'm a great machinator. Nothing happens with me that I don't want to happen.

Cliff

My views on religion [in 1963] are much stronger than they were. It's probably Licorice and his influence. As you know, he left to join the Jehovah Witness organization. I think everyone has to decide about this and it's an individual choice. But he brought to my mind that if you never held grudges, never argued, turned the other cheek, everything would be that much better. I tended to curse every now and again, swear a little bit and I've managed to stop completely. In fact I just don't swear. I think this helps people's lives. (1963)

BELOW
Cliff pictured outside Rookswood, his first large detached house, which was in the village of Nazeing, Essex

Bill Latham (mentor)

Jay Norris got stirred up when she heard that Cliff and the family were asking questions about the Jehovah Witnesses. She thought I might be able to help sort them out. I suppose it was a deliberate ploy that in July 1964 Cliff was assigned to my car in a rally that Jay organized. It never crossed my mind that there would be any development from this

meeting. I don't actually think we did a lot that day because there were a lot of other people around. The next time we met I think it was at Rookswood, his home in Essex, and it was just him and his mum and sisters. Then there was another meeting at Rookswood when I took Graham Disbrey, who was a fellow teacher at Cheshunt who I'd grown up with in Finchley.

BELOW
Cliff at home at Rookswood with his mother and sisters (left to right): Joan, Donna and Jacqui.

Cliff

I was reading and thinking and talking to people from lots of different denominations. Among the orthodox Christians that I spoke to were two masters at my old school: Bill Latham and Graham Disbrey. My youngest sister, Joan, was now a pupil there and since my father had died I'd become very parental towards her. It was on one of her open days that I went back to the school to discuss her work and met these two teachers. (1979)

Graham Disbrey (teacher)

I met Bill when I was about 13 through the Crusaders. The leader of the Crusader class was a man called Cecil Poulter and he was very astute. He recognized the talent that was in Bill and before he was 21 he had made him a helper and then a leader in the class. In our teens, Bill and I attended different Crusader camps, but when we became tent officers we would invariably end up at the same camps and would travel down in my car. We went to different churches, but Cecil Poulter had an open house on a Saturday night and Bill and I became regulars. I think there was a compulsory Bible study beforehand! At that age you have best friends, and I'm sure that Bill and I would have regarded one another as best friends.

Jay Norris

It didn't occur to me that they might not have much in common. I knew two chaps. I knew Cliff very well and I knew Bill very well and those were the two people I thought would get on well in a jolly way. I didn't think Cliff had a lot of ordinary, nice friends. He was stuck in the pop world where the people were quite often very second-rate and Bill had a lot of Christian friends. I actually thought that Bill had much more to offer Cliff [than he] had to offer Bill. Being a pop star can be very lonely and dull.

Graham Disbrey

I was at the car rally in 1964 and I think that after that we went back to Jay's home for refreshments and that's where the conversation really got going. By the end of the evening there were still 15 or 20 people left and there was some fairly interesting talking going on, but whether Bill ever spoke in any depth of spiritual matters that day I don't know. Cliff seemed quite on edge that evening, but Bill was a very easy guy to get on with. Bill was a very good and popular teacher. He'd worked as a journalist for a short time before he went into teaching and that meant that he was a very good communicator. The next time we met, at Cliff's home, he wanted to get straight into the Bible and we talked into the early hours.

Cliff

My conversion took years and it would probably take almost as long to describe it. I became very dissatisfied with things eight or nine years ago, during the heyday of my career, so I began to get serious-minded about a lot of other things, and religious topics kept coming up. I then followed this up and spoke to Jews. I talked to members of a sect called Jehovah's Witnesses, and finally met up with people who waved no other banner than that they were Christians, and for the first time encountered people who talked about Jesus in relevant terms. The Jesus they spoke about was very, very real and alive. (1973)

Graham Disbrey

I feel that Cliff had been going through a difficult time. Not in terms of success; he had obviously been doing extremely well in his career. But I had the feeling that there were not many people in his life that he could trust. He was actually quite lonely, despite the crowds around him. From what I had gathered there had been some unhappy sexual experience. He had also been taken advantage of financially. I felt that God had been active in his life, contriving a situation where he was open to Bill as a person and to the things we were sharing with him. He was in a world where everyone was making a great fuss of him and yet the youngsters in our Crusader group got used to him in two weeks flat and treated him just like everyone else. They were impressed with his cars and cameras but on a personal level they treated him very ordinarily and I think he revelled in that. He enjoyed being ordinary again.

ABOVE
Cliff with Hank Marvin at the London Palladium in Aladdin and His Lamp, *December 1964. The music was written by The Shadows*

BELOW
Cliff with 19-year-old Vivienne Ventura, his co-star in his 1966 film Finders Keepers

Bill Latham

Our discussions from the word go were very high-powered and with my pretty limited Crusader theology I found myself on thin ice in terms of answering questions on the divinity of Christ and all those red herrings. I thought I was floundering and needed to bring in people with more authority than I had. That came initially through Graham Disbrey but I then went to David Winter, who I had met at St Paul's Church in Finchley where we were both lay readers. David was editing *Crusade* magazine at the time and later went on to work at the BBC.

Graham Disbrey

It was after that meeting at Rookswood that the relationship really developed. Cliff was doing the pantomime *Aladdin and His Lamp* at the Palladium, and he'd leave and go straight to Bill's house in Finchley. He started to become disillusioned with Rookswood, even though it was a big house, and started to see Finchley as his home. I think he felt isolated in Essex. There was a big gap in his life after his dad died.

Cliff

My father's death was a great loss to my mother, and she began seeing Derek Bodkin who had worked as a driver for me. Although he was much younger than her, he seemed to be a stabilizing influence. It meant I felt free to leave home and make a life of my own. At that time we had quite a large house, and when my mother and my sisters left, there was nothing to keep me there. At the time I was making *Finders Keepers* at Pinewood and it used to take me an hour and a half to drive there. Bill Latham lived much closer to the studios and offered to put me up while I was filming. I accepted. I stayed with him and his mother, Mamie, for six weeks. It so happened that they were about to move and so I suggested that we move together because we all got on so well. They agreed and we found a nice house in Totteridge, north London. Bill's mother virtually adopted me. It was like having a second mother. (1976)

Graham Disbrey

Cliff began to get integrated into all the Christian activities we were involved in. There is no doubt that the spiritual issue became his main priority. He started coming to church and attending Crusader meetings.

Mike Conlin (tour manager)

We used a car-hire firm in north London. The head of the firm drove Cliff's Cadillac to the opening of *The Young Ones*. Derek Bodkin was one of the guys who worked for him and sometimes turned up as one of the drivers if the main man couldn't come. If Mrs Webb wanted a car or wanted to go anywhere at any time she would ring this firm and get a car. She met Derek like that and that was the beginning of it. Apparently she became keen to take up badminton and if there was no one to play with, Derek would play with her. You don't consider that someone who you see now and again as a driver might move in with your mother.

Olive Gregory (Cliff's aunt)

I don't think anyone was keen on the relationship with Derek Bodkin. She came to see me in Manchester and Derek had driven her up and that was the first time I had seen him. I was thinking, "Surely not! He's younger than Cliff." I was a little bit worried because she hadn't said anything about marrying him, but by certain things that were said I could tell something was going on.

Ray Mackender

We went up to see Cliff play near Manchester. We drove up on the Saturday and stayed with his Aunt Olive in a prefabricated house near the music hall. Then Dorothy suddenly remembered that she had left a joint in the oven at home. When we came back the next day it was shrivelled to the size of a chestnut. She had a habit of doing that. Once Derek drove us to Harrods on a Saturday and she suddenly remembered she had left a chicken in the oven so Derek was immediately dispatched back to Essex to turn the gas off.

ABOVE
After selling Rookswood, Cliff bought a more modest home in Totteridge, north London, which he shared with his spiritual mentor, Bill Latham, and Bill's mother, Mamie

Tony Meehan (drummer)

I think his mother's relationship with Derek Bodkin really freaked him out. It did his head in completely that someone was having sex with his mother. I don't think she let Cliff know what was happening because Derek was over 20 years younger than she was and he worked for Cliff. It was initially a clandestine affair, and so, to him, it felt like a betrayal. Those are the facts. When it all eventually broke up, it just wasn't talked about. It was like a death in the family.

Derek Bodkin (chauffeur)

I suppose I have taken over Cliff's place in Dorothy's life, in as much as he used to be the man of the house and now I am. Where she used to ask his advice, she now asks mine. But I certainly don't treat Cliff like a son or try to give him advice. If he wants any, he asks for it. (1966)

Graham Disbrey

Bill's dad had died and his sister was no longer living at home. There was space. Cliff could have his own room. He gave the impression of being very happy to join in Bill's lifestyle. It was difficult for his mother to see him join another family, though. It was compounded by the Christian dimension because she was increasingly into the Jehovah Witnesses. I think the apprehension was tempered by the fact that everyone liked each other. There were never any rows. I think Joan liked Bill as a teacher and Jacqui got on well with him. I know that Cliff's mother voiced her apprehension to other people, though, and Bill's mother knew about it and was quite upset.

BELOW
Derek Bodkin (left) was a 23-year-old driver when he began dating Cliff's recently widowed mother. The relationship is believed to have had a profound effect on Cliff

Ray Mackender

Cliff made a mistake in dedicating one of his books to Mamie "my second mother". That really hurt Dorothy. It caused a rift for quite a while.

Graham Disbrey

During the Easter break of 1965, he came on a Crusader holiday to the Norfolk Broads. We drove down to Roxham, picked up three or four boats and then we'd cruise around and sleep on the boats. There would be two leaders for each boat and then a crowd of youngsters. This was where Cliff started to muck in. He enjoyed being involved in the cut-and-thrust. He needed a role and interestingly enough the role he picked was that of cook and his speciality was shepherd's pie, which he would spend a long time getting just right. As a celebrity Cliff was under great pressure, but here he could just do the things he liked doing. Every evening there would be meetings aimed at introducing the kids to the Gospel or building them up in the faith and Cliff would play his guitar along to the choruses.

Peter Graves (university lecturer and Crusaders' member)

I first met Cliff in September 1965. The people he was now mixing with were extremely normal and he wasn't put on a pedestal. There were a lot of insults flying between us, a lot of banter, and Cliff was caught up in all this. He was not given any special status. Once we had got over the initial excitement of meeting him and having the first photograph with him, we became ordinary friends. That appealed to him. Bruce and Hank found that very hard to understand. I think Cliff wants to be accepted as a normal person.

Cliff

I was going to Crusaders and would have called myself a Christian, but I think all that was happening was that I wanted to say I was a Christian because I was British, I wasn't an atheist and I wasn't a nasty person.

Graham Disbrey

We went to a Whitsun camp in Lewes and we got into some serious discussion. Because he identified with the Christian position constantly, I challenged him as to how he could be sure that he was a Christian. We were standing outside his tent one evening when I challenged him directly. Despite the apparent certainty and confidence, I have a niggling suspicion that he had doubts as to where he stood. I didn't realize the significance of this event until many years later.

Peter Graves

By the autumn of 1965, the general feeling among those of us in Crusaders was that Cliff was definitely interested in Christian things. But as far as we knew there had been no definite Christian commitment. There had certainly been no public announcement. He was, however, interested in asking lots of questions.

BELOW
Cliff became an in-demand performer at church functions and evangelistic concerts, and allowed Bill Latham to interview him publicly aabout aspects of his faith

LEFT
A small pamphlet that marked Cliff's first tentative step in writing about his beliefs

my faith *Cliff Richard*

Cliff

In time I learned from my new friends that it was not sufficient just to believe in
God. You had to live on a personal basis with God, and the only way to Him was
through Christ. It meant rediscovering Christ personally and it eventually came to
the point where one day I opened my heart and mind to Him and asked Him to
come in. I was lying in bed, actually, and I just said to God, "Look, I know you're out
there. Would you mind moving in and taking over my life?" It was like being reborn
and it has been my main preoccupation ever since. (1979)

Hank Marvin (guitarist)

It didn't bother me when Cliff became a Christian because I'm pretty tolerant. I feel
that everyone has the right to believe what they want to believe. I certainly believe
that he came under some undue influence, and that for years he has remained under
that undue influence. That's my feeling. It didn't worry me. It worried other people.
It worried Bruce, who thought that Cliff was going round the twist.

Tony Meehan

I think Christianity gave him a place to go. Up to that point he must have wondered
why he didn't feel that emotion that other people felt towards the opposite sex. Most
of his songs are about wanting a person and loving a person. He was holding himself

up as an object which women were meant to desire and then he was saying, "Well, you can't have it, because I'm not giving it." That's an odd situation.

Ray Mackender

The wedding between Dorothy and Derek Bodkin was a family affair. There was a balcony above the front door of Rookswood and we collected rose petals and gently dropped then on the couple as they walked underneath.

Cliff

I knew that my mum and Derek had become an item, but I suppose the wedding did come as a bit of a shock. She did say to me that she'd like me to know that she and Derek were going to get married. I didn't go to the wedding because they were a bit worried and didn't want crowds. I stayed at home with Joan, I think.

Bruce Welch (guitarist and producer)

I think it was due to his father dying and his mum marrying the chauffeur. He suddenly had a stepfather who was younger than him. It didn't help. He lost his father at the height of his fame and had always been close to his mother. At one point he was going to give everything up and go train to be a schoolteacher. He thought there was a conflict between being a star and being a Christian. Bill Latham soon found a way around that.

Cliff

I intend to give up one day. I'm not quite sure when, though. I can remember one time relying on show business. If I couldn't be in show business I thought I would commit suicide, but Christianity has give me something much more stable and I feel now that if the time comes that I want to go and teach, then I'll be able to do it. All I have to do is choose the time. (1966)

John Davey (friend and Crusaders' member)

He got the idea that he would have to give up show business. I think it was seeing Christian people he respected doing things that he felt were more "Christian". He explored the possibility of becoming a teacher. He sat an O-level GCE in religion at Lewes Grammar School and then approached Trent Park Training College. He got as far as talking to the principal about the implications. The principal said he was more interested in people committed to teaching than those with academic qualifications, so he left with a positive feeling, but within six months his career had thrown up possibilities of doing fulfilling things as a Christian within his chosen profession.

Cliff

I didn't think I could remain within my career and be a Christian because the Christians I knew were busy being Christians either on the mission field or teaching religion in schools or working for aid organizations. So I thought, "This is what Christians do. If I'm a Christian, I need to do something like this." I thought I'd have to leave show business. But then I was invited to do gospel television shows, questions about my faith came up constantly in interviews and I realized that I could remain where I was and be a Christian. As I went on I became more relaxed because I thought what could anyone possibly say to me or throw at me that would change my mind, and the answer was nothing. There is nothing that anyone can say to me now that can change my mind about my faith.

John Davey

I think he thought of teaching because a lot of us were teachers and he also felt that being a Christian was incompatible with what he saw going on around him in the world of show business. He felt he could make a difference as a teacher. He recognized the superficiality of pop stardom and realized that many young people idolized him, spent a lot of money on his music and looked up to him. These moral issues worried him. I don't think we were very encouraging about him staying in show business. We said, "Look, you don't have to worry about financial stability." However, our position changed. We thought it would be a loss to show business if he quit and a loss to Christianity if he didn't take advantage of the opportunities he had because of his position. We thought that some might think his conversion was a gimmick and that possibly his popularity could wane as a result. We talked about the lyrics of certain songs in his repertoire. There is no doubt that rock 'n' roll in those days had questionable moral overtones which Cliff was very worried about.

David Bryce (road manager)

I can remember him struggling with the decision. I was with him in the dressing room at *Talk of the Town* and I said, "Think of what you'd be giving up. If you don't want it for yourself, at least you can use it to do a lot of good for a lot of people." At that time he didn't think he could be both a Christian and a rock star.

Cliff

There was an American Christian who was a filmmaker named Jim Collier and he told me that I shouldn't give up. He told me that I was in a unique position. I had thought I couldn't really be an active Christian within show business. The Christian examples that I knew were people like Bill who was teaching religious studies in a secondary school.

Gerald Coates (pastor)

I think Cliff knows that if it wasn't for Bill Latham he probably would have become a school teacher and Wembley Stadium, world tours and singing for the Queen wouldn't have happened. It was Bill, more than anyone else who advised him not to quit.

Cliff

When the Billy Graham organization asked me to give my testimony I jumped at the chance because it's every Christians wish to say that he's a Christian to as many people as he can. It's an opportunity God gave to me and I took it. I performed a gospel song called "It Is No Secret." (1966)

Billy Graham (evangelist)

In this country quite a bit of cynicism has grown over the years about religion in general and evangelicalism in particular, and I think Cliff's identification with an American evangelist at that moment in his career might have put elements of his future in jeopardy. But, in other ways, I think it might have strengthened it. For us, I'm sure it was a tremendous contribution to the crusade itself and also the film that we would later make. The thing that has thrilled me about it is that Cliff has stuck with it. Not only stuck with it, but grown tremendously.

BELOW
At the Earl's Court rally of American evangelist Billy Graham, Cliff made his first public announcement about his Christian commitment on a night devoted to youth

Mike Conlin

The office was definitely worried about what was happening with Cliff. We had already had the trouble with Licorice Locking. It was a vague worry rather than a fretful worry. They thought that if he gets into that kind of rubbish we'll have to watch him like a hawk, otherwise he'll be knocking on doors.

David Bryce

We don't "let" Cliff do things. He's his own man. We thought it would probably do more harm than good to his career, but we'd all been together long enough and cared about each other deeply enough that you did whatever made you happy. It wasn't until Norrie spoke to him about doing a gospel album that he saw what he could do. He had a lot of respect for Norrie.

David Winter (biographer, broadcaster and friend)

At a human level, he loved performing. He loved being out there. People used to wonder what he did instead of sex and the answer was that he performed on stage. It gave him amazing satisfaction. To take that away would have been quite destructive to him as a person. The question was whether he could walk as a Christian and still do that job. Once he had discovered that it was possible, that Peter Gormley didn't throw his hands up and that his popularity wasn't destroyed, he felt comfortable about staying in show business. Then, in addition, he found that he could use his faith in his career.

Nigel Goodwin (actor)

When I became a Christian in 1962 I had gone to work at *Crusade* magazine, where I met David Winter, and a group of artists began to form. Each of us was asking how we could survive in the business while remaining Christian. I met Cliff after speaking at St Paul's, north Finchley, and being asked back to David's house. At that time he was thinking about being a teacher. There were people in his office who felt that if he came out and started confessing Christ, he would lose his audience. Cliff wanted to know whether he could stick at doing what he was good at and yet be unashamedly Christian. He didn't want to feel that he'd always have to be apologizing for his faith. In the end, Cliff listened to those he felt had some understanding of the arts and media, people he felt knew what they were talking about. I would have asked Cliff, "What is your calling? What is your gift? Is it God telling you to leave or is it other people?" I had always been appalled at what had happened to an actor called John Byron who was the first *Hamlet* on BBC TV. He had become a Christian in the 1950s but then went to a church where he was told that he couldn't be an actor and a Christian. He then spent 20 years as a missionary in Africa. When he returned to England he realized that he should have stayed as an actor. Through advice like that he lost 20 years of his life.

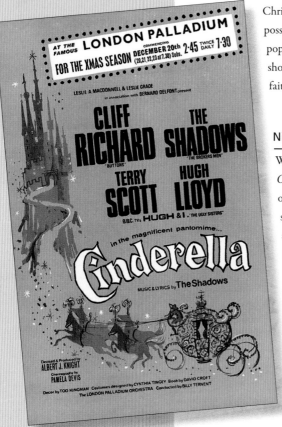

BELOW
Cinderella, *a Christmas pantomime at the London Palladium, was Cliff's first major public production after identifying with Christianity*

David Winter

I was hired as a script consultant on the Billy Graham film *Two a Penny*, and then wrote the book of the film. Billy Graham was very impressed with Cliff, and the director Jim Collier came up with the idea of making a film. He then got the screenwriter Stella Linden to come up with a story-line. Jim and I then worked on the screenplay and wrote in extra scenes like the one set in the National Gallery looking at a painting of God creating the universe and others that made an intellectual link that the film previously had lacked. I was very keen that it shouldn't be a whiz-bang "bloke gets converted at a Billy Graham rally" type of thing. Cliff was very anxious not to play a goody goody.

Billy Graham

One of the good things about *Two a Penny* was that it left people to make up their own minds. That was what people remarked on. It that sense it was a new dimension in our filmmaking.

Cliff

The part I played in *Two a Penny* was quite irreligious, really. It was the story of a young couple who were in love and then one of them is converted. It's the story of what happens to them. The girl is converted and I'm very much not converted. It's an interesting film because that must happen daily. It can make a relationship taut and tense.

Paul Jones (vocalist with Manfred Mann)

Because I was an outspoken atheist at the time, I was put on television with Cliff to challenge him about his beliefs. I had no time for Cliff. I thought he was an old has-been. Robert Kee, the interviewer, was blatantly partial to my side of the argument. I don't really remember much of what was said except that Cliff never really got a chance to talk about his faith because what he had to talk about was Billy Graham. In the wake of the film *Privilege*, which I had starred in, I was putting down Christianity and Christians at every opportunity. After it was over I just thought what a smart cookie I was and that I'd won the argument to my satisfaction. The only relief I can obtain from that now is that the Lord had the last laugh.

ABOVE
Two a Penny was an evangelistic film featuring Cliff as a minor drug pusher whose girlfriend becomes a Christian. Convent-educated Ann Holloway (shown above) played the girlfriend

Billy Graham

I had a luncheon here in London to which I invited several interesting people like Lord Home, Princess Alexandra and Cliff. There were just a few of us sitting around and we got to talking about the deity of Christ, and Cliff gave the finest exposition from the Bible. They all pricked up their ears because they expected me to say it. They hadn't expected Cliff to say it.

The Cliff Richard Story

NEW SINGER, NEW SONG | DAVID WINTER

Tony Meehan

It's understandable that when he became a Christian his career took a back seat because he had led such a vacuous sort of life. When he found some meaning in God, it took over the area of his life that you would normally devote to wife and children.

Bruce Welch

He's obviously not a family man with kids and a mortgage. He's not into that and never will be. His career and God took the place of that. He's a one-off who remains an enigma. Normal humans can't believe that a guy could live like that, but he did. His career was enormous, but even bigger than that was God.

Cliff

I'd always had religion with me, to an extent, but I wasn't a Christian. I always believed in God. There is so much more commitment in being a Christian in contrast to just believing in God. It's given me a positive reason for living. I've built my life around it and it takes first place. That's the big difference. Everything else takes second place. (1966)

Billy Graham

If Cliff had asked me about the compatibility of his career and his faith I would have told him that it's a matter between him and God. I cannot tell him what to do.

Dave Foster (evangelist)

I first met Cliff on the set when he was making *Two a Penny*. He was still talking about leaving show business and that this film might be the last thing he did. He said he was doing it for God but it could well be his swansong. I talked about the idea of staying on and he wanted to know what he could do in the milieu he was in. Off the top of my head I said, "Why not gospel concerts?" It was then that David Winter came up with the concert theme of *Help, Hope and Hallelujah.* It was three sections of songs, the first section being about human longing, the second section about Christ and the third section a celebration. It wasn't long after that he contacted me and said that he'd found a group he could do these concerts with. They were called The Settlers.

Cindy Kent (singer with The Settlers)

I met Cliff at a church in Barnet and he suggested that St Paul's in Finchley would be a good church for me to attend because they would understand my lifestyle, which involved a lot of travelling and a lot of missed Sundays due to work. After I'd started going to St Paul's I was doing a concert with The Settlers at the Royal Festival Hall and Cliff came along. David Bowie was also in the audience that night! Cliff had been offered the chance of doing these gospel concerts and needed a group to take with him. He wanted a group that would not only back him but make their own contribution to the evening.

ABOVE
Cindy Kent (right) was a Christian who performed with the folk group The Settlers. They accompanied Cliff on his first gospel tour

Dave Foster

Peter Gormley wondered about the wisdom of these concerts. He had real doubts about a pop singer doing gospel concerts. He worried that they might fall flat, which is why we didn't do them in England at first and instead went to places like Stockholm, The Hague and Zagreb. We did a lot in Germany. Then we did one in Paris which Peter flew over to see. He was bowled over by it, so when it came to do a second series, Peter agreed that we could do them in England. I spoke to George Hoffman of the charity Tearfund and we put on a concert at the Royal Albert Hall for charity.

George Hoffman (founder and director of Tearfund)

It was very much a venture of faith on Cliff's part to support Tearfund because there was no way that he was identifying with an organization that was established or prestigious. There was only Bill Latham, me, a secretary and a lot of enthusiasm. At the time Tearfund was really a manila folder on my desk at Evangelical Alliance. It was one of five jobs that I had.

Nigel Goodwin

The Evangelical Alliance had published a report called *On the Other Side* that looked at why evangelicals were not involved in different areas of our culture. Famine relief was one of these areas and the arts were another area.

George Hoffman

After having helped raise money for Tearfund, Cliff was keen to go abroad and visit some of the projects we were sponsoring. The first visit was to Bangladesh. What hit him when he arrived was the total contrast between this and the world he was used to. He was just stunned by the density of the population, the smell, the heat and the noise. But he has this ability to see right through to the individual, whether it was Mother Theresa or a child in the gutter. When he was confronted by these people it was as if nothing else mattered for that moment. He gave himself wholly to that and when he had finished he would smile. I've been on other Tearfund trips with Cliff and there's no doubt that this one affected him the most. It was the birth of a new country and it was enduring civil upheaval and natural disaster. Everything hit them at once. I think it had an effect on him from which he never recovered. He's never been the same person since. Every night after visiting with people we would come back to be with the workers and I would lead a Bible study. We would pray and talk until late and those discussions were very meaningful for Cliff. People become overwhelmed when they come into situations like this and Cliff was no different. They go back home to their normal lives and wonder why on earth they're working in a bank or whatever. They can't see what difference they are making. In one of the Bible studies, I was working through I John and had gone through the passage "He who doesn't love his brother who he can see, cannot love God who he can't see." I stressed this command to love one another. Cliff told me afterwards that he had never seen it in that sense before. I was stressing that we're commanded to love in just the same way that we're commanded to believe. He said, "That makes sense, because there are times when you don't feel like loving." I said, "I know. There are times when as a married person you don't feel particularly married but you're married and it's your responsibility to love. It's out of this commitment to Christ that we're commanded to love." I think that helped him think that through. He's always had this Biblical mind. He wants to find things out and think them through clearly.

Cliff

Having seen the situation in Bangladesh it's pretty obvious that that country needs the love of the rest of the world. I've come back thinking it's not a matter of whether I can love these people without actually knowing them; I have *got* to love them. It's not just the situation, it's the people. I have to do it as best I can. I'm not qualified to be a nurse or a doctor but I can't shelve the responsibility. Compared to those people there is no one in Britain who is not wealthy. (1973)

ABOVE

Cliff began making low-key appearances accompanied only by his guitar where he sang only hymns, gospel songs and pop material with questioning lyrics

Liz Hutchison (Tearfund worker)

I think it had a profound effect on him. We had a Volkswagen minibus which he drove to the camp. We had a daily routine and he just wanted to see what we did. The first thing was to pick up these severely malnourished children and bundle them into the van. There were maybe 25–30 of these children. Then we took them to the centre to bathe them, feed them and give them any medicines they needed. I know that one thing that happened to him was particularly meaningful. He always says that when he looked at these children he couldn't bear the thought of touching them. Then he accidentally trod on a child's hand. The child screamed and his immediate reaction was to pick it up. This child absolutely clung to him.

Cliff

My first impression when I visited my first camp was that I didn't want to touch anyone. It was so filthy. Someone once said of India that it's like one great toilet. And it is. In certain parts of the camp you'd need boots because you'd be walking through human excreta. But two hours after I arrived, and it seemed like a lifetime, things had changed. I went to a feeding programme for babies and someone in our party accidentally trod on the fingers of one of thee little mites and there was a bellow and I don't know what it was but I just reached down and grabbed this little kid. It stopped crying instantly and grabbed hold of me. It was the bear-hug of all bear-hugs and it sobbed. If ever you think about love these people are so devoid of it. The babies know that they're not loved. (1973)

David Winter

The Tearfund involvement was important. Boy pop stars are really rather spoiled, and his conversion changed him. He had to learn to put up with opposition from both the secular and Christian press. The visits to refugee camps were important in helping him grow up. I think it's very much an Anglo-Indian thing. You're taught to look after yourself and look after your family. It's your fault if you don't do well. But he has become very sensitive to those whose poverty is obviously not their own fault, like those who live in the undeveloped world.

Liz Hutchison

Each day Cliff went with a different nurse to a different project because he wanted to see as much of what we were doing as he could. When he came to our houses in the evening he would bring his guitar and would sing some of his songs. He was very relaxed around us, which was good because when we heard he was coming, some of us had mixed feelings. We thought it might be a publicity stunt. What impressed us all was that he made us all feel comfortable. You could tell it was having an impact on him by the things that he said and the genuine interest he had in what we were doing. I think he felt that what he was doing with his life wasn't as meaningful as what we were doing. A lot of foreigners would come and say that they wished they could help, but unless you're actually trained, you can't be of much help. What Cliff has done is amazing. Nobody will ever know the significance of his contribution.

Peter Graves

I led the first ever Tearfund work party in Israel and Cliff was doing some concert dates out there at the same time. Bill was working with Tearfund by then so he came out at the tail-end and we turned it into a bit of a holiday. We spent 10 days in Jerusalem then went to Tiberius on the Lake of Galilee for a further 10 days. Cliff had been to Israel before with Dave Foster and he had made the film *His Land* out there with Billy Graham. While we were staying at Tiberius we went up to the Golan Heights close to the border with Syria.

David Winter

We did a series for Tyne Tees TV called "Life with Johnny", for which I wrote most of the story-lines. They were modernized versions of parables done as musical dramas. They were half-hour shows and Cliff was Johnny. For each show Cliff, The Settlers and me wrote three or four new songs. I think there were seven programmes in total.

Cindy Kent

Johnny had three girlfriends. I was the got-to-get-married-if-it's-serious one, Una Stubbs was the flighty, sexy one and Linda Marshall (now the well-known writer Lynda La Plante) was the straight one who got him in the end. Peter Gormley's wife was one of the dancers. It was an interesting series in that we were breaking new ground in religious broadcasting.

Nigel Goodwin

I think Cliff began to change when he realized he had songs written by Christians that were good enough to be included in his non-gospel concerts. I think Larry Norman, who wrote "Why Should the Devil Have all the Good Music?" and "I Wish We'd All Been Ready" was important in this. In some ways, he became too important, because he was the only one who was writing good stuff and who was unashamedly Christian.

Larry Norman (singer-songwriter)

I think I met Cliff at an arts conference in England and then we both took part in a big concert in Hyde Park for the Festival of Light. I think he was already singing my songs at that point because he asked me what I was singing so that he didn't sing the same song. He later spoke to me of the dilemma he felt in having to sing songs from his past, the future and gospel music. He wasn't sure what was the most credible and dignified way to present the songs he really cared about. I found him very wise and thoughtful.

Cliff

People like Larry Norman are the greatest exponents of rock 'n' roll but all they do is Christian music. The general public don't know about Larry but he's the guv'nor. He writes incredible songs and I do three of them. He did a song called "Why Should the Devil Have All the Good Music?" He had this thing about "Why does the church consider rock 'n' roll to be sinful? It's great music. The devil doesn't own it. It belongs to me." I tried to get him to come on my TV show but he didn't think it would be the right thing. (1976)

Larry Norman

Cliff told an Australian reporter that I could have reached so many more people if I had sung more love songs and done more pop music instead of concentrating on the direct communication of theology.

ABOVE
Cindy Kent from The Settlers (above) became one his co-stars in "Life with Johnny", a TV series loosely based on New Testament parables

Cliff

I was at a Christian conference in Morecambe and was asked to go to a Christian meeting in the town. I went along and got the message that the Gay Liberation Front was coming along, too. I couldn't believe it. It was the first time I'd really come into contact with this movement and they came flying in with make-up on and wearing chiffon robes. They just screamed around the place. I met a couple of them afterwards and one of them apologized for their behaviour. (1979)

Bill Latham

There were a few tough experiences for him when he got involved in the Nationwide Festival of Light. It was early days for Cliff as far as his Christian life was concerned and suddenly he was pitched into a public experience of opposition that most of us never have to confront in a lifetime.

Cliff

The Festival of Light is not allowed to say it's against permissiveness in terms of sexuality. But why not? If we're really permissive we should be all out to do our thing, but it doesn't work. (1973)

David Bryce

His popularity didn't go away. He did his gospel album *Good News*, he did *Life with Johnny*, and then there were his gospel concerts. But when he started recording he did ballads which, although successful, weren't as exciting as the music he'd done before. I think it took him time to work it all out.

ABOVE
Californian singer Larry Norman, one of the first Christian artists to fuse the energy and natural rebelliousness of rock 'n' roll with the outlook of Christianity. Cliff became a big fan of his work and covered several of his songs

Bruce Welch

By the late 1960s Cliff was up against much more competition and times were less innocent. People like The Beatles, The Stones and Bob Dylan were making statements through their music. This was pop music on a much different level than the pop music when Cliff got into the business in 1958.

Graham Disbrey

Cliff started to take his holidays with us. The first was in Portugal and the second was to America. We flew to LA and the film company that had made *Two a Penny* had provided us with an apartment in Burbank and a huge estate car to drive around in. Cliff had only taken the Equity minimum payment for his role and so they insisted that he accepted this offer of free hospitality. We went to Disneyland and Universal Studios. We saw The Animals in concert at the Hollywood Bowl and then Tony Bennett at the Copacabana.

John Davey

We were introduced to Tony Bennett. Then Colonel Parker, Elvis Presley's manager, arranged for us to stay at the Dunes Hotel on Las Vegas. We stayed there for three or four days. Back in LA we had a VIP tour of Universal Studios. Cliff enjoyed the anonymity, but on the other hand, it was a permanent frustration that he had never really cracked the American market with his music.

Cliff

Bill's friendship is not only special, but consistent. Although I don't feel lonely because of Christianity, I can feel alone, so Bill and my friends are very important to me. I enjoy loving my friends and being loved by them in a platonic way. (1989)

Bill Latham

I can never understand society's assumption that if someone is single after a certain age then they must be homosexual. I suppose the assumption is that if two men share a home they have to be having a sexual relationship.

Cliff

Crumbs, we all know homosexuals, don't we – nowadays? It's incredible, but we do. But homosexuality will never be normality to my mind, because I can see that normality means a man and a woman and procreating. (1977)

ABOVE
In the early 1970s, Cliff became embroiled in Britain's culture wars over issues of homosexuality, pornography, censorship and the permissive society. He became an ally of television clean-up campaigner Mary Whitehouse (right)

The Rock Connection 1968–79

From the late 1960s through to the mid-1970s, Cliff's career went through its most unsettled and least artistically satisfying period. The sales of his singles slumped, his albums were lacklustre and the only film he made was a box-office dud. Successive waves of musical fashion – psychedelia, heavy metal, glam rock, punk – seemed to make him seem more and more irrelevant.

Not that Cliff fretted too much about this. As far as he was concerned he had already proved himself and he wanted to explore avenues that wouldn't have been feasible when he was Britain's number-one star. He took roles in small provincial theatre productions, played cabaret clubs in the north of England and toured as a gospel artist. He even recorded the British entry to the Eurovision song contest and was pushed into second place by the entry from Spain.

Unattached now since his break-up from Jackie Irving in 1964, there was speculation that he must be gay, something that he had always strenuously denied. His explanation for his singleness was that he hadn't found the right girl. The right girl for many onlookers was Olivia Newton-John, who appeared many times on his TV shows in the early 1970s. Although they looked good together, they never shared a romance, and Olivia later moved to America, where she starred in the film of the musical *Grease* with John Travolta and became an international celebrity.

It was Bruce Welch who revived Cliff's career when he came in to produce the album *I'm Nearly Famous* in 1976. The grittier approach to recording and the wider choice of songs pushed Cliff to new heights. The single "Devil Woman" became a hit in America and it suddenly became OK to like Cliff again.

Bill Martin (songwriter)

I was an aficionado of the great songwriters, and Irving Berlin had done everything from "White Christmas" to "Easter Parade", but no one had ever done anything with "congratulations". Songwriters get titles in their heads, and this was one I had been carrying around with me. My writing partner, Phil Coulter, and I recorded a demo of "Congratulations" and we just felt that it had to win Eurovision.

Cliff

I was more than happy to do Eurovision because it was watched by more than 400 million people. I told my band that we'd go out there and we'd play the best show that we'd ever played. It was obvious that the British public was going to pick "Congratulations" as the song they wanted me to do in the final. I would have much preferred "Help It Along". I still prefer "Help It Along" it as a song, but I knew that [with] the British public having decided on "Congratulations", it would go on to be a big hit. I was right. I think it sold over two million copies.

Bill Martin

I think that we were cheated in the Eurovision song contest. We were taken backstage to win it and to this day I'm convinced that when it came second by one vote, it was because they couldn't afford to give it (to the UK) for a second year running. We had won it with "Puppet on a String" and so the BBC had to be the hosts, and if we'd won it again, they would have had to host it again. I'm convinced it was a fiddle because Cliff had walked it and it became number one everywhere in the world, with the exception of America.

Hank Marvin (guitarist)

The specials and TV series that we worked on in 1969 and 1970 were a lot of fun for me. We got on well, a lot of our musical tastes were similar and we were on the same wavelength. He really put a lot of effort into his work. He had to learn new songs, dance routines and comedy sketches. On the music scene he was drifting away, as he was expecting success to happen almost by accident. It was big family entertainment. Keeping in mind his image as a Christian, the content couldn't be smutty, and by then I was coming along with my own study of the Bible and trying to make changes in my life and also didn't want to be involved with smut, so the programmes were a good vehicle for both of us. The idea was to appeal to the whole family, who could sit down at teatime without having to be embarrassed by anything. That was the whole concept

ABOVE
Cliff with The Breakaways (Vicki Haseman, Jean Ryder, Margo Quantrell) while rehearsing "Congratulations" for the 1968 Eurovision Song Contest

BELOW
Poster for the Cliff Richard show at Fairfield Hall, Croydon, in November 1969

of those shows and they got big audiences. Funnily enough, some of the press slagged us off for not having enough lavatory humour. It was getting him away from what was street credible at the time: Deep Purple, Led Zep. It was miles away from that, but Cliff is anyway. He's never going to be Led Zeppelin and his fans wouldn't want him to be.

Cliff

We reached up to 15 million viewers with my show, 17 million at one point, and the one thing about the show was that it was totally devoid of any kind of political or sexual connotations. The viewing figures must prove that people don't dislike that sort of thing. The letters I got said, "It's so great to be able to switch on at 6.15 p.m. and sit with my family and not feel embarrassed." It's wrong to assume that everybody is for the permissive society, whatever that is. (1973)

David Bowie (rock singer, songwriter, actor)

I'm very into shock tactics. I want to stretch people and get a reaction. When people tell me I'm having an immoral effect on the youth of the nation, I just laugh. I'm not a very responsible person. (1973)

Cliff

I did see reports on a David Bowie concert and I've seen him on television and his audience was incredibly young – sometimes 13 or 14, and he seems to me to be portraying something that's quite unnatural and could be indirectly dangerous. Heaven help us if going on stage in drag becomes the normality. I don't really care for Women's Lib or Men's Lib or whatever because there is a vital difference between man and woman, and unless we keep that difference there are going to all sorts of confused psychological problems. I'm violently against the sort of thing that sometimes happens on stage.
.

Olivia Newton-John (singer and friend)

I met Cliff because we shared the same manager, Peter Gormley. He was looking for someone to be in a pantomime with, but for various reasons that didn't work out. But about a year later I went on his TV show with my first record. That went well, and I started doing duets with him and was asked to stay on for the whole series. So, Cliff was responsible for giving me my breakthrough in England.

Bruce Welch (guitarist and producer)

Olivia's wonderful – she's tremendous. You can't help but like her. What you see is what you get. She came to fame on this show by doing one song a week. Maybe people thought something was happening between her and Cliff, but there was certainly no romance between the two of them while I was with her. By then, she was a star in her own right.

Olivia Newton-John

I learned a lot about presenting a song from Cliff. He's very professional and his songs all tell a story. He acts them out rather than just sings them, and I used to watch him every night. He has a wonderful voice with incredible pitch. I don't think I've ever heard him sing out of tune and he has great taste in the songs he chooses.

Muriel Young (TV presenter)

I think Cliff fell in love with Olivia when they worked together, but Olivia was engaged to Bruce so he couldn't follow it up. He was very fond of her, without a doubt. She knew he was fond of her and she was fond of him. Cliff was such a true-blue chap that he could never have poached her. When Olivia broke off the engagement to Bruce, Cliff was too decent to step in because Bruce was his friend.

ABOVE
Although the public, and Cliff's mother, thought Olivia was the ideal partner for Cliff, their close relationship never took a romantic turn. She became engaged to Bruce Welch (above) before leaving for America

Cliff

Olivia Newton-John is lovely. I think the world of her and like her very much, but she's not a girlfriend. Actually, she already has a boyfriend, so we won't be marrying, although we do socialize when we're in London. She's a sweet girl. (1973)

Graham Disbrey (teacher and Crusaders' member)

He was very, very fond of Olivia. I got the impression that, in a way, he worshipped her. She was a most attractive girl. Yes, I think he did have a great affection for her.

Cliff

I hold to the teaching that you shouldn't have sex outside of marriage because it's a Christian teaching. There are a lot of things that are difficult about Christianity. When you're not a Christian you can believe anything you want, because there is no law. The one thing I hate doing is to enforce a Christian doctrine or belief onto a non-Christian. But what you're asking is whether I believe it, and as a Christian I do believe it. The girls know I'm a Christian before we go out and usually the kind of girls I keep company with now would be Christians as well, and they wouldn't want it any other way. (1973)

ABOVE
Cliff rehearsing with Pam Denton for Five Finger Exercise *at the New Theatre, Bromley, in 1970. It was Cliff's first serious acting role on stage*

BELOW
Peter Shaffer wrote Five Finger Exercise *in 1958. He went on to write* Equus *(1973) and* Amadeus *(1979)*

Eddie Purse (pastor)

Cliff's mother told me that the only person he had really had any heart for was Olivia Newton-John, and that all finished when she wouldn't accept his Christianity and he wouldn't go down that road. I don't think that he really knows how to have someone close to him.

Dorothy Webb (Cliff's mother)

Knowing all the girls and knowing Cliff, I think that if he was going to marry, Olivia would have been the girl.

Cliff

Mothers have their ideas about what their sons should do and who they should marry!

Olivia Newton-John

I don't think Cliff's fans felt threatened by me, because in England at the time I had very much the same kind of image as he did. I was kind of "too good to be true". Actually, the fans have always been very nice to me and have accepted me. I can see why women find him very endearing, though. He's a very gentle and kind person. He's fun to be with and he has a great sense of humour.

William Gaunt (actor)

The New Theatre in Bromley was being run by a guy called David Poulson, who was also about to direct *Five Finger Exercise*, a play written by Peter Shaffer. Cliff was approached to play the part of a young fellow who has a relationship with a young German tutor who was played by me. It was quite controversial at the time because although it was only hinted at, it was about homosexual attraction. It was unusual that Cliff accepted the role, although I don't remember him ever discussing the implications. He just wanted to get on with it. The extraordinary thing about it was that we thought it would be completely boring to Cliff's teeny audience, but in fact they all turned up and the theatre was always absolutely packed with teenage girls.

Cliff

It was one of the most exciting things I'd done in my career. I had to act and I had to get out of myself. We got fantastic reviews. Even papers like *The Times* and *The Daily Telegraph* were nice to us, and they don't throw compliments away. They said good things about the play and I felt really proud. *(1972)*

Kenneth Harper (film producer)

There was a long gap between *Finders Keepers* and *Take Me High* because we'd run out of ideas for films. *Take Me High* was set in Birmingham and it was pure music. We wanted to prove that you could do a musical film without the dancing, and the answer is that you can't. The scripting was rushed and the filming was rushed. A lot of great directors can take an unpolished script and invent something that's better than anything in the script, but this time, it just didn't happen. The fellow who wrote the music was absolutely marvellous, but unfortunately we blew it. It wasn't a successful film. It didn't make its money back.

Cliff

It was really different from the other films. In those there was always The Shadows or Una Stubbs. This is the first time with a completely new team. I play a sharp merchant banker who moves to Birmingham – the last place he wants to be – and falls in love with a girl. Debbie Watling, who plays the girl, is fantastic. We kiss in four different ways for about half a minute. The cameras merge this into one big kiss. It's a fabulous kiss, and it was all my idea. (1974)

Anthony Andrews (actor)

It was a great honour to work with Cliff in *Take Me High*. I had grown up with his music and films and it was tremendous to suddenly step in there and do one of those musicals like the ones I'd seen him in. I was slightly disappointed when I saw it because it was so much fun to do and yet looked so dated. When you look back at it, the whole thing seems like a hangover from another era. It was a film that missed its moment.

ABOVE
Take Me High, *set in Birmingham, was the least successful of Cliff's movies, both critically and financially*

Eric Hall (Head of Promotions, EMI)

The movie was terrible. It was the old Cliff. I don't think Cliff was tearing his hair out about it and threatening suicide, but he certainly felt that even if his career wasn't exactly going backwards, it was at least standing still.

Trevor Spencer (musician)

When artists like Cliff become incredibly powerful, it is sometimes hard for them to work out where their success came from. Obviously they have a gift, but their careers need to be carefully guided in order for them to maintain credibility. The songs for the *Take Me High* soundtrack just weren't very good. They were written by Tony Cole, who was a discovery of Dave Mackay. At that time, Neil Diamond was quite big in England, and I think Tony Cole thought he was Neil Diamond and David believed him. It was that style of writing: lyrics stuffed with synonyms.

Dave Mackay (record producer)

Tony Cole was an Australian writer. He was signed to Festival Music and Peter Gormley had asked me to produce an album with him, which I did. It was a really good album that had a lot of good material. Peter liked the way that Tony wrote, and that's why, when the *Take Me High* film came up, they negotiated a deal for him to do it and I was asked to produce and arrange it.

ABOVE
The Shadows disbanded in 1968 and didn't come together again until 1974, when John Farrar (far left) joined Hank Marvin and Bruce Welch

Tony Meehan (drummer)

I came in as a musical advisor for six months. I didn't really fit into that whole set-up. I was listening to people like Crosby, Stills and Nash and all that music coming out of America. That's where the idea of Marvin, Welch and Farrar came from. They unashamedly lifted it and started doing three-part harmonies. They had never heard of Crosby, Stills and Nash until I played the records to Hank. They were very out of touch. They had been big for so long and thought that they were unassailable. It came as a nasty shock to suddenly find that they were yesterday's papers. I also tried to turn Cliff away from the pink Cadillac, bobby-socks sort of thing. Norrie Paramor seemed to have lost his direction. They brought me in to help Cliff find a new direction. I was supposed to carve a niche for myself, but after having been one thing in the organization in the past, it was hard to come back as something else.

Tony Clark (EMI studio engineer)

I joined Abbey Road in 1965. Producers in those days were like father figures. It was their job to pick the songs, pick the keys and do the arrangements. It was very structured. I wouldn't say that Cliff had lost his touch, but music had started to move. He was always professional and competent. It was just that everything else had started to change, and Norrie was still carrying on in the only way he knew how to make records.

Trevor Spencer

Cliff was in the era of performing songs like "Flying Machine" and "Goodbye Sam, Hello Samantha". It was all a bit iffy. I'd come to England from Australia in 1969 with the musicians Kevin Peek and Alan Tarney. The three of us were in a band together in Adelaide. Terry Britten was in an opposition band called The Twilights. We played Hendrix and Queen covers, whereas Terry's band played Beatles and Hollies covers. When I got a band together in England with Kevin and Alan, we asked Terry to join. Through Terry we had a connection with Dave Mackay.

Mike Conlin (tour manager)

After Cliff became a Christian, he started going out on tour less and less, and so I started going on the road with Frank Ifield. Then Peter Gormley had an enquiry from EMI Australia, who were looking for someone to manage The Twilights, who were Australia's top group. So, I jumped at the chance and went out to Australia for three years. When I came back, the guitarist from The Twilights, Terry Britten, came back with me.

ABOVE
Cliff with Debbie Watling who starred with him in Take Me High. *She was better known for her role as Victoria Waterfield in the TV series "Doctor Who"*

Dave Mackay

I came over from Australia and was brought in by Peter Gormley to produce Cliff after Norrie Paramor left London and moved to Birmingham. The first single I did with him, "A Brand New Song", wasn't a hit. "Power to All Our Friends" set us back a bit as well as far as his career direction was concerned, but we had no control over what won the contest for Britain's Eurovision entry. Just as we were trying to break new ground with him, we were landed with a song like that. I had very mixed feelings about it. The fact was that I knew we would get a hit with it and he very much needed a hit at that time. However, I also knew that it wasn't the right thing to do artistically.

Cliff

I've had my first flop in 14-and-a-half years. "A Brand New Song" is my first record not to get into the charts. I really can't understand why, because I played it to my mother and she was sure it would be a hit. (1973)

Terry Britten (guitarist and songwriter)

I was in a band called The Twilights and for a while we were managed by Mike Conlin, who used to work for Cliff. I then came to England in 1969 and formed a group called Quartet with Alan Tarney, Kevin Peek and Trevor Spencer. From that came a lot of session work, a lot of it with Dave Mackay. I was backing The New Seekers one night at *Talk of the Town* when Cliff came backstage and asked me if I'd like to work with him. My first memories of working with him were of tours around Britain playing places like the Fiesta Club in Sheffield and Batley Variety Club.

Cliff

I wanted to make a career out of one-night stands in nightclubs. I thought the atmosphere was great, and so I told Peter Gormley that that's what I wanted to do. I didn't think I was aiming low. The audiences were magnificent and I enjoyed the nightclub scene.

Trevor Spencer

It was horrible. We used to refer to it as "The Scumbag World Tour". We were actually going to have some T-shirts with this printed on them. Cliff used a lot of pick-up musicians, especially in the brass, string and woodwind sections, and these guys were often more interested in getting drunk than playing and hence became known as "scumbags". Cliff's office thought all musicians were tarred with the same brush. Kevin Peek was notorious for having fallen asleep on stage when we played the Albert Hall. He was a really good guitarist, but he'd been demoted to rhythm guitar because of his acoustic playing and he used to nod off a bit.

Terry Britten

We felt like hired helps. My heart wasn't really in it. It was just a job.

Trevor Spencer

We would be playing places like the Fiesta in Sheffield and the Golden Garter in Manchester. The entrance to the stages was invariably through the kitchens, and you'd slip on some cooking oil before you made your entrance. That's what entertainment was like during that period. Cliff's album *The 31ˢᵗ of February Street* marked the beginning of a change.

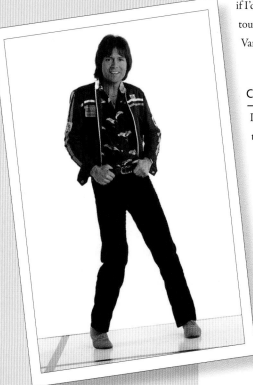

ABOVE
*Cliff photographed during his mid-1970s'
renaissance when he shed his tortoiseshell
spectacles and corduroy jackets for something
a little more contemporary*

Tony Clark

Dave Mackay, who produced *The 31ˢᵗ of February Street*, had a relationship with the musicians on the album, and because of that, things started to change. You felt that a group atmosphere was starting to develop. It wasn't so much Cliff the solo artist; he had a say as well. Dave was allowing Cliff openings to say how he felt.

Dave Mackay

He wrote all the songs for *The 31ˢᵗ of February Street* by himself and played a lot of guitar on it which he had never done before. He also sang on the backing tracks. He'd never worked like this before because he had never had to. He just used to turn up and sing. I always remember Bruce saying to me that if Cliff didn't have three hits in the can by 10.30 p.m. he thought he'd had a bad day. He would turn up at the studio, he'd be handed some lyric sheets and then he'd go in and sing the songs through perfectly. Then it would be good-night. He'd put the lyric sheets in his bag and leave. It had just become a mind-set for him. When you've had that much success over that long a period, you don't feel the need to change. But then you start to see that it's becoming less and less successful. You also see that other people are coming around you who are doing great things, and what you're doing is rather pedestrian in contrast. It was a long, hard slog to turn him around. It was during this period that he met people like Terry Britten and Alan Tarney because we were working on his stage numbers, trying to rearrange the old hits so that he could go out on stage and perform them with a new coat of paint. This was happening just as he emerged from those years of terrible variety shows on TV which were just so mindless and horrible.

Trevor Spencer

Cliff had started to do a gospel tour every year and we enjoyed those because, surprisingly enough, the gospel material had a bit more meat to it. His secular songs, by contrast, were pretty fluffy. During the concerts Cliff would talk between numbers and it would be the same every night. Barrie Guard, who was conducting the orchestra, had a tendency to fall asleep during these bits and I used to have to do a drumroll to wake him up. I had to make sure it was never too big a jolt for him, because if that happened, he would wake up and count everybody in even though Cliff was in the middle of a speech.

Barrie Guard (musical director and arranger)

When I first started, we had an 18-piece orchestra, but then the music changed and synthesizers came in. I started playing percussion and synthesizers instead of waving my arms at six people. I did the arrangements, counted the band in and played away. On the gospel tours we played in church halls and gymnasiums. There was very minimal lighting and so forth.

Trevor Spencer

Barrie didn't come from the same place as the band, musically speaking. He was like a structural engineer who played saxophone, and he seemed to see everything as a musical equation that needed solving.

Barrie Guard

I went to Japan twice with Cliff during this period and once to Australia for the opening of the Sydney Opera House. I didn't think that this was a particularly low point in his career, although there was a feeling that he was never again going to be as big as he'd once been. It was as if he had found a comfortable niche and that things would go on like this forever. He certainly didn't give the impression that he was taking a back seat. He was as excited about his work as he'd ever been.

Trevor Spencer

We would do six-week stints at the London Palladium, with two shows a day and three on a Wednesday. As a band we were not only playing for Cliff, but for Olivia Newton-John and Marvin, Welch and Farrar. By the end of each day we didn't know what we were playing. We couldn't tell the first half of the second show from the second half of the first show. It was so bad for us that everything seemed to run together. I can remember being in the middle of one show and there was a point at which the curtains would open, Cliff would bow and we would perform three numbers, the third of which was "Do You Wanna Dance?" All Barrie used to do was to lean towards me, put his arm out in a "take-it-away" sort of gesture and I would start to play "Do You Wanna Dance?" So Barrie put his arm out this particular night and I just nodded as if to say, "Right, Barrie, right." But I didn't play anything. He did it again but my mind was totally blank. I was thinking that he was telling me that I'd just played well on the last number and I'm going, "Thanks Barrie." He did it again and Cliff stood there in this total silence. Then Barrie stood up and said, "Play something!" He had no idea what the third song was, either. It was just the third song!

Terry Britten

We had lots of discussions on different subjects, but I wouldn't say I ever got to know Cliff. You're only ever involved at the level of business, music or studio. It's the same with a lot of famous people. They're up there.

Cliff Hall (keyboard player)

The band members don't normally knock about with the star of the show. We were all very friendly with Cliff, but he's not the sort of person you'd wake up to ask what he was doing that day.

Barrie Guard

I suppose I got to know Cliff as well as anybody did. I sat next to him on planes for four or five hours at a time. We all found that we could only take religious discussions with him so far because he wasn't open to other ideas. We had exploratory points of view on spiritual things, whereas Cliff's view was very fixed. He probably got the feeling of where we each stood on religion, and as it wasn't quite where he stood, it wasn't worth discussing.

Graham Todd (keyboard player)

He was a friend for as long as it suited him. It was also a business arrangement. He came round my place two or three times, but it was almost as if it was the right thing to do. It was showing deference to a player.

Trevor Spencer

People used to go to the toilet to swear if Cliff was around. It wasn't that they thought Cliff would say anything to them about it, but it would have been like swearing in front of your mum. There was a funny time when we were rehearsing at Twickenham for a tour of Australia. Terry Britten was playing around with his guitar sound and had a polished aluminium fuzz-box that had a shadowy face printed on it and the trade name Big Muff. Cliff came over, looked at it and said "Big Muff. What a great name for my next album. Instead of that shadowy face, I'll have my face. Big Muff. What a great idea." The musicians could hardly control themselves. The backing vocalist John Perry had just become a Christian himself and so he took Cliff off in

a corner, put his arm round his shoulder and explained to him the sexual innuendo. Cliff turned round and said, "Oh drat! You can't say anything these days."

BELOW
Cliff's need to be near London's airport saw him move from north London to Weybridge in Surrey, close to the former homes of Tom Jones, John Lennon and Ringo Starr

Tony Rivers (backing vocalist)

He was very naïve. We were playing a live gig at the Palladium and the backing singers were in front and we'd be given acoustic guitars and we did "Theme for a Dream" and "Spanish Harlem". As the roadie came out to give us a guitar each, I got my guitar and Cliff put his on. He looked at my guitar and then looked at his and said, "I've got a bigger one than you." I looked at him. I didn't say a word but the audience fell apart. I thought, "If I don't say anything I'll be wrong, and if I do say anything I'll be wrong." So Cliff, again, says, "Oh, you just can't say anything these days!"

Terry Britten

I think you have to respect what people believe. The worst thing was when people would say "Oh, Christ!" just out of habit. When they were around Cliff they'd become more aware of what they were saying. You'd find yourself saying "Christ!" and then you'd hear a voice saying, "Right name. Wrong context."

David Bryce

When we had an early flight I used to suggest to Cliff that he stayed with me and my wife, Jean, because we were only 20 minutes away from the airport. So he used to do that and one day he said to Jean, "I really like it down here. Why don't you find me a house?" Within a week she had found this house called Feather Green on the St George's Hill estate in Weybridge. She told him, "It's not the greatest-looking house in the world, but the location is perfect."

Bill Latham (mentor and friend)

While we were living in Totteridge we'd been going to St Paul's Church in Finchley, but when we moved to Weybridge we started attending Guildford Baptist Church.

David Pawson (minister)

I think he wanted to be an ordinary person among ordinary people. I think it was the one place he could come where he wasn't treated as someone special. He didn't come to any meeting other than the Sunday-evening service, but at one time we set up a small group of about half a dozen people, some of whom hated his music, just to support and pray for him.

Cliff

This was the time in my life when I was settling in to being a Christian.

David Pawson

The only embarrassment we ever had was girls arriving with one-way tickets from Australia or New Zealand who God had told to marry Cliff. Not a single one of them ever got through to him. Clearly God wanted Cliff to be a polygamist!

Cliff

There was a fan who turned up on my doorstep recently with a couple of suitcases and announced she'd come to stay. She said that she had been told "by the Lord" that I needed her. So, at considerable expense, she'd obeyed the Lord, and here she was! I tried to explain that I was surprised that the Lord hadn't told me what he had in mind so that I could have at least have prepared the spare room. But she wasn't impressed. It took a couple of policemen to get her out of the house. (1978)

Bruce Welch

Cliff had come through a time where he was making crap movies, putting out crap singles and hadn't had a hit single in a year. When someone said that there was a chance of producing Cliff if I could find the songs, I went out and found the songs. At that time, he wasn't into himself or his career to anything like the degree he later became involved.

Cliff

When Terry Britten gave me a demo cassette of "Devil Woman" I thought, 'Crikey! That's fantastic!' I had it for a year-and-a-half before I recorded it. I thought I could never do it because it would have been such a change for me.

ABOVE

Although Bruce Welch rarely saw eye-to-eye with Cliff, it was his capabilities as a producer that revived Cliff's career with I'm Nearly Famous

Bruce Welch

Cliff has a great voice – it has great quality. All his fans are women and they think he's singing only to them. That's the way it was for Elvis and Sinatra. That's what a song like "Miss You Nights" does. I took him "Devil Woman", "Miss You Nights" and "I Can't Ask for Any More Than You"; when we recorded them no one could believe it was Cliff.

ABOVE
Christine Holmes, a former children's TV presenter, wrote the lyric for "Devil Woman", the song that put Cliff back on the music map in 1976

Cliff

Bruce knows what I can and can't do. I can't sing like Robert Plant, so I don't even try. But I can do a rocky number like "Devil Woman" and a soft ballad like "Miss You Nights". Those are the two extremes of any kind of music. Bruce knew what I was capable of, it was just a matter of finding the right material. The trouble was, people were still sending me songs that sounded like "Congratulations" and so Bruce didn't tell anyone who he was collecting for. He knew what he wanted and he went out looking for it.

Terry Britten

I had the music for "Devil Woman" and didn't quite know what I was going to do with it. Someone introduced it to a writer who was stronger on lyrics, Christine Holmes, and she gave it the title and came up with the story.

Christine Holmes (singer and lyricist)

I had this idea of doing a fortune-telling song and it was going to be the story of a guy going to the fortune-teller and the fortune-teller predicting that he would meet a tall, dark stranger and that she would be that stranger. In other words, the fortune-teller fancied him. It was based on my observations of women. I'm Piscean, so I'm the most sensitive sun sign. I'm a very good observer. I watch relationships very closely. "Devil Woman" is an observation of what women can be like when they're trying to get a guy.

Cliff

Actually the lyric is anti-spiritualism. It's a warning : beware. I'm not trying to preach at anyone but black magic and spiritualism are very dangerous areas. When we recorded I was worried about one line that said "And I knew just what I came here for" so I altered it to "I wondered what I came here for". (1976)

Bruce Welch

Cliff thought "Devil Woman" was about something else. That's because he didn't know. There was a line in it about "neighbourhood strays" and he thought it was about cats!

Dave Townsend (songwriter)

I wrote "Miss You Nights" in August 1974. I was in England and an old flame of mine, Sally Lewis, was away on holiday in Spain. I think it was a case of exaggerating my feelings, of using something in my life and taking it one step further. I was missing her and the phrase "miss you nights" and the melody came together. When she came back from the holiday, I gave her a copy of the lyrics.

Sally Lewis (Dave Townsend's girlfriend)

When I got back from Majorca, Dave came over to see me. He sat at the kitchen table saying how much he'd missed me and told me that he'd written a song for me. Then he gave me a piece of paper on which he'd written the lyrics. We parted not long after that, and then I remember getting a call from Bruce Welch's secretary asking if I could read the song over the phone because Cliff was going to record it and they wanted to be sure they'd got the lyrics exactly right.

Cliff

I think that is one of the nicest songs I ever made. When I heard Dave Townsend's version I thought it was terrific. We just stole the whole thing and he was pleased for us to do that. I mean, anyone could have recorded that song and it would have been a hit. (1976)

Tony Clark

"Miss You Nights" was another exciting session. It was done in Studio 2 at Abbey Road and had live orchestration and a live vocal. When we had a playback session after the third or fourth take, you could feel the emotion in the control room and my assistant, the late John Barrett, picked up on this. He slipped out of the room without anybody knowing, soaked a handkerchief under a tap, and when he came back started mopping his eyes with all this water splashing down as if he was crying.

Graham Todd

A lot of new guys came in to play on that album and they put a lot of enthusiasm into it. Previously Cliff had become very show-biz. He'd go into the studio, do his vocals and then leave for a dinner appointment. Suddenly he got into the sessions. It rekindled his enthusiasm.

Bruce Welch

Those three songs turned into *I'm Nearly Famous* and gave him credibility. He got great reviews and big hits. Highly respected people in the industry were sending me congratulatory telegrams. Suddenly the world was into Cliff. Elizabeth Taylor wore an *I'm Nearly Famous* badge. Elton John wore one. I gave Cliff his credibility back, I know I did. From that moment on it just grew and grew. His gigs got bigger. His money got bigger.

ABOVE
Elton John negotiated an American release for "Devil Woman" on his Rocket label. The record became Cliff's first major breakthrough in the US charts

Cliff

When we handed the tapes to the people at EMI they went wild. I was amazed. I thought, "You mean they actually like it?" When it came out, I wondered if the press would knock me, but they liked it, too. I was bowled over.

Eric Hall

I was involved in what turned out to be a change of image for Cliff. It wasn't easy. It was a whole relaunch. It was mainly my idea to do the T-shirts and the badges. Every day I would go out with a bag full of badges and I'd stick them on whoever I met.

Tony King (Executive VP, Rocket Records)

Elton John absolutely loved "Miss You Nights". He thought that would be the hit that would help Cliff crack America. He had to negotiate with EMI to allow Rocket to release the record in America and EMI was happy because they'd never really been able to do anything for Cliff in America. I was then put in charge of promoting the record. We did three albums in America with Cliff, the last one being *Green Light*, and then Rocket Records virtually vanished. After I had listened to *I'm Nearly Famous*, I realized that "Devil Woman" was the better track for America. We tinkered with it a little bit to master in a little hotter for American radio, and then I hired a press officer to promote him.

Cliff

When I went to America with "Devil Woman" it sold 1.4 million copies. When I came back people said to me, "You've cracked America!" The only thing I could think of was that 249 million people did not buy it. (1993)

Tony King

We took him out on a promotional tour of America. We went to Boston, Atlanta, Memphis, New York, Detroit and LA. We had media parties in each city. The only angle we used was to stress Cliff's musical credibility and stay off the Christian side of things. We had to treat it as a fresh start rather than going on about the past. I remember we were travelling first class on a plane and Kris Kristofferson was sitting a few seats ahead of us. Cliff wanted to talk to him but I said we'd better leave him alone. Anyway, when we arrived at the airport, there was Kris waiting for his luggage and as soon as he saw Cliff he came over and said, "You're Cliff Richard aren't you? You're one of my idols. I wish I'd known you were on the plane. I would love to have talked to you."

Cliff

The visit did me a lot of good. I've had a top-five hit over there with "Devil Woman". I did a lot of radio stations and was knocked out that some of the black stations were playing "Can't Ask for Any More Than You", which has been released as a single. (1976)

Tony King

Another big admirer of Cliff's was Freddie Mercury. I took Cliff to an after-gig party at the Roof Garden in Kensington where there were nudes covered in paint waiting for guests in the elevators. Freddie asked me to bring Cliff back to his house after the party and there was all sorts of madness going on there, but Cliff was completely non-judgemental. He relaxed, accepted Freddie at face value and they got on extremely well. Freddie had been educated in India so they had that connection as well.

ABOVE
Cliff pictured at a party with Queen singer Freddie Mercury (left) and Rocket Records executive Tony King (right)

David Bryce

We broke out of doing cabaret clubs in Britain. We started doing the Odeons, Gaumonts and Essoldos. The lighting became more complex. Strangely enough, the development in our light and sound happened through the gospel concerts. We got to one venue and there was no sound, and so we called Cliff Cooper of Orange. Then we were at another venue and there were no lights, so we called Peter Clarke of SuperMick and suddenly a van turned up with three Genie towers. Things just got bigger and bigger after that.

Ron King (tour manager and later personal assistant to Cliff)

The tours changed when we booked the biggest theatres in the towns and instead of playing one night we played two. Eventually we were doing a whole week in places like Birmingham, Manchester and London. Then we thought, "If he can play four nights at the Hammersmith Odeon, which is to almost 14,000 people, then there is no reason why we can't play Wembley Arena." That marked the change from theatres to venues.

Bob Hellyer (lighting engineer)

For years they had used whatever lights were available in the theatres and David Bryce would operate them. It wasn't so much a show as a musical entertainment, but as time passed people began to expect more. It was in 1976 that he first brought in his own lighting. It was after he had been through that strange period when he didn't know whether he was a film star, a television presenter or a singer.

Cliff

I love what I'm doing now so much better than what I did in the early days, although I love the memories of when I started out. I've sat down with Bruce and Hank and laughed about the terrible old blue Bedford bus we travelled in, but I couldn't bear to go around the country that way again. The important considerations when putting on a concert today are the lighting, great sound equipment and arriving at the venue in good shape rather than being totally drained. It takes me at least a half-hour just to loosen everything up before a show.

Bob Hellyer

Designing the lighting was always a team effort. Cliff would say, "In this part of the song could I have this sort of effect?" and we'd chat it over. He became more interested in theatrical effects. He saw an effect in *Starlight Express* – a curtain of rain made with lasers – and he asked me to go and see that because that's what he wanted. His shows are semi-rock 'n' roll and semi-theatrical because he likes to choreograph numbers. He likes to be at a certain point on the stage at a certain time and for a certain effect to happen. He likes things to be very precise. He knows exactly what he wants. In Europe, we transport all our own equipment. In the Far East and Australia, we have to pick up equipment over there.

Cliff

We were on a tour of Japan with Olivia and Pat and John Farrar were with us. It was coming up to Olivia's birthday and I got really drunk on sake. Someone told me not to change my drink and I'd be OK. I naïvely drank more that I should have done of this sake stuff. The next day they all said to me "That was great. You were really one of the lads." They didn't become Christians or anything. Nothing changed. They were just thrilled that I had got drunk. I thought, "Are they admiring me, or what?" I felt dreadful. I hated it. I've only once succumbed since and that was one night I came home in a limo and they provided smoked salmon sandwiches and Champagne – I thought this sounded wonderful as I hadn't eaten all day. But the Champagne made me really sick that night. So when people pat me on the back for these slip-ups I think it's dreadful. It's not something I want to repeat. If someone is able to say, "Oh, Cliff got drunk" it's not going to make any difference to them. It just means that I made the same mistake they made.

Trevor Spencer

When we were on tour in Japan Cliff drank too much sake and accidentally got drunk. We had a picture of him on the bullet train covered in a blanket with his tongue hanging out like a sleeping lizard. The purple tongue and the orange blanket clashed horribly! It was the closest we ever got to any evidence of dishevelment.

David Bryce

We started playing Southeast Asia because we were on our way to Japan. So we took in places like Kuala Lumpur, Singapore and Hong Kong. His major territories are Australia, New Zealand, Europe, Scandinavia and the UK. He's never really made it big in Canada, He can't run around the world trying to build markets in places he can only get to once every two years. Europe as a whole is his biggest market. Per capita, Denmark is the biggest in Scandinavia. If you don't have the consistent hit singles, album sales will fall.

Brian Bennett (drummer)

It was wonderful when we played in Russia. I was the MD for that. It was the first time a Western act had played Russia, but Cliff's office underplayed it. We were a week in Moscow and a week in Leningrad. The audiences didn't scream. I think if anyone had screamed they would have been marched out. One guy came diving over a car at the stage door to get an autograph and he was promptly seriously manhandled and arrested.

Cliff

I had an amazing reception in Russia. I think it proved that rock 'n' roll is the international language. We played a normal two-hour set and by the end they were all up on their feet, clapping and stamping, and they'd rushed to the front of the stalls. The stage was invaded, and I got a couple of bear-hugs from enormous bearded Russians. It was a fantastic reception. (1976)

Trevor Spencer

Cliff's passport still said "Harry Webb" and so when they checked in the hotel in Moscow and showed their passports, he was given this dorky room while Cliff Hall was given was given a suite with a gold-painted piano! So, it was down to Cliff Hall's room for a party every night!

ABOVE
Cilla Black (left) and Lulu (right), two of Cliff's longest-standing female friends from the pop world. They both started their chart careers in 1964, by which time Cliff was already a veteran

ABOVE
Cliff at London's Capital Radio in September 1978, promoting his new album Green Light, *the third to be produced by Bruce Welch*

Cliff

I've come to the conclusion that in England in particular, the middle-of-the-road audience is much larger than the audiences at either extreme. It's an incredible market. So I think it would be stupid for me to say that all I was ever going to do from now on was "Devil Woman". That song crossed the line somewhere because middle-aged neighbours of mine have come up to me when I've been walking the dog and told me what a great song they thought it was. You don't expect that from that age group, but it came. I think that's because "Devil Woman" was a classic rock song. I get sick of singing "Living Doll", but I don't think I'll tire as easily of "Devil Woman" because of its qualities as a song. I don't want to cut the grandparents out. It's good if they hear what I'm doing now and enjoy it like I do.

Bruce Welch

I changed the way he recorded. I told him, "However you used to record, that was then. This is now." I changed the way he sang, especially his vocal range. He had never sung falsetto before. He told me that he could never sing like that. I said, "Yes you can." He had never tried it. Now he does it all the time. I gave Cliff his credibility with albums and singles. The business accepted him.

Cliff

After the success of *I'm Nearly Famous*, Bruce found it easier to find the second batch of songs because suddenly people were sending him new material. I think that for *Every Face Tells a Story* we had about 50 great songs to choose from.

Alan Tarney (songwriter, musician and producer)

I had two songs on *Every Face Tells a Story*. In fact, I'd had a hit back in 1972 with Cliff on a song called "Living in Harmony". I was in a group called Quartet, and when that split up I retained a partnership with Trevor Spencer, the drummer, and together we signed a recording deal with A&M. We wanted a career ourselves, and before we signed to A&M we gave some songs to Bruce Welch. As Tarney and Spencer, Trevor and I had a couple of minor hits.

Cliff

With *Small Corners* I wanted to prove that pop songs with words about God didn't have to be anything like people's preconceived ideas of gospel music. But I'm not trying to convert anyone to Christianity. The title was taken from an old children's hymn which ends with the line "You in your small corner and I in mine." I thought it was an apt title because I felt that I was doing my own thing in my own small corner. I really feel that the album is a part of me. It is also the first album that I've ever produced. (1976)

Bruce Welch

I was offered the opportunity to produce *Small Corners* but I turned it down. I thought the timing was wrong. It was as though he was thinking, "Wow. It's all happening. Let's do a religious album."

Tony Clark

Because of the success that Bruce was having with the albums, it seemed inevitable that he would do the gospel album, but when he was asked, he turned it down because he said he didn't have anything to offer a spiritual album. Cliff was obviously determined to do it anyway.

ABOVE
Cliff with veterans from another era: forces sweetheart Vera Lynn and ex-Goon Harry Secombe

Terry Britten

I started writing with B. A. Robertson and six of those songs ended up on *Rock 'n' Roll Juvenile*. I wrote "Carrie" with B. A. I had the music and a chorus and a few lines I liked the sound of. I realized that it would take someone who knew what they were doing to make it into a proper story, so B. A. did the rest of the song. I had always just liked the name "Carrie", but it wasn't written with anyone specific in mind.

B. A. Robertson (songwriter)

Carrie was quite a strong song. It makes you think, "Is she homeless? Is she squatting?" You don't know whether the narrator is Carrie's husband, boyfriend, lover, brother or father. Nowhere in the song does it say what the relationship is between Carrie and the singer. It's a very mysterious song in that way and musically it has a "Heard It Through the Grapevine" groove.

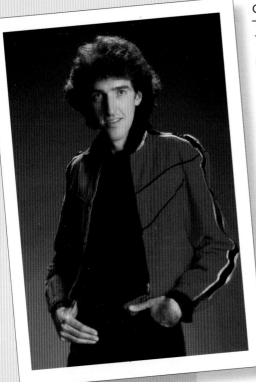

ABOVE
B. A. Robertson, who went on to have a career as a singer, co-wrote Cliff's hits "Carrie", "Hot Shot" and "Wired for Sound"

Cliff

You wouldn't make your next album if you didn't think it was at least as good as, if not better than, the last album. As far as I'm concerned, my next album, which will be called *Rock 'n' Roll Juvenile*, is the best album I've ever done. (1976)

Bruce Welch

I produced *I'm Nearly Famous*, which had taken me a long time in terms of looking for songs. I'd turned down *Small Corners*, then I'd done *Every Face Tells a Story* and *Green Light*. My next job was to start collecting songs over a nine-month period for the follow-up. My manager was Peter Gormley, who was also Cliff's manager. I was at Abbey Road one day with the engineers when Tony Clark said, "See you next week in Paris." I said, "What do you mean, Paris?" Tony said, "For the new Cliff album." I said, "What new Cliff album?" My manager hadn't told me. Cliff hadn't told me.

Cliff

People sometimes assume that, because they've worked with me, they have a contract for life. I'm not tied to anyone anymore. I made up my mind I wanted to work with Terry Britten because I wanted to co-produce for the first time. I had no idea that Bruce was out collecting songs.

Bruce Welch

They never explained what happened. Basically, Peter ceased to be my manager from that point on. We still kept in touch, but we were no longer close. As they finished recording *Rock 'n' Roll Juvenile* in Paris I was working with Alan Tarney on an album for Charlie Dore. I was doing the session and I'd always recorded Alan's songs. Olivia had recorded his songs. "Green Light" was one of his songs. So Alan came in the studio with "We Don't Talk Anymore". I said, "This is a terrific song." I played it to Cliff, who agreed that it was great. We recorded in two days using three different studios.

Cliff

One thing I gained from new-wave music when it came to recording *Rock 'n' Roll Juvenile* was a fantastic energy. I took my band with me to Paris, we stayed in the same hotel for a fortnight, we did nothing but eat and talk music and I think we captured a sort of energy that maybe was lacking on some of my past albums.

Alan Tarney

Cliff had just finished recording *Rock 'n' Roll Juvenile*, which was an album he'd really wanted to do, and all of a sudden Bruce appeared and took a tape of "We Don't Talk Anymore" to Peter Gormley. Peter played it to Cliff and Cliff couldn't really understand why they both wanted him to do this song when he'd just recorded an album. When he eventually did record it, he started by just going through the motions. It was only on the third chorus that he really started to get into it.

Bruce Welch

It became his biggest hit ever and I think it was EMI who forced him to include it on *Rock 'n' Roll Juvenile* as the only song on the album not produced by Terry Britten.

Cliff

"We Don't Talk Anymore" wasn't actually scheduled for the album. It was a stop-gap single because we didn't have anything from the album ready. When it got the reaction that it did, we made sure it went on the album because it seemed silly not to include it.

Alan Tarney

It's a debatable point as to who really produced that single. I played every instrument except the drums, which Trevor Spencer played. I also mixed it. There's a book that includes a photo of the tape box, and if you look at it, you can see that Bruce asked the engineer to cross my name off and put his name on as producer. All he really had to do with it was finding the song. He was the "producer" inasmuch as he took it to Peter Gormley.

Cliff

"We Don't Talk Anymore" is really a sad song. It's been a big hit and I can't help smiling when I sing it, but really I ought not to because it's a song about two people who don't talk to each other. It's a pathetic situation.

ABOVE
Cliff posing for the cover session of his 1979 album Rock 'n' Roll Juvenile

Love Songs 1980–86

Cliff's return to commercial success in the mid-1970s was unexpected. For the first time in his career, he began to focus on the craft of making albums rather than simply adding his voice to pre-recorded tracks. He interacted more with the musicians, showed a keener interest in the selection of songs and began to develop his stage shows through more elaborate staging and the expansion of light shows.

He had resolved the apparent contradiction between his religious beliefs with his role as an entertainer and was now increasingly merging his secular and sacred careers. He would happily sing a gospel song in his regular concerts or sing his old hits in a religious venue. He began to scout for young musicians and songwriters who were Christians that he could sign to his publishing company and record label.

For a brief period, his love-life became a focus of attention as he was spotted in the company of British tennis star Sue Barker. Unlike his appearances with Olivia Newton-John this seemed like the real thing and Cliff at one point even boasted that he and Sue were "the new Charles and Di". Unfortunately, this was true. Like the royal couple, they broke up and went their separate ways.

A less welcome intrusion into his romantic potential was the newspaper revelation by Carol Costa that Cliff had enjoyed an affair with her while she was still married to Jet Harris back in 1960. The headline in the *Daily Star* was "Cliff – My Secret Lover". Although the story was true, it upset Cliff that Carol had chosen to sell the information so long after the event.

His recording career went from strength to strength. "We Don't Talk Anymore" had been his biggest hit ever and resulted in him employing its writer, Alan Tarney, to produce his albums *I'm No Hero* and *Wired for Sound*.

Tony Meehan (drummer)

He was dead for six or seven years. He was like yesterday's papers. The fact that he bounced back in the 1970s shows how strong-willed he is. I think it shows the nature of his motivation in that he never got silly or lazy. He stuck with it. He never gave in. I think that he is much more intense than comes across and I think he has staked his life completely on his career.

Cliff

There was a time when I almost lost interest because I was stuck in such an incredible middle-of-the-road bag. I did it at the time because it sold records, even though I disliked them. I've always been honest about it – I'm in the business to sell records. But rock 'n' roll is what it's all about. It keeps you young. If you have some affinity for it you should be able to do it forever – as long as you have the energy. (1979)

Graham Todd (keyboard player)

He would never relax when we were on tour. There was always this feeling that he was slightly on guard and that he was careful to be Cliff Richard and not to be Harry Webb. I would have liked to have seen him let his hair down a bit. It's a bit like dealing with a corporation.

John Perry (backing vocalist)

When he's your boss, it's just "Yes, boss," and "No, boss." There was segregation because we wouldn't always travel the same way. Cliff was the star and we were the backing group. The raciest I ever saw him get was when a woman sent a note over to him that must have been a bit dodgy. He looked over to her, ripped the note up and then slapped the back of his hand as if to say, "Naughty!"

Mark Griffiths (guitarist)

He's a nice guy, but I don't know him even though I played with him for 10 years. I've had dinner with him, but I've never had an in-depth conversation about anything other than tennis or the latest show. He doesn't really talk about the normal things in life. He doesn't seem aware of them. If you told him that your daughter had to be rushed to hospital and you had to wait all day to see a doctor he would never ask you what it was like. It's all just sucked in and then it's gone. I once had my arm in plaster for a tour and my wrist was giving me a lot of pain and it was four or five days before he even noticed! I was actually doing the gigs with him. Another time I was in bed for two days while we were on tour. Fortunately we didn't have any gigs on those days. Anyway, when I eventually got off my bed I saw Cliff coming back from a game of tennis. He noticed me and said, "I hear you've been sick. Did you have to get a doctor in? By the way, the new single has just gone in the charts at number 26."

ABOVE
Cliff began to develop the staging for his shows as he moved from cabaret clubs into theatres. The sound, lighting and choreography were all improved

Cliff

The one thing I'd criticize people for in the business is that they're terribly narrow-minded. All they talk about is the business, and their records, but there is a place for all that. Everybody goes home except us. We seem to be the only ones who don't. I've spent some really boring times with showbiz people. (1976)

Mick Mullins (backing vocalist)

I think Cliff lives in a dream-world, but he knows exactly what he's doing business-wise. Because he has never worked, as such, he'll sometimes say dumb things like, "Why do people who live in blocks of flats get violent?" How would he know? All his waking life he's been famous.

Tony Rivers (backing vocalist)

You would expect to know a normal person after working with them for 10 years, but Cliff isn't normal. I've had conversations with him where he says he's perfectly normal because he shops at the local supermarket in Weybridge. He hasn't got a clue. I'd say, "You haven't got a clue what real life is like. Try being a worker in a factory in Sheffield getting up at 5.00 a.m. to get to work by 6.00 a.m. and not having enough money." I remember walking back from an Indian restaurant after a gig in Wellington, walking along by the sea back to our hotel, and saying, "Don't you ever want to get married and have kids? Don't you want someone to carry on your name?" He said, "Oh, no. I like the way I live at the moment." I can't imagine life without my son, Anthony, but he just wasn't interested in passing his genes on.

Mike Read (DJ and friend)

Sometimes his naïvety makes me laugh. Because he has been successful the whole of his adult life, there are areas where there are streaks of naïvety, almost a childlike naïvety, which can be endearing. Inevitably he gets locked into what he's doing and sometimes, because of that, he can be a bit vague. You think he's being unfriendly, but he's preoccupied. He looks a bit glazed-over. He would never in a million years dream of being rude.

George Hoffman (founder and director of Tearfund)

We went to Haiti together for Tearfund. It was an awful place. They found these two children who had torn each others hair out so that they could eat it and then they had both died. That was on the island of La Gonave, where Napoleon had sent all his exiled prisoners. On the boat over to the islands Cliff wrote a song in order to stop himself being sick from the movement of the sea and the thumping of the motors. That was another deep experience for him. We were both very conscious of the presence of evil there. On La Gonave itself we stayed in a missionary bungalow, but at Port au Prince, on the mainland, we stayed in a small hotel located in a quiet place on a mountain.

John Muggleton (documentary filmmaker)

There was definitely a dark spirit about Haiti and a lot of that was to do with voodoo. Baby Doc was in power, so it was relatively stable politically, but spiritually it was oppressive. However, evangelical Christians were tolerated because generally they were involved in different sorts of social work.

Cliff

When I went to Haiti I "adopted" a boy called Louismar and his mother. It's one of the poorest countries in the world, so £10 a week is enough to feed, educate and clothe a child. I've never made a big thing about it because I hadn't gone there to find out whether I could "adopt" someone. It was just one of those emotional spur-of-the-moment things. (1990)

George Hoffman

On another trip we went to Calcutta, a city he knew from his early years. He remembered many of the places quite vividly. We went to the area around Howrah station where his parents had had their apartment. The locals bought him a big kite which reminded him of the kite-flying as a child. He was mobbed when he was there. We had to have a special security agent who never let us out of his sight. We spent a day with Mother Theresa while we were there. We just spoke with her, listened to her, prayed and read the Bible with her.

Cliff

I did solo gospel concerts in Bombay and Calcutta and then went on to Bangladesh on behalf of Tearfund. The reception I got to my gospel concerts was amazing. There was even a letter in *The Statesman* newspaper in Calcutta where the writer said, "I've been a Hindu all my life. I went to the Cliff Richard concert and I have to admit in print that I have to look into this Jesus thing." I was amazed. The Indians seemed so open.

ABOVE
An informal performance at Mother Theresa's celebrated hospice in Calcutta. This was Cliff's first journey back to the city of his childhood since leaving in 1948

BELOW
Mother Theresa and other members of the Missionaries of Charity listen to Cliff in Calcutta

Bill Latham (mentor and friend)

Cliff is involved in a very self-centred profession. I think it's inevitable that there is a greater degree of self-absorption for a pop star than there is for the rest of us. I think it is commendable that Cliff has taught himself, or forced himself, to concern himself to be aware of others. I don't know if this would have happened if he hadn't embraced the Christian faith.

Cliff

To be honest, I don't care what I'm worth. All I know is that the money comes in and I support, up to my ears, the charity called Tearfund. I've been praying for a long time that God would help me use my money correctly. Maybe it'll come to the point where I'll just sign away everything as I earn it. I'm quite prepared to do that if God tells me. I believe in tithing. I feel that my money should be used for God's work. I don't know exactly how much I tithe, whether it's 10 per cent or more likely 20 per cent. (1972, 1974)

ABOVE
Cliff with his friend, mentor, press officer and charity affairs manager Bill Latham. Latham gave Cliff necessary stability and guidance for most of his career

Jill Frost (fan)

The fans just adore Cliff. They think he's wonderful. A lot of women obviously see him as their ideal man. They see him as sensitive, caring, compassionate and gentle. I don't think they look at him as a bodice-ripping hero. There might be some more disturbed ladies who view him in that way [but] with most of them, it's not a sexual thing. I think most of them would be absolutely horrified if Cliff made an advance to them. It would destroy all their illusions. He is the unobtainable ideal.

Tony Meehan

The girls used to be outside the theatres screaming, "We want Cliff! We want Cliff!" and Jet would open the dressing room window and shout out "Cliff's queer and he hates his fans." That was Jet's line! It was a joke, but there was probably some substance to it that made it so funny. There was never any serious attempt on his part to bed a lady. I've never seen him respond to provocation from the opposite sex. I don't think men identify with Cliff at all. He was a girl's idea of how a boy should be – terribly attentive, well-mannered and never touching them. He had all the money, power and status that he could ever want and yet he didn't want sex. When the real business started, he didn't deliver. That was where it became rather baffling to the women because they would then think, "What's wrong with me?"

Cliff

I'm not naïve about this thing. The whole world revolves around man/ boy and girl/man and all that kind of thing. I grew up and became a man, and I'm obviously aware that there is this attraction that remains throughout our lives no matter what we do. We rather enjoy the company of the opposite sex. The same goes for an artist. If you're a man, you tend to have a lot of female followers. (1973)

Carol Costa (ex-wife of Jet Harris, Cliff's former girlfriend)

Jet got in touch with me after 20 years and the idea was to write something nice about Cliff, but then when I sat down with him and Tony they were trying to make out that Cliff was gay. When I heard them saying these sorts of things I said, "I'm not having it." I didn't want to know. That was when I sold the story of our affair to a newspaper. I was approached by people who said that if I went public it would squash the rumour. I was trying to put things right. I did write to Cliff and I told him my reasons for doing so. Tony and Jet set that up in the first place but then I decided to go out on my own.

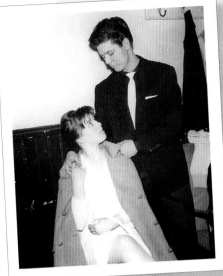

Cliff

I wasn't sure why Carol had brought it all up other than that she was short of money. I felt disappointed and for that reason I never bring her name up in interviews. If someone asks me about her I don't like to follow it through too much.

Sue Barker (TV presenter, former girlfriend)

I met Cliff through Alan Godson of Christians in Sport, who I'd been put in touch with through the commentator Gerald Williams. Alan gave Cliff my number and I think I spoke to him for the first time the night after I won the Brighton Tournament in October 1981.

Cliff

I saw Sue win the tournament on TV, and then when I went to see The Shadows at the Dominion in Tottenham Court Road, Sue was a guest of theirs, sitting in one of the boxes. Hank had met her in Brighton and invited her along. I had no idea she was going to be there. Then she played some exhibition matches and I asked if I could come along to watch.

Hank Marvin (guitarist)

We were on tour and bumped into her at the hotel. I think I spoke to her first and we chatted and she left us some tickets for a tennis tournament. It was in Brighton and we went along and saw her win. We met her afterwards, got chatting and kept in touch.

Sue Barker

Cliff wasn't really into tennis that much. He loved watching it and would get carried away about British people not doing well in tennis. That's why he went on to create The Tennis Trail. It all happened that evening. We talked about it and Cliff decided he wanted to do something.

Cliff

Once Sue and I started dating, the natural thing was to play tennis. Before that I had dabbled. I'd be lucky to play four times in a year. Then I started playing with Sue at the David Lloyd Club and realized that when you play it properly it's really good! She then introduced me to a lot of other people.

ABOVE
British tennis star Sue Barker was Cliff's first girlfriend in 18 years. The press followed their every move

Sue Barker

He loved the challenge of timing a ball and hitting winners. Tennis is a sport where you actually battle with someone, and he saw it both as a challenge and an enjoyable way to keep fit. We also used to eat out a lot. We'd watch videos and I'd cook something. A couple of times we went to the cinema. I remember seeing *Tootsie* somewhere in Leicester Square. We used to go to the theatre. Most of the time we were together we went out to dinner. But I was out of the country a lot, so it wasn't as if we were seeing each other all of the time.

Charles Haswell (tennis partner)

I met Cliff through Anne Hobbs, who was a friend of Sue Barker's. He was looking for someone to play with and I was delighted to do so. He's a good all-rounder. He has a good forehand, he's experimented with the double-handed backhand and he really is a very good server. Most amateurs have a strong first serve and then just pop the second one over the net, but that's not Cliff. He has a very good second serve and will quite often ace people with that. He gets very involved in the game. He's keen to go after the ball. I think Cliff loved meeting the tennis crowd because they were very ordinary, straightforward, nice people. He thrives on that.

Cliff

I felt quite besotted with Sue almost immediately. I just liked her as a person, admired her as a tennis player and found her very attractive physically. Funnily enough, I have never usually liked blonde girls.

Sue Barker

I never knew anything about Cliff's life before and he wasn't very forthcoming with that. He didn't want to talk about the past at all. I once asked him if he'd ever been close to getting married and he sort of said "Yes," but it just wasn't something he wanted to talk about. He wasn't going to volunteer information. The more I got to know him, the more I realized that he is very private and likes to keep everything that way.

BELOW
Cliff publicly announced that he and Barker were "the new Charles and Di." Like Charles and Di, they did not stay together

Cliff

My relationship with Sue resulted in a good many sleepless nights, and there were numerous instances when the distortions and fantasies of certain newspapers caused embarrassment and, sometimes, real hurt. If we had got married, I think it would have been a mistake. (1990)

Sue Barker

He spoke about "getting married" in articles about us, but we certainly never discussed it. When I read these comments they came as total news to me. When we got back together after a long time apart, both of us were very happy even though the relationship was no longer the same. Sometimes we became closer and sometimes further apart, but we never regained the intensity of 1982. It probably all happened too quickly. We were riding on this high for a few months and it was like, "Mmm. Maybe we're rushing it." The funny thing us, I don't remember a particular conversation to say, "This is it."

Mark Griffiths

I read into it at the time that it was good for Cliff to have a famous person on his arm. If it had been Tracy from Dagenham it might not have happened. Sue's a great girl and I know they got on really well. Tennis was the link.

Graham Todd

I think it was useful for his career to apparently have a girlfriend. I think Sue was a lot more earnest and sincere about it than Cliff was. I always felt he was leading her on a bit. She was such a nice girl.

Tito Burns (manager)

All the talk about Sue Barker was a lot of rubbish. But it was understandable. It's show business. You've got to make the man seem macho. There's nothing wrong with that.

Gerald Coates (evangelist and spiritual mentor)

I think Cliff likes the company of women. I think he appreciates feminine beauty and charm. He had a relationship with Sue Barker, but he made it quite clear from the very beginning that marriage was out. But I think Sue thought, "Well, give it a few months." Cliff can be quite intransigent once his mind is made up.

Sue Barker

For me, it was certainly a romantic relationship, especially for the first year, but then it just petered out. The next year was just up and down, and then we saw each other less and less until it was just down to seeing each other every now and then for dinner. I think we had both served a purpose in each other's lives. It was good for me to be with someone who wasn't in tennis, and I think it was good for him to be with someone who wasn't in show business.

Jill Clarke (flatmate of Sue Barker, Bill Latham's girlfriend)

He believed that if he were to marry, his wife would have to be number one. He couldn't do that, so he decided it was better to have no one rather than make somebody his number two. Cliff was just too busy to have a proper relationship with Sue. They went out for meals and spent a lot of time together, but I'm not sure how far the relationship went. (1999)

BELOW
Sue Barker encouraged Cliff in his love of tennis. Cliff later devised a scheme for training young British tennis hopefuls

MIXED DOUBLES

The Brighton Centre
19 December 1983

Mark Griffiths

The relationship was frustrating for her because she knew that there would never be anything else because Cliff was married to his career.

Sue Barker

I certainly felt I needed to put the brakes on but I didn't want the relationship to fizzle out. I think he thought it was going too fast. There was a period when he wouldn't phone me. He wouldn't speak to me. It was almost as if he didn't want to front it in the same way that he hadn't wanted to front it with Jackie Irving back in the 1960s. When I got back from my tennis engagements, it had gone to a different stage without us ever having sat down together and discussed it. It had slowed down to a point where there was no romance at all.

Cliff

When the relationship was dying I was abroad and Sue and I discussed it on the phone. I felt awful, really responsible and treacherous, even though I'd never asked Sue to marry me. (1989)

Alan Godson (vicar)

The relationship didn't happen and it's regrettable. There was the problem with Sue of, "Why is this happening to me?" Both she and Cliff were Christians, so she couldn't see how it could turn out this way. There had been a good possibility of a good relationship there. My initial concern had been purely for her to be given some spiritual input by a mature Christian.

Peter Graves (friend and Crusaders' member)

He is married to his lifestyle and that is more important to him than any woman could ever be.

Cliff

I'm not married to my career. We're just engaged.

ABOVE
Both Cliff and Sue revealed their feelings for each other in press interviews. This led to a series of misunderstandings that would eventually weaken the romantic side of their relationship

Sue Barker

Cliff says that we had to decide about marriage, but we never thought that. It was never going there. Yes, we were romantically involved, but it was only for a few months when I was playing and he was doing an album. If you added all the time up that we were together, it would probably be about three-and-a-half weeks. But it was almost as if he then had to decide whether we were going to marry or not.

Alan Godson

She wasn't a starlet swooning over a big star. The good thing was that Cliff had met someone who didn't care that he was the great Cliff Richard.

Cliff

If I had married Sue I could have made it work, but the love went before it got that far. I really want to fall "in like" with somebody – that's more important than the romance. And I'm not worried about being celibate. (1989)

Sue Barker

I think a lot of it was blown out of proportion. I certainly don't consider it one of my more serious relationships, even as far as seeing and being with someone. Some people just hide their feelings. A lot of people just don't like to display their emotions in front of other people. It just sorted of drifted in and out of my life. It wasn't one of my most serious relationships.

Cliff

Halfway through our relationship I did think of marrying her. I really believed that if it was that good and it carried on, we would marry. But then my feelings of love disappeared. I can't really say why. I couldn't get married unless I felt it was for life and maybe I am too selfish to commit myself. (1989)

Graham Todd

Cliff went out on an American tour in 1981. We had a tour manager who was a Vietnam veteran. He had a plate in his head, smoked pot and would sometimes go a bit strange. We had a date in Baltimore and as we were drawing close in the tour bus this guy realized that he'd left his briefcase behind in the town we'd just left. It had all the information about the event, the venue and the promoter. So we had no idea where we were due to play that night. We had to drive around town looking for Cliff Richard posters to see where we were expected. We got there only half an hour before the show only to find that the revolving stage wasn't working.

David Bryce (tour manager)

The worst thing that ever happened to us on tour happened to us on that tour. All of our equipment was stolen from a trailer outside our hotel. Mart Jenner had a left-handed guitar that he had modified. He was heartbroken. John Clarke had a special guitar. The drummer had a modified kit. It was horrific because it was the weekend and we were playing in the city on the Monday. We had to call all the music shops in Los Angeles to ask them to stay open late so that we could re-equip ourselves. By the time we got to Seattle, the band all had long faces and it was so pathetic that I just said to Cliff, "I want to stop this rehearsal." I went up to the band and screamed at them. I said, "The gear is gone. You're not gonna get it back. We're gonna complete this tour but with the gear you've now got. Now go home and have a good night's sleep." I used some bad language as well. They went home and came back and started rehearsals the next day. The only bit of equipment that was ever recovered was a piece of the lighting.

ABOVE
A quick sound-check in Baltimore, 1981, showing keyboard player Graham Todd (left) and lead guitarist John Clark (right)

LEFT
Cliff in concert during 1981, with Graham Jarvis (drums), Mart Jenner (guitar), Stu Calver and Tony Rivers (backing vocals)

Olivia Newton-John (singer and friend)

When I was making the movie *Xanadu*, there was a duet written for the film and the producer wanted a named singer to do it with me because it was going to used over an action sequence. So Cliff was the ideal person. It was a big kick to be able to ask him to do "Suddenly" with me because it was like returning a favour a long time later.

Graham Todd

Terry Britten was a great man for a riff and a dynamic sound. We used to have this thing called "The Brown Nose Award". We actually had this nose like a clown's nose that was brown and it was always given to the band member who could cringe the most in front of Cliff. Terry normally won the award and it would be presented to him while he grovelled on his knees. Terry was smart. He would work out good riffs which he'd then play at sound checks so that Cliff would come over and say, "That was nice, Terry." Terry would say, "Oh, it's just something I'm working on," and Cliff would say, "That would make a nice song, that would." He was very smart in that respect. That was one way Terry got his songs away with Cliff.

BELOW
The sign outside a concert venue in Baltimore, 1981. The crowd was mostly made up of Brits living in America who waved Union Jacks and cheered his hits

Terry Britten (songwriter)

Alan Tarney had great success with "We Don't Talk Anymore" so, as happens in this business, he became flavour of the month. I also found that I was moving away from Cliff musically. I got into writing with B. A. Robertson and this seemed to cruise along. I had kids and that took up more time. Then I was involved in writing for Tina Turner and when that sort of thing happens you think more of America and you get opportunities to write for a lot of other well-known people. It's hard not to put your creative energies in that direction. I honestly believe that Cliff is best-suited by the sort of songs that Alan writes.

Alan Tarney (producer, musician, songwriter)

Because of the success of "We Don't Talk Anymore", Peter Gormley asked me if I would do more tracks with Cliff. I ended up doing the albums *I'm No Hero* and then *Wired for Sound*.

B. A. Robertson (songwriter)

Alan gave me the backing track on a tape. It sounded a bit like something Robert Palmer would have recorded. When I played it, the title "Wired for Sound" came to me. It seemed a bit of a peculiar title, so I called Alan and said, "I know this sounds a little bit daft, but I think this song is called 'Wired for Sound.'" Then, a couple of hours later, I had the whole lyric. I called him back and read it down the phone.

Aleksander Mezek (songwriter)

I think Cliff became more demanding on songwriters as time went on. Sometimes he had ideas on specific subjects and he'd ask several people to write songs on this subject. So as a writer you found you were competing against other writers even though you were unaware of it at the time. If he has something on his mind at any particular time, he usually tells the writers and they try to come up with something to match.

ABOVE
Cliff with Garth Hewitt (left) and Nutshell members (left to right): Mo McCafferty, Annie McCaig and Paul Field. Cliff produced records for both Hewitt and Nutshell

Garth Hewitt (singer)

I was an honorary curate at a church in Ealing while at the same time working for the Church Pastoral Aid Society as a temporary gospel singer. This created a few problems administratively; I think that was when Bill Latham expressed interest in managing me. Then a guy called Phil Lloyd, who worked in the Imports Division of EMI International, heard a record of mine that his niece was playing. Out of that Phil made some enquiries, and with Cliff's help created a label called Patch that had a picture of a dog on it.

Phil Lloyd (EMI; manager of Patch record label)

I was very taken with Garth's obvious concern for the Third World. One of my sisters is married to a pastor and I heard his daughter playing Garth's records. I realized from this that he already had a market. The idea with Patch was to create a label that could be used by these Christian artists who were working with Cliff. I thought we could have a certain number of sales in the Christian market and then turn to the commercial market. We very nearly broke Garth. His album was "Record of the Week" on BBC Radio 1, we had posters on the sides of London buses and the effect was totally disproportionate to the money we had put into it.

Garth Hewitt

Cliff produced my album *Did He Jump...* EMI really went to town on it. He sang all the backing vocals, and posters were put up in major cities. But right at that time graffiti began appearing outside EMI's headquarters in Manchester Square that said "THE PARTY'S OVER". A lot of redundancies took place, and basically the whole of EMI International was out of work – including Phil Lloyd. This was after my album came out, but before the single. Having Cliff produce it was, I think on reflection, a mistake because EMI will back up what an artist like Cliff gets involved in, whether they have any enthusiasm for the project or not. I was basically a singer-songwriter and albums were my best vehicle, yet I was being pushed into recording singles. There was an automatic tension. But it led to a TV series called *Pop Gospel*, which I did some presenting for, and *Pop Gospel* later became *Rock Gospel*.

Muriel Young (TV presenter)

I think I first heard a Garth Hewitt record and then I found out that Bill Latham was his manager as well as being Cliff's adviser. I got on to Bill, and between us we created *Pop Gospel*. It was wonderful music, we had great dancers and it was a fizzing sort of show. Garth presented. Cliff only ever came on as a guest. I thought the format would work because everything else on the music scene was getting a bit rotten and I hated punk. I loved the sounds of the sixties and early seventies. The programmes I worked on tended to be aimed at younger viewers and I couldn't include a lot of the contemporary songs because they were just plain filthy. I thought it would be rather nice to go in absolutely the opposite direction and do *Pop Gospel*.

BELOW
Gospel artist Sheila Walsh was produced by Cliff and recorded a duet with him. She fronted a Granada TV series "Pop Gospel", later becaming a personality on American religious television

Sheila Walsh (gospel singer)

Bill Latham started to manage me, and then Cliff heard a couple of songs I was getting ready to record for an album and he suggested doing a duet. He ended up co-producing the album. We sang together on the single "Drifting", which was not a commercial success. I don't know why. He has such boundless energy and incredible enthusiasm and had a great belief that it would be a smash hit – although when it wasn't a hit I never felt that he thought I'd dented his singles' record. It was just "Well, that didn't work. Never mind. Whatever we do next is going to be incredible." He produced my album with Craig Pruess and it was the most fun record I've ever worked on. It was the first time I had worked with anyone who made me feel that my vocals were going to be the most important thing on the album. He did most of the backing vocals himself and got a real kick out of it. He was totally enthusiastic.

Craig Pruess (producer)

Cliff wanted to fuse his beliefs with his professionalism and make a great album. I met him at his house and started listening to material. We started 18 tracks for that album, which became *Now You See Me*, and chose the 10 that were strongest. We talked a lot about the devotional aspects. When the songs really connect, it's when they connect with what someone feels, whether that be love for an individual or love for God.

Paul Field (singer and songwriter)

I think Bill Latham came with Cliff to see Nutshell in concert at Richmond. At the start, Cliff didn't have much to do with it, but he was obviously consulted. I imagine he had a say in whoever Bill took on. Through Cliff's connections we got a deal with EMI. The first single we did was "Last Train Home" and then Cliff produced "Dangerous Game" for us. Both singles bombed. It was the old-boys' network. Mike Read played them a couple of times on Radio 1 and that was it. The singles weren't very good. Production is not Cliff's strong point.

Chris Eaton (singer and songwriter)

I met Cliff when I was 20 years old and I then sent him some of my songs on a tape. I didn't hear from him for 18 months, and then I was told that Cliff was recording four of the five songs. He did "Summer Rain" and "Lost in a Lonely World" which both went on *Wired For Sound*. Then he did "Take Me Where I Wanna Go" in concert for a long time. I'd come from the Christian scene and I was aware that Cliff was taking a risk on me in using me as the person he felt could channel his faith through onto his pop albums.

ABOVE
Cover photo session for his 1982 album,
Now You See Me ... Now You Don't

Paul Field

It became a bit self-defeating for us. We were doing all these gigs with Cliff, so the only places people ever saw us was playing with Cliff. We got less calls for gigs on our own because people assumed we were now desperately expensive. We got less and less gigs and therefore Bill Latham had to charge more for the few gigs we had. There are only so many places you can play in Gospel Land and I think audiences became tired of us.

Garth Hewitt

I launched my album *Under the Influence* at Claridges, and for some reason Pat Boone came long. There were pictures in the music press of me, Cliff and Pat grinning dementedly at the camera and I realized that it was getting to the point where I didn't quite know what was going on. It was all becoming very frightening. My reaction was to release a compilation album called *Record of the Weak* that was unashamedly about caring for the poor. It clarified my thinking. It's important to decide which area of music you're in, and I thought I had something more serious to say than could be said within glossy pop.

Gerald Coates

Over a two- or three-year period in the 1980s, Cliff clearly identified with what was then called Cobham Christian Fellowship. It later became Pioneer People. He would sometimes come with Bill, sometimes without. He enjoyed the worship and the teaching. During that time, Cliff and I would get together privately and talk and pray. Bill encouraged those meetings. I think Cliff liked our style. He welcomes the charismatic approach. He was very much at home meeting with us. Between David Pawson's church in Guildford and coming to us, he did go for a short time to Walton Baptist Church, but it just didn't give him what he needed.

BELOW
Gerald Coates (right) with his wife Anona, Bill Latham and Cliff. For a short time Cliff attended church at the Cobham Christian Fellowship, where Coates was pastor

Cliff

Bill and I only go to church from time to time. Not regularly. We haven't been members of a church for a long time. This is something I sort of regret but rationalize by saying that it doesn't seem to be possible. There is no church in the area that we live where we could go and sit at the feet of a leader.

Dave Cooke (keyboard player)

Graham Jarvis was a real clown. He always made everyone laugh. John Clark was the quiet one who would sit in his room trying to save up his daily allowances. On one tour he saved so much that he was able to buy all his central heating when he got home. The pranksters were me, Mark Griffiths and Alan Park. Mart Jenner was a bit of a hooligan. I lasted from the end of 1980 until a few months after Graham Jarvis died in December 1985.

Stu Calver (backing vocalist)

In 1986, Cliff got rid of a lot of his long-established musicians. That was me, John Perry, Tony Rivers, Dave Cooke and Mart Jenner. Graham Todd had gone a couple of years before and Graham Jarvis the drummer had died in the January.

Bob Hellyer (lighting technician)

On his last tour, Jarvis was yellow. Even the whites of his eyes were yellow. He was not in a good state and, although we didn't realize it, he was getting through a bottle of vodka before each show and a bottle of vodka afterwards. We knew he was unwell. We used to have what we called "alternative tea breaks" where we'd have Champagne rather than tea but we didn't realize what he was putting away when he wasn't with us. He died of cirrhosis of the liver. If the truth be known, the management liked to keep Cliff in the dark for as long as possible about things like this. In their opinion, he shouldn't be bothered with the details.

ABOVE
The Grand Knockout Tournament was a one-off televised event organized in 1987 by Prince Edward (right) that pitted younger members of the Royal Family against competitors from the worlds of sport and show business

Dave Cooke

Jarvis died on New Year's Eve. I called him the day before and we'd agreed that I would come over the next morning to play some backgammon with him. I called at 8.30 a.m. to check that it was still alright, and the nurse passed me over to his wife who was in tears. She said that he'd died half an hour ago. Even though we knew his health was bad, no one thought his life was in danger. It was around March 1986 that I had a call to say that they were creating a new band. The way it was put was, "We're putting a new band together because if we all got together in the same way as before we'd all be bursting into tears because Jarvis isn't there." In fact, it wasn't really a new band. It was three of the old band along with six new people.

ABOVE
*Cliff's band remained steady for almost a
decade, then the musicians were all "released"
at the end of 1985, when Cliff decided it was
time for a change*

Mark Griffiths

Things started to change when Jarvis died. He had been the M.D. and that band had remained fairly consistent for four or five years. A lot of people got dropped on the scrapheap. People like John Perry and Tony Rivers, who'd done 10 years' service, were just dropped like that. A lot of times these changes are made to suit Cliff's new image. Although David Bryce does the firing, Cliff knows all about it.

Tony Rivers

We all left because Cliff was going to be doing the musical *Time*. I think the last gig was on December 16, 1985. After the show, all the band were in tears because they all realized that this was probably the last gig we'd all do together. There's a picture of us in the dressing room and we've all got red eyes and Cliff's smiling! That says it all, really. For Cliff, it was the start of bigger and better things.

David Bryce

That's what I do. If I have to let somebody go, I let them go. I never do it unfairly. I've been asked to fire people like a young boy on the crew who got drunk too much and I'll say, "No. Give him a chance." Sometimes we have 60 people on a tour, but if something goes wrong Cliff can't scream at the lighting operator or the sound engineer. He'll scream at me. I become the whipping boy. I don't expect him to go round having verbal matches with people. He comes and tells me what's wrong and I go and sort it out.

LEFT
David Bryce (right) played a vital role in Cliff's success. He chose songs, hired and fired musicians, organized tours and was in charge of Cliff's personal protection

Cliff

My manager and I always say that we never have an audition for musicians. We only have a personality test.

Tony Meehan

His conviction in himself is enormous. I always felt that. He's the sort of man who you can't tell that certain things can't be done. He is a very strong man and it's this that a lot of people underestimate in him. He's a leader and has a lot of vitality and strength. In the best sense of the word, he is egotistical. You are looking at a highly complex man, and for that reason it is easier to take the image that he offers than to go deeper and analyse what makes him tick.

BELOW
Cliff's pop career is only six years shorter than Queen Elizabeth's reign over Britain. They've met so many times she longer has to ask him what he does

From a Distance 1987–99

Although Cliff's career was still on a roll, he chose the second half of the 1980s and a good part of the 1990s to fulfil his dream of starring in musicals. He had starred in musical films, acted in straight theatre and appeared in pantomime, but he'd never been in a West End musical.

It seemed the logical next step as his concerts became increasingly technically sophisticated. He was interested in the development of laser lighting and enjoyed acting out songs such as "Devil Woman" and "Green Light." *Time* and *Heathcliff*, both of which were staged in London, were commercial hits that were mauled by the critics. Not that Cliff minded. To him, bums on seats were a better indicator of success than stars in reviews.

The character of Heathcliff had fascinated Cliff ever since he read Emily Brontë's *Wuthering Heights* while at school. He'd nurtured the idea of playing him since his earliest days in show business. In 1964, he told the *Daily Express*: "I'd like to do a dramatic film when I'm ready for it. I'd love to play Heathcliff in *Wuthering Heights*, although I don't suppose I ever will. Not until I'm about 30, anyway."

It was also a period of great change in his personal life. The regular church going that had started in the mid-sixties petered out when Sunday became his only day off from the theatre. Bill Latham, his mentor in all things Christian, became so seriously involved with Jill Clarke, a girl he'd met in South Africa in 1980, that she moved into "Charters", the Weybridge home Cliff shared with Bill. Soon after that relationship ended abruptly, Latham became involved with Pia Hoffman, a German fan of Cliff's who had been a stage-door habitué at *Time*.

Latham eventually left Charters to set up home with Hoffman, leaving Cliff alone at home for the first time in his life. Around the same time, Cliff's mother began to lose her memory and had to move into a care home. Although she didn't die until 2007, Cliff felt that he had already lost her. Then, in 1999, Peter Gormley, the man who had so successfully managed Cliff's career since 1960, passed away at the age of 79.

It seemed that all his moorings were coming loose and close friends began to worry about him. What would he do without Gormley's advice, Latham's companionship and his mother's loving approval? The changes were to signal a serious period of re-evaluation that would lead to a sabbatical. The upcoming millennium would prove to be a turning point.

Dave Clark (Producer, *Time*)

I first had the idea for the musical *Time* at the end of the 1970s, after The Dave Clark Five had finished. I grew a beard, went round the world and generally got back into being Dave Clark the person. During this period I realized that music is perhaps the one universal thing. Going to non-English-speaking countries like China and Japan, I noticed that records were played in English, whereas English films and TV programmes were subtitled. So, I thought it would be good to do something with this idea of music as communication. I'd always wanted to do something in theatre because I had spent three years studying drama, but it had to be the right thing. It had to be something that I had a passion for. I worked on this germ of an idea in 1980. I thought it would be good if someone had to stand trial on behalf of the earth. The natural thing would have been to make such a representative a politician, a well-read person or someone older, but I thought it should be someone that the young could understand because it's the young who have to change things. We can plant the seed, but they have to make it grow. I wrote a chunk of it in California, where I had a house. The original idea was mine and then I brought in a co-writer, David Soames, because I needed to work with someone who had experience in the theatre. He had a guy called Jeff Daniels helping him.

BELOW
David Soames co-wrote a musical called The Time Lord *with Jeff Daniels in 1974. This was eventually incorporated into* Time *by Dave Clark*

David Soames (scriptwriter and lyricist for *Time*)

Jeff and I wrote *The Time Lord* in 1974 and it was put on at the Overground Theatre in Kingston in 1978. We met Dave Clark in 1980, and he'd been working on a similar science-fiction idea. When he heard what we had done, we were introduced and we put the two ideas together and that was how *Time* was born. Dave never saw the production, but he heard tapes and saw the script.

Dave Clark

I made a demo of the whole of the album. I then played it to a few friends. Stevie Wonder was the first; he offered to record a few of the songs. Then Julian Lennon did one. Then came Dionne Warwick. It just went on and on like that.

David Soames

It was Dave's idea to have a rock star speaking on behalf of the earth. We had something along those lines. We had someone who sang with a small band. Dave said it had to be someone who had power on earth. We had had it as a woman, but Dave said it had to be a man. In *The Time Lord*, the Time Lord was just a man whose name was Melchizedek.

BELOW
Cliff performing as pop star Chris Wilder, the central character in the musical Time

Dave Clark

I had known Cliff for a long time. Two of his sisters had run my fan club. The Dave Clark Five was playing at the Royal in Tottenham before we had ever made any records, and two girls called Joan and Jacqui Webb came and asked me if they could start a fan club. I thought this was great. Then a year later, after we'd released our first single, it came out that they were Cliff Richard's sisters. Cliff was very kind and generous. He sent me a cable congratulating us on our first hit and then invited me over to his house. We've been friends ever since.

David Soames

Half of the songs in *Time* were written by me, Jeff Daniels and Dave Clark. The other half were brought in. The song "It's in Every One of Us", written by David Pomerance, had been lying around for a couple of years. Dave wrote a couple of songs with John Christie.

Dave Clark

When I was writing *Time*, I didn't have Cliff in mind at all. When I came to think of the musical opening in England, Cliff became an obvious choice because he is such an institution. I couldn't think of any other major star who had lasted so long and who had attracted generation after generation. Theatre is about attracting people across the generations and across the social spectrum, and so Cliff became my first choice for this country. At that time he was tied up for at least two years with tours. The next time we met, I had the tracks recorded by Stevie Wonder, and when Cliff heard them he committed on the spot. He said that he'd love to do it. I had to remind him that it would not just be a year out of his life when it opened in the West End, but an additional six months to take in preparation time, rehearsals and previews.

Cliff

When I decided to do a year in a show everyone told me that I'd get bored, but I wasn't at all. I didn't miss a show. It was just a fabulous experience. It was so visually startling that it was actually doing something that no other show was doing. It was the first of the high-tech shows. We had unbelievable lighting rigs, and people came down from the ceiling on ropes. It was stunning.

David Soames

The holographic head of Akash was something that Dave came up with.

Dave Clark

I sent the script to Lawrence Olivier's agent for him to consider the part of Akash but it was turned down. I then asked a friend of mine who knew him to make sure he actually read the script. I wanted to make sure. I then got an invitation to tea and he had obviously now read it. He'd creased every page. He asked me very in-depth questions about different parts and it was a wonderful meeting. He said, "I'll have to drop my voice at least an octave like I did in *Othello*." Then he said, "Forget the tea, let's have a drink." He was so into the project. It wasn't for the money, I can tell you that. He did it because he wanted to.

Sonya Jones (backing vocalist)

Time took up six days a week, with matinees on a Wednesday and Saturday. We rehearsed it for about six weeks before it opened.

Jodie Wilson (actress)

I think 250 girls auditioned and I got an offer right after the first audition. The director, Larry Fuller, said that unfortunately the lead role had already gone but he'd love me to be the understudy. Five days before the opening night I was asked to take over as they'd become unhappy about the actress they'd chosen for that role. She was doing pantomime in Scotland and she had to be flown to and from rehearsals every day so while this was happening I was learning the part with Cliff and I think he got used to working with me. When she was there it was difficult. Opening in the show was exciting to me as well as very nerve-wracking.

Roger Bruce (company manager)

I'd been with Cameron Mackintosh and Andrew Lloyd Webber for over seven years working on all the big musicals. I was working on bringing

ABOVE
*Cliff as Chris Wilder with Jodie Wilson
as Louise in* Time, *1986*

Les Miserables from the Barbican to the West End when Dave Clark offered me the job on *Time*, I had to beg Cameron to release me and that's how I met Cliff.

Dave Clark

It was a musical about caring about what happens to people. That's the simplest way to put it. If you're happy within yourself, that happiness radiates towards others. The character played by Olivier philosophizes what I feel.

Jodie Wilson

Cliff was lovely. I had a birthday party during the run and I invited the whole company along. It was on a Sunday, which was everyone's day off, so only Rosemarie Ford, Clinton Derricks-Carrol and a couple of the dancers could come. I was really disappointed. Cliff came to my dressing room on the Saturday night to tell me that he couldn't come, and as I'd already had a lot of people saying the same thing I was practically in tears. Cliff said, "Don't worry. I'll take you out for your birthday." So he took me out on the Tuesday and it was so nice. It was something he didn't have to do, but he wanted to make up to me. He bought me a little jewellery jar. I haven't got a bad word to say about him.

Cliff

When it was all over I missed *Time* terribly. Straightaway I went on holiday to the Caribbean and found that I was in bed for about 10 or 11 hours a day. I didn't know I was that tired. When I did the show I felt really good every night, but when I stopped I suddenly became aware and my body was telling me, "Wait a minute..."

David Bryce (manager)

I think Cliff did well with Alan Tarney because a lot of people can write songs, but there aren't many who can write albums. Alan actually knows how to make albums. What he produces becomes more than just 10 tracks.

Alan Tarney (producer and songwriter)

I felt that I had never recorded the definitive album with Cliff, so I got together with David Bryce on a casual basis and we started discussing it. Cliff at that time had gone off to work with Craig Pruess. He does this from time to time. He goes off and makes his own records with a producer he feels he can dominate. He then chooses his own material which, quite frankly, always sounds a bit inane. The idea with *Always Guaranteed* was to do something a bit more special.

Gerry Kitchingham (studio engineer)

I would say that half the tracks on *Always Guaranteed* were written by Alan in the studio. He tends to write his better songs towards the end of a writing period. It's almost as though he feels he works best when he's got a good proportion of the project under his belt. He would always do a guide vocal and when Cliff came in to puts his vocal on it didn't necessarily mean that the track was completely finished. Alan was at his peak on that album. Everything just came together.

Alan Tarney

The way I write is to do a song a day. I sit with a blank piece of paper and start writing with a guitar or a keyboard. I usually have the title and a chorus first. The really important thing is to finish it by the end of the day. I couldn't let it run over. When I'm away from the studio I become more relaxed, and I can't reach the peaks that you need to reach to write great songs. To write well, I need to be in an unnatural situation where I'm eating, breathing and sleeping music. They say that the best songs are written in 10 minutes, but the thing is that you never know when that 10 minutes is going to come. So, you have to sit there writing songs seven days a week, and eventually the 10 minutes come along. *Always Guaranteed* was the closest Cliff got to a *Thriller* album. There were four hits on it.

Gerry Kitchingham

From an engineer's point of view, Cliff has a very good voice. He has brilliant microphone technique although he doesn't have terrific dynamic range. There are some singers who belt it out and you have to compress the vocal too much. He has very good control. The low end of his vocal is particularly good. You can EQ [equalise] quite a bit of the middle-top end into the vocal if you like without it going really thin because the initial sound is very full. I use a valve microphone, which tends to emphasize that low end of warmth. He also has the ability to listen to a playback and immediately know what's needed to improve it.

ABOVE
Cliff's second home in Weybridge with its extensive landscaped gardens, swimming pool and tennis court. He lived here until 2006

Alan Tarney

It goes in cycles. Cliff does one album which is very successful and then the next album, which should continue in the same vein, doesn't. Cliff comes in with 25 different songs and you realize that it's just going to be one of those hodgepodge albums again. We set a precedent with *Always Guaranteed* which we should have built on, but for some reason Cliff undermined it. I've never been able to understand why he does this. I think he possibly feels that the producer is having too much control and he resents that. I think it's a shame, as far as the listening public is concerned, that we aren't allowed to take it as far as we possibly can. I had the whole of the follow-up album written and had given Cliff the tape. The idea was to go into the studio and just complete these 10 tracks. Then Cliff started pulling in these outside songs that he wanted to do. I couldn't understand why he wanted to include "The Best of Me" and "Joanna" on *Stronger*.

Paul Moessl (songwriter and producer)

I played on three tracks on *Stronger* and Cliff let me arrange two of the tracks: "The Best of Me" and "Joanna". What I didn't know at the time was that I was on trial. Cliff wanted to see what I was like to work with in the studio. I then co-produced "Mistletoe and Wine" with Cliff. The first track I produced totally on my own was the single "Saviour's Day".

BELOW
Cliff at the rear of Charters in Weybridge. It was built for the writer Leslie Charteris, creator of Simon Templar, alias "The Saint"

Cliff

I've always got my eye open for a Christmas song, but I don't chase it. Sometimes I get a song sent to me and I just can't resist it. Christmas has become something special because, as the years progressed, we discovered that more records are sold between October and December than the rest of the year put together. Everybody and their mother releases a record at Christmas, so if you have a number-one, it's a real coup. (2006)

Chris Eaton (songwriter)

Cliff tends to go on a first listen. The personal touch means everything to him. "Joanna", which I got on the *Stronger* album, was just a piano/vocal, but my idea was to have it done in the style of Richard Marx, which is how I explained it to Paul Moessl, who produced it. I actually went down to Esher and played "Joanna" to Cliff. I told him that I loved it but wanted to record it myself. I played him other songs, but because I had said I wanted to keep that one, he liked it. He really got into it but I don't think it really hit the mark. He's much cleaner-cut in his sound than I am in my soul. I'll write a song and I'll want a certain groove on it, but it's not what comes out.

Alan Tarney

The people to be most wary of in this business are the friends of the artist. The producer can make the most fantastic record, the artist can tell you it's brilliant, then they play it to their friends who don't happen to like it and the artist will come back and say he's gone off it, and you. The reason for the change of heart is because they played it to their friends. Friends wield enormous power.

Cliff

I feel that if I gave up singing today I could say that my career has been a success. The pressure is off. However, I feel that 1989 is going to be another highlight. At Christmas I was at the top of the video, album, compact disc and record charts with *Private Collection*. This year I will be releasing my 100th single. I've only had nine singles that haven't made the charts and I feel I can't complain if one of my records only makes it to 27, for example. There are people who would give their right arm for just that. I just hope there is more for me to enjoy and it isn't downhill from now on. (1988)

Mel Bush (concert promoter)

I knew Brian Goode, who used to manage The Shadows, and one day I told him that I thought it would be great if Cliff was to do a large outdoor event. He mentioned this to Cliff's office and at first they were unsure. They liked the idea, but were a little reticent because Cliff had never played outdoors in Britain before. They didn't know if it was the right career move.

ABOVE
Bruce Welch and Hank Marvin join Cliff on stage at "The Event", Wembley Stadium, 1989

BELOW
The Vernons Girls reunited for the "Oh Boy!" section of "The Event", 30 years after they'd last performed on the acclaimed TV show

Cliff

I didn't think that people would come out in those sorts of numbers to see me. Also, I'm a working musician, which means that I always go to people's home towns. I go to their towns and they come to see me. When Mel mooted the idea, I thought it was ridiculous.

Mel Bush

I managed to convince them that it would really be a success. I told them that it couldn't just be announced as a concert; it had to be a celebration of his 30 years in show business and a way of saying thank-you to his marvellous fans for being with him for so long. The more I spoke with Cliff, the more he saw the possibility and thought it would be good to bring in artists he had worked with over those years.

Cliff

When we agreed to it I thought up the idea of the show that became "The Event". Mel was the one who said, "Look, I've got my idea to the ground and it's definitely your time and you can do this." They opened up the box office for just one of the dates and it sold out over the weekend. He phoned me to tell me that one whole concert had been sold out.

Mel Bush

Most of the production came from my side, but the form of the show came from Cliff. I'd always wanted to reduce Wembley from a cavernous stadium with a stage at one end. We actually made a proscenium arch out of one end of it. We put the stage across the end and built scaffolding from the grass to the underside of the stand and screened the whole lot with drapes. It looked like an auditorium.

Cliff

I didn't want it to be another history lesson, as it is whenever I reunite with The Shadows. I love working with The Shadows; we have great fun and the public love it, but we don't really go anywhere. That's when I got the idea for doing the "Oh Boy!" section. It was a way of telling my fans that, although a lot of people have done this sort of event before, I haven't, and I'm going to give you a special day.

Maggie Stredder (Vernons Girls)

There had been a total of 18 girls in the Vernons Girls and I managed to get 12 together for "The Event". Two had died, two couldn't be traced and two weren't in the group when it was really famous. They looked great. We started rehearsals two weeks before. It was amazing. It was the high spot of their lives. Most of them were now mums and grandmothers, working in shops or doing their little part-time jobs.

Mel Bush

If you look at the facts and figures for England, Cliff is actually the biggest-drawing act. The last tour we did drew over 400,000. If he had the time and wanted to I think he would have absolutely no problem in playing to a million people in England. No problem at all. To reach 400,000 people we have only had to play in four arenas.

Cliff

The Shadows disappointed me a bit because they wouldn't do the "Oh Boy! "section. They wanted to save their appearance for their own set. My argument was that we're above that. I was starring in the show and I was doing the lot. It wouldn't spoil my later entrance by also coming on in the middle of the show. I think The Shadows are bigger than that as well.

Bruce Welch (guitarist)

We didn't want to play during the "Oh Boy!" set because we're current, not has-beens. Also, it would have detracted from the half-hour set we were going to do as The Shadows and the half-hour we were going to do as Cliff and The Shadows.

Cliff

When The Shadows told me this, and then I found I couldn't get Marty Wilde, I felt a bit desperate. I had no idea how to contact The Kalin Twins, but then they bumped into one of my road crew who gave them my number and I suddenly got a call. They told me that they'd love to be on it. I nearly died! It was fantastic.

BELOW
The jacket of Cliff's white suit that he wore at "The Event" was sewn with 2,000 diamantés that sparkled in the stage lights

Hal Kalin (one-half of pop duo The Kalin Twins)

I was in a bar and a guy who was playing the organ and singing finished his set came over and was introduced to me. He told me that he had a close friend who worked with Cliff and that he knew Cliff was planning this huge concert at Wembley. He asked if he could pass on my number. I said, "Sure." That's when we made contact. I'd been working for the criminal-justice system and my brother, Herb, had become a probation officer. We'd given up singing professionally in the late 1960s and were only doing small time things. To suddenly be invited to London and work at Wembley Stadium in front of 70,000 people was amazing.

Cliff

It was because The Shadows decided not to do the "Oh Boy!" section that I had the idea of getting together with Tony Meehan and Jet Harris. It was slight pique. I thought, "I'll show them," and got hold of two of the original members of The Shadows. The Searchers and Gerry and The Pacemakers had nothing to do with my career, but they were people we fought against in the sixties and survived in spite of them. Of course, they offer great value for money.

Paul Moessl

Cliff likes to keep things fresh, which is the reason the band members tend to change a lot. It's purely an image thing. He wants a different look, so he changes some of the faces on stage. When he switched to a band singing on stage with no additional backing vocalists it was because he wanted something more rock 'n' roll. The band we had was excellent. Musically, there was nothing wrong with it whatsoever. He just wanted a change, and being a star he can do exactly what he wants. It was rather awkward for me because many of those who were sacked thought that I had instigated it. If they had told them upfront what was going to happen, it would have been a lot less messy.

Mark Griffiths (guitarist)

The sackings that took place at the Knebworth gig in 1990 were bad because the musicians were only going to be told after they had finished two shows. I found out because I had already said I couldn't do any more shows that year due to my commitment to The Shadows and had a deputy sorted for Cliff's autumn tour. I sensed something was wrong at the rehearsals. I got a funny feeling from the crew and other people I knew. I probed a bit and was told what was going to happen. When the other guys found out, there was hell to pay. The backing singers had been promised a rise once they joined the band, but when the contracts finally came through the day before the tour started, it was for the old money. They then said that they weren't going out unless they got the same money as us. They got their money but that's when the idea for the clear-out began. Some of the guys were very bitter about it. One of them had moved house on the strength of what he was going to earn and he got into big trouble with his mortgage.

Bruce Welch

During rehearsals for Knebworth, I saw David Bryce and Cliff in a corner and I went over to them and said, "You do realize that the band all know, don't you?" They said, "Know what?" I said "They all know that you're going to sack them." They said "They can't possibly know." I said "They know." The way of hiring and firing, of getting rid of people, of friends who've been with him for years and helped his career, really sucks. They're treated like crap.

Trevor Spencer (drummer)

Cliff used management in the way it should be used, I suppose. Keep the persona clean and delegate the nasties.

Cliff

We don't really sack people. We terminate their contracts or we don't renew them.

Mick Mullins (backing vocalist)

It was a bit cheap the way it was done. We were all sitting around in the band room and Cliff came in and said, "Well, I don't know how you found out but, yes, I'm trying out something new, so this is the last gig, chaps." He wouldn't have come to tell us if we hadn't found out beforehand. He was put in a position where he had to face it on his own instead of getting Mr Nasty to do it. When you're in his band, it's as though butter wouldn't melt in his mouth and any of the crap that is dealt out comes only from David Bryce. But Cliff's not daft. He decides what's going on. That's the bottom line.

Bob Hellyer (lighting technician)

I think the "Knebworth shuffle" was down to people asking for more money. They gave John Clark the sack for asking for too much, but had to bring him back because they couldn't find a comparable guitarist. Because working with Cliff is regular work, they use this fact to argue – well, maybe you could earn more elsewhere, but this is stable employment.

Cliff

It wasn't a sacking. I just needed a change. That vocal group was probably the best I've had on stage. I just wanted a different look. I wanted a band that sang, not a separate vocal group.

Van Morrison (singer, songwriter)

We were sitting around in the studio and someone said, "We should get Cliff to do a vocal on this one." We were having a laugh. Next thing I know, some guy has contacted him. I didn't know. A couple of weeks later I was told Cliff was ready to do it. By then, I'd completely forgotten about it. He did a great job, though. He's a good singer – very good. He's a professional. He just goes in and does it. It's great working with someone like that.

Paul Moessl

"Saviour's Day" was the first record of Cliff's that I produced alone.

Chris Eaton

He did "Saviour's Day" because I went down to a
Christmas party at Cliff's office in 1989. He had done
"Mistletoe and Wine" for Christmas 1988 and in 1989
he had done the song with Band Aid and one with Van
Morrison. He was talking about "From a Distance" as
his Christmas record for 1990. I played him "Saviour's
Day" in his Rolls Royce and told him I felt strongly
about it. After he'd heard it he turned round and said,
"This is a number-one song."

Paul Moessl

After co-producing the Christmas album *Together With
Cliff Richard*, we worked in the same way on *Cliff Richard:
The Album*. Cliff doesn't normally go for a full album, a
record that begins at track one and flows right through
to the end. That doesn't really enter his head. Because of
this, the person choosing the songs has to be in complete
control. When Cliff is left to do it alone, the continuity goes
all wrong.

Cliff

My favourite book when I was at school was *Wuthering
Heights.* When I did *Time* in the West End, I felt really
good working in the theatre and I wanted to do something
else. I spoke to a friend of mine, who was the director of the Edinburgh Festival
for a number of years, about my idea of playing *Heathcliff* in a musical version of
Wuthering Heights and he really thought that was good. He thought it would be
different and for me it would be unexpected. I got Tim Rice interested in writing
the lyrics and John Farrar in writing the music.

Jay Norris (teacher)

He only failed his English literature GCE O Level by two marks and passed in
English Language. I thought he would have got the English literature. We had done
Shakespeare's *Julius Caesar*, *Wuthering Heights* and a poetry anthology that included
a poem by D. H. Lawrence. I must have done a good job, because *Wuthering
Heights* went on to be his favourite work of fiction. That's because if you understand
something which is good, you enjoy it more. I remember him reading Lawrence's
poem "The Snake" and Coleridge's "Khubla Khan" onto a tape.

ABOVE
*Cliff and Dame Diana Rigg following a "Joy
To the World" concert at London's Royal Albert
Hall in December 1997*

ABOVE
Tim Rice, best known for his work on such musicals as Jesus Christ Superstar, *was invited by Cliff to supply the lyrics for a musical based on Emily Brontë's* Wuthering Heights

BELOW
John Farrar, seen here with Olivia Newton-John, wrote the music for Heathcliff. *He had played guitar with Cliff in the 1970s*

Cliff

People tend to think of Heathcliff in romantic terms and, of course, the love between Heathcliff and Cathy was strong, but it points out the danger of an obsessive love. When Cathy dies, Heathcliff is so obsessed, so filled with hatred that she married someone else, that he returns as a vengeful character and spends most of the rest of the book destroying everyone else. Everyone was telling me, "Well, you're the nice guy – how can you play this role?" I would tell them that this has nothing to do with it. Some of the most shocking things are done by some of the nicest people, or those who you think of as the nicest people.

Tim Rice (lyricist for *Jesus Christ Superstar, Evita*, and others)

I was thrilled to have been asked to write some songs by Cliff. I really took orders from Cliff and the writer of the book, Frank Dunlop. At times I worked together with John Farrar if I was in LA, but at other times he would send me over a tape of a tune and I would fax him back a lyric. I've never sat in a room, writing with someone. I suppose that might happen if both writers were doing words and music, but not if you're doing separate jobs.

Cliff

There was a point at which it seemed that it wouldn't happen. Neither Tim nor John Farrar like being rushed, and the words and music weren't finished in time for me to tour with it as I had planned. The venues were booked and there would have been a £1.5 million deficit if I hadn't done something, so I did *The Hit List* tour instead. I used the same halls. It was a sell-out tour and in the concerts I sang three of the songs from *Heathcliff.* As soon as the public heard them, bookings for the musical skyrocketed. A lot of people thought I was going to do *The Sound of Music* because that was the public concept of a musical. I don't think rock 'n' roll had made it to the theatre. I wanted to be true to the music. I was and it worked. The public loved it. Over a period of seven months, nearly half a million people saw it and the album went platinum.

Tim Rice

The last thing I want to do is to criticize the musical, but I think there were one or two flaws in it. I talked to Cliff and David Bryce about it. I thought we had the germ of something pretty good. It worked superbly for Cliff. It was a big hit. But I don't think anybody else would ever take it on. From my point of view it fell between two stools. The music was very rock 'n' roll, and yet the rest of the show was very traditional. Most of the songs I was very pleased with, but they never stood a chance because they were delivered in a rather pop-rock way, and some of the words were hard to make out. I mean, it worked wonderfully for Cliff, but it never got beyond being a Cliff Richard show.

Cliff

Heathcliff took up five years of my life. I'd like to see it become a musical in which someone else could take over the lead role, but it would have to be someone who could sing and act. There is no way you could put in a singer with no stage experience. There is an incredible discipline involved in the thespian world that sometimes rockers don't bother with. It's interesting. When I announced *Heathcliff*, people said I could never do it. Now that I've done it the same people are saying, "Well, no one else could do it. It's Cliff's show." Of course, there are loads of people who could do it. They would just do it in a different way.

Tim Rice

I had nothing to do with the production. The thing was, the critics were vicious but the punters loved it; it was sold out. One of the problems that Cliff had was that he was producing it, helping to write the book and starring in it. What it needed was someone else strong to be in control the way that Cameron Mackintosh takes control of his musicals.

Cliff

The reviews were horrific. Bill Latham rang me and said, "Don't read the reviews." So I never read them. I couldn't be bothered. There's no point reading them now. They were totally wrong. The amazing thing is, my sisters Jacqui and Joan went to the press night in Birmingham and they overheard journalists saying how much they liked it and how it was so much better than they thought it would be. But not one of them wrote it. The press were wrong about *Phantom of the Opera*, *Cats*, *Les Miserables* and

ABOVE
Cliff played the role of Heathcliff on the London stage for a year, starting in October 1996

ABOVE
Cliff received his knighthood from the Queen on October 25, 1995. He had been awarded the OBE in 1980

Starlight Express; three of these musicals are the longest running shows in the West End! It's obvious to me that the critics have no concept of what the public actually wants and therefore they don't know what we're trying to do. I'm not interested in doing something that only me and one critic likes; I've never run my career like that. That's why they've written me off so often but it's probably why I'm still here. I'm written off because I don't do what people think is "the thing to do".

Graham Disbrey (teacher, Crusaders' member)

He is very much an establishment figure now. He has become very accepted. He meets with royalty. He lives his social life on a very elevated level.

Cliff

When I received my knighthood I joined a group of people who were going to become knights. There were three or four of us. There was a stool with an armrest on the right hand side. An official talks you through the procedure. He said, "You walk to the centre of the platform, turn left and there the Queen would be. You'll then see the stool. You have to go forward and kneel on your right knee. She dubs one shoulder, then the other, and you stand up. You then lean forward so that she can put the medal around your neck. She will then speak to you and that's the only time you are allowed to say anything." I told my sisters afterwards that I bet she wished she'd given the knighthood to a doctor or someone because I just mumbled. I was so overwhelmed.

Mike Read (DJ and friend)

The royals will be relaxed with you if they feel there's not going to be any comeback. I danced with Diana for half an hour at the Royal Albert Hall and the papers came to me and said, "What did you talk about?" I would say, "Nothing" because the royals would hate to think that you went away and related conversations that they'd had with you. When we were in Austria one time, Charles and Diana were at the same resort and we met up with a lot of people from their party one night and they wanted Cliff to sing. He ended up in the bar singing all these obscure B-sides and they had a great time. The next day they say that Diana had been really upset that she wasn't there and she wanted Cliff to have dinner with her and Charles the next day and then to organize another sing-song. Unfortunately, Diana's father died that afternoon and they were rushed home.

Charles Haswell (friend)

Charles and Diana were at the same hotel. I had
already met her through several charity events. On
the Friday night we had a little sing-song with the
private detectives, and obviously word got back
to the prince and princess and we were asked to
repeat the performance on the Sunday. It was so
sad. We were asked to meet at eight o'clock and
the news of her father's death came in at about
three o'clock in the afternoon.

Cliff

Since getting the knighthood I'm invited to more royal functions.
The more you meet the Royal Family, though, the more you realize that the only
difference between them and us is that they're royal. We all go through the same
things. They're either interesting or not interesting. The Queen would never ask me
about my tours or recordings, but Diana used to. When I met her in Australia in
1988, during the country's bicentennial celebrations, she spoke to me and knew the
Always Guaranteed album by name. She was more in touch and interested. Before
her death, opinion seemed equally divided between those who thought she was
manipulative and those who thought she was wonderful. Afterwards, things swung
100 per cent in her favour. I've sat next to her at dinner parties where she has been
saying, "What am I going to do? The press are getting worse. I can't go anywhere
without bodyguards and detectives and I hate it." I just said, "You're going to have
to swing with it." She ended up just doing her own thing and letting everyone know
where she was going. Charities need publicity. They need the fundraising effort to be
publicised and so charities manipulate situations by using people like me or Diana.
That's what it's about. But then it's crazy to say
that she was manipulative. She was there to raise
the profiles of these different organizations.

ABOVE
*Cliff is presented to Princess Diana at the
Royal Albert Hall following the "Joy to the
World" concert in December 1991*

BELOW
*Cliff chats informally to Diana while watching
tennis at Wimbledon. Virginia Wade, who won
the women's singles title in 1977, is on the left*

Chris Eaton

Musically, I couldn't see where he was going. It
became more disappointing to write for him. He
was getting embarrassingly "pretty" and I didn't like
that side of it. It's understandable that he can't put
the soul behind some of the tracks he sings because
he has never experienced what he's singing about. He
doesn't know about the heartbreak. I'm sure he may
have been through it, but he never talks about it.

Cliff

Real as I Wanna Be is a very diverse album. We've got one really sentimental but brilliant song, a couple of funky things, some menacing things, a happy dance-able song that I'm going to get remixed and one track where I sound like a new boy band. The song always dictates the way you will record it. "Miss You Nights" and "Devil Woman" fit on the same album because they were by the same artist and used the same producer. There is cohesion because we did them at the same time. In the end, the song tells you what to do. (1997)

Peter Wolf (producer)

The idea was to make an album that was honest. It had to be what Cliff was. There was no grand plan other than to produce good music and present it in the most straight-ahead way possible.

Cliff

We did not know there was anything wrong with [my mother]. We thought her memory was going. We used to joke about it. She'd say, "I'm getting so stupid. I can't remember," and I would say; "Oh, come on, I can't remember what I'm doing tomorrow. I'm not stupid; I've just got a bad memory." If only we had known. My sister Joan looked after her and there was a point where she'd say: "Mother is being so belligerent," and they'd get into arguments. Now my sister says, "If only we had known early on that this is what it was. I would have just said, 'Yes, Mum, no, Mum' and just made her happy, because that's all we can do."

ABOVE
In the 1990s, Cliff's mother succumbed to a form of Alzheimer's disease that would eventually lead to her death

Gerald Coates (evangelist and spiritual mentor)

I think Bill's attitude is, "Look, Cliff: you've got fame, you've got wealth, you can go away with friends... What have I got? You go to America for a month and I'm left here twiddling my thumbs." Jill [Clarke] filled a very necessary gap. I think Cliff would find it very hard if Bill and Jill married and were living in the same house together. That would be difficult. I don't think he would be adverse to Bill marrying Jill, but he wouldn't want to be a lodger in Jill's house.

Jill Clarke (Bill Latham's ex-girlfriend)

To begin with, I lived with Sue Barker – Cliff was still going out with her at the time, but after he broke up with her I rented a flat of my own. I spent more and more time at Cliff's and eventually moved in … In my heart I was committed to [Bill Latham]. I felt I was married to him without having a piece of paper to prove it. (1999)

Sunday Mirror

Right from the start it was Cliff who laid down the house rules. Jill was forced to become celibate and sleep in a separate bedroom from Bill because of Cliff's Christian beliefs. And it was Jill who had to stay at home alone to look after Cliff's pet dogs while he took bachelor-boy holidays with Bill. Then finally, when Bill found another woman, it was Cliff who broke the bad news. (1999)

Jill Clarke

[Bill] wrote me a letter which I found while he and Cliff had gone away to film a TV show. It was just left there for me to find on the bed. I was absolutely shattered and didn't stop crying for a month… It was Cliff who had to speak to me. He said, "We need to find somewhere for you to go." Initially he said that it would be a place nearby so that I could see the dogs. The dogs are my saving grace now. I get all the love I need from them.

Daily Mail

Now a new face – that of Pia Hoffmann – has joined Cliff and Bill at the breakfast table. (February 13, 1999)

Bill Latham (mentor and friend)

[Pia Hoffmann's] motives are not devious. Cliff doesn't have fans in his home. I have been dealing with them for many years and I know that many, in their enthusiasm and determination to get to Cliff, will say all sorts of things. Pia is not one of them, and I'm not just a kid who is easily manipulated. I haven't

BELOW
When Bill Latham set up home with Pia Hoffman (centre) it marked the end of 35 years of house-sharing with Cliff

RIGHT
*Pia Hoffman, a Cliff fan from
Germany, lived at Charters before
she and Bill moved to another house
in Weybridge. This left Cliff living
alone for the first time*

been taken in. We're in love. Pia was a very active fan as a kid, and like a lot of other teenagers, she had a great crush on Cliff. She and some girlfriends in Germany would go and see his concerts all over the place. But she decided that when she grew up that great adventure ended. Since the age of 19, she has been a successful student, has been successful in her profession and has lived a totally normal, Cliff-free life until I met her in the course of her profession and began a relationship with her. (1999)

BBC News

BBC Television presenter Jill Dando has died after she was shot in the head on the doorstep of her home. Ms Dando, 37, who presented *Crimewatch UK* and *Holiday*, suffered a fatal brain injury in the attack in Fulham, west London. She was taken to nearby Charing Cross Hospital, where she was confirmed dead on arrival at 1303 BST (1203 GMT). Her post-mortem examination later revealed that she had received a single gunshot wound to the head. (April 26, 1999)

Cliff

[Jill] was a very beautiful woman and she just seemed to be a very genuine person, and it was really nice to get to know her. She seemed to have a chemistry where more people liked her than is normal. She was also a very funny person. Her murder is very difficult to understand and I find it all very confusing at the moment. (1999)

Sir John Birt (Director-General, BBC)

Jill had a schoolgirl crush on Cliff, which never wholly went away. The "Holiday" team gave her a marvellous surprise. When she was filming at the magnificent Opera Ball in Vienna, Cliff stepped out of the crowd to whisk her away onto the dance floor. She wrung her hands in disbelief, almost overcome by her excitement. Cliff became a good and valued friend. She learned tennis so she could partner him at his tournament. When he came to dinner at her home, she hid most of her vast collection of his recordings to disguise from him just how great a fan she really was! (Address given at Jill Dando's Memorial Service, September 28, 1999)

ABOVE
Popular TV presenter Jill Dando (left) had grown up as a fan of Cliff's music. The two became close friends, and her murder in 1999 had a devastating effect on Cliff

Cliff

I believe that free will allows us to choose to do good or bad. The person who killed Jill carried out a despicable act – a bad, evil thing – and poor Jill was the victim of his anger. But she had a strong faith. I believe that Satan was smirking on that day. Jill was not perfect, but I truly believe she is in a better place. With regard to my faith, I cannot say why it happened to Jill, but one day we will know. (2002)

Don't Stop Me Now 2000–07

In the year 2000, Cliff fulfilled a longstanding ambition of clearing his diary. He spent his time travelling, visiting old friends and relishing the kind of anonymity he'd left behind when "Move It" became a hit in 1958. It was obviously a time for him to organize the next stage of his career. He was, after all, on the verge of his sixtieth birthday, a time when many of his contemporaries were retiring from work.

He had consistently said, ever since the early 1960s, that he would go on singing for as long as his voice held out and there was an audience willing to pay to hear him. He wasn't about to change his mind, but wanted a bit more slack in his life. The constant cycle of recording, promoting, rehearsing and touring left very little time for the ordinary pleasures of life. Ordinarily he could travel, but not explore; meet people but not make friends; talk but not reflect. He needed time to relax and absorb.

One of his few appearances in 2000 was on board the Seabourn *Goddess*, where he hosted 60th birthday celebrations for 87 friends as they cruised the Mediterranean. The celebration was paid for by *OK* magazine in return for exclusive coverage and it signalled a change of attitude. In the past he had steered clear of ostentation but now, dressed in his Alistair McQueen coat, he seemed to embrace the glamour and glitz.

He began to get more involved in other business interests, creating his own wine, Vida Nova; investing in a hotel with Indian businessman Surinder Arora; and developing a range of fragrances named after his hit songs. He bought a plot of land in Barbados and had a luxury home built overlooking the Caribbean sea. He later sold his house in Weybridge and bought a smaller house in Wentworth, an apartment in New York and a luxury penthouse suite near Ascot.

Some credit this change of direction to the arrival into his life of John McElynn, a former priest he met in New York in 1999 who now shares Cliff's homes, is his constant travelling companion and has taken on many of the "gatekeeping" roles once occupied by Bill Latham. McElynn organizes his diary, answers his phone and opens his emails.

Although Cliff continued to record and tour, his impact on the charts had waned. This was partly attributable to lack of airplay.

Radio stations keen to pursue listeners with the most disposable income didn't view Cliff fans as their target audience. This frustrated Cliff, who saw no point in releasing singles if the music wasn't going to be broadcast.

But while his record sales dipped, his social cachet increased. He became a natural choice as a guest for major national celebrations, socialized with the rich, powerful and famous and was frequently photographed at first nights, charity events and openings. Almost half a century after his first single, he became the first British pop star to loan his home to a prime minister.

BELOW
Performing "Move It" with Queen guitarist Brian May at "Party at the Palace", June 3, 2002

Cliff

I think there has to be a re-evaluation about my position in the music industry. I don't intend to make records that aren't played. If they're not played, one assumes there won't be any hits. The only stations that would play the tracks of *Heathcliff* were BBC Radio 2 and Heart FM. We can't waste our time doing those things. (1998)

Simon Sadler (Head of Music, Kiss 100 FM)

Cliff does have a point. Some stations are prejudiced. I have to say that, if I did see his name on a record, I'd find it very difficult to play it. (1998)

Cliff

"Millennium Prayer" is nothing more than a collection of positive thoughts for the millennium – that we are fed, that we are kept away from evil, and that we are more forgiving at this special time. I think that's why people have responded to it. But then people say it's controversial. What is so controversial about it? To find "Millennium Prayer" controversial, it seems to me that you'd have to be an absolute devil-worshipper. (1999)

George Michael (singer and songwriter)

Just knowing that there has been a Christian campaign for it – I think it is so exploitative of people's religion. It really is. I think there are people out there who feel it is their duty to buy this record on the eve of the millennium. That is a really horrible reason for a number-one record. (1999)

Cliff

"Well, here I am at 60 and I'm number one! So, stuff them all. Rock 'n' roll music has got nothing to do with age or religious beliefs. I'm not trying to change the world; I'm just a pop singer. So I find it really disturbing that all these people are having a go at me. I have never heard of an artist who gets to number one and then gets slagged off by others. What are their motives?" (1999)

George Michael

Cliff is always taking his hat off to himself, telling you how many hits he's had. Yes, absolutely great achievement. But I think the single and the way it has been dealt with has been vile. (1999)

Cliff

Besides my charity concerts, the concert for Jill Dando and events for my 60th birthday, I won't be making any appearances next year. I've made a lot of friends all over the world and during my tours I'm not able to get to see them. Now I'm planning to visit these people in different places around the world. The last few years have been so busy with *Heathcliff*, the Albert Hall concerts, the Hyde Park shows and the upcoming millennium shows in Birmingham that I really need some holiday. But after 2000, I promise to come back refreshed. (1999)

Aleksander Mezek (singer and songwrier)

As far as I know, he was actually considering disbanding his office. Everyone was expecting him to do this at that stage. It was a bit of a crisis point for him. It was partly do with the fact that Bill wanted to get married to Pia and she was living at Cliff's house and Cliff decided that this arrangement could no longer go on. I also think it was around that time that he was finding it difficult because his mother was starting not to recognize him. He told me that once when he was leaving the home where she's living, she turned to a nurse that was looking after her and said, "Do you know who that was? That was Cliff Richard." That got to him. It was a big shock. His mother obviously knew who he was, but she didn't recognize him as her own son, she recognized him as a pop star. Everything just came to a head for him. It was during his year off, while he was in New York, that he met (the American priest) John McElynn and they got on really well. He was really happy to be introduced to John's family and felt really at home there. He found a circle of friends.

Nigel Goodwin (actor)

In finding John, I think Cliff found a family. There was John, his mum and his sisters and I think that was very important to Cliff. The other thing is that he can be in America without being hassled. He can shop in Macy's without someone shoving a camera in his face or a piece of paper in his hand.

Aleksander Mezek

Cliff is used to having a personal assistant. He always had that in Bill and I'm sure that Bill is still very important for Cliff to have around because he knows so much about what Cliff requires. I think John is more like someone who can arrange his private diary and take care of his private contacts rather than the business ones.

Cliff

My year off from touring has been one huge lesson. I was beginning to believe it was impossible for me to lead a normal life and then I spent some time in America and realized that I could. I met some people through mutual friends who had never heard of me and it wasn't until I played them "Devil Woman" and "We Don't Talk Anymore" that they said: "We know those songs, but we've never known who sang them." (2004)

ABOVE
Former priest John McElynn (right) met Cliff in 1999 and moved into his home shortly afterwards. McElynn, a New Yorker, now manages Cliff's private diary

Stuart Ongley (music publisher)

He loves the fact that he can be relatively anonymous in America. He can live more of a normal life there. He can go around unnoticed. I think that, after all the pressure he's been under for all his life, he really enjoys that.

Gloria Hunniford (TV presenter)

I think Cliff has spread his wings.

Nigel Goodwin

Cliff is enjoying his life more. He's enjoying using his money and he's constantly diversifying. I think he's experiencing a new freedom and there's a new sense of having fun.

Aleksander Mezek

He's become more settled. The year 2000 was definitely his low point. I saw him at the Royal Albert Hall in 1999 and he looked really drained. He's in a much happier place now and he's looking at his career in a different light. When you've survived for so long, the career almost works for you. He understands what his place is in the British music business. People give him credit for it and he's pleased with that.

Cliff

It's an ideal time for me to take it easy. I've had a wonderful career. I've been really lucky in what is a very tough business. Nevertheless, I've had to work hard, too, because none of this comes easy. Feeling happy and content is very important to me. Right now, I'm especially at ease with my life and that's the best place to be. (2000)

Steve Chalke (Christian leader and social activist)

Has Cliff changed? I think there's a yes and a no to that. I think he's changed a lot in the way he spends his time and the things he gets involved in. He doesn't do the amount of church-related stuff that he used to, and his relationship to Bill has changed as well. In another way he hasn't changed at all. I interviewed him on stage at an event for the centenary of Crusaders and he's still really clear, articulate and engaging about his faith.

Martin Townsend (Editor, *OK!* magazine)

We wanted to do something for Cliff's 60th because he's always really popular with *OK!* readers and so Bill Latham came in and we asked him what Cliff would really like to do. He said that his dream was to take all his best friends from over the years on a cruise ship. So we started to look at different ways in which we might do this. At one stage we thought we might get Cliff to perform on the *QE2* in return for a few days on one of P&O's smaller boats. In the end we were able to get his favourite cruise line, Seabourn. They have small ships that are quite intimate where you can get to know everyone on board. We basically hired one of their ships for him, and in return we got an interview with him before he left, coverage of his 60th birthday party and a follow-up story using pictures taken by Gloria Hunniford's husband, Stephen Way.

Nigel Goodwin

The birthday cruise was a lot of fun. It was organized really well. It started with a champagne breakfast at Heathrow, after which we flew to Nice, where we were piped onboard by Cliff, who was dressed in a naval uniform. The boat then sailed to Monaco where Cliff celebrated his birthday onboard. By then, a gale was blowing up. We were supposed to sail to Portofino, but the weather was too bad so we headed back along the French coast to San Tropez. We had a day there, then went to Barcelona, Las Palmas and finally to Málaga, where we all caught the plane home.

Cliff

The people onboard are all very special in my life. That may be unimportant to anyone else, but it's my birthday and it was important to me to surround myself with people who have meant a great deal to me over the years. It was very difficult to come up with a guest-list. My first one had about 500 people on it, all of whom I would have liked to have here, but I had to trim it down to 80 by using different criteria. (2000)

Martin Townsend

We joined the ship in Monaco and Shirley Bassey, who lives there, came down on the first night. There were lots of his mates there: Bobby Davro, Gloria Hunniford, Mike Read, Bruce Welch, Olivia Newton-John. Before we went on the boat we went up the hill at Monaco to a fantastic restaurant where a group of us had dinner. The only problem was that it absolutely poured with rain that day. We had a massive party on the first night and Shirley Bassey sang "Happy Birthday" to him, which was fantastic. Then Cliff gave a speech and then those of us from the magazine who'd come to cover the party left the ship and left them to it. Gloria's husband took loads of photographs which we used. We didn't want to accompany him every minute of the day so he just went off and had a fantastic cruise.

Nigel Goodwin

The band played every night. Cliff sang, Olivia sang and different people did their things. Cliff was very much present and took time to sit with each group and be with them. The different groups of people represented different parts of his life. There were the musicians he was then working with, personal friends, people he knew from the Christian community, management, some people from British Airways that he'd befriended, tennis players and some fellow entertainers.

Aleksander Mezek

Cliff loves warm climates, and I think that's what appealed to him when he was offered the opportunity to build a home in Barbados. I was at his home in Weybridge when he had the plans drawn up, and I think it was a really good investment opportunity for him. I think it was an exceptionally good deal for a

BELOW
Cliff began to diversify his business interests in the 21st century, launching a range of fragrances named after some of his best-known songs

prime plot of land. Barbados has a pretty even temperature all year round, the social calendar is similar to that in Britain and a lot of his friends have houses there. It also has the advantage of being close to America, which is where he is spending a lot more of his time.

Cliff

I was offered the pick of the plots in Barbados and I didn't hesitate in choosing the one with the best view. Every morning I wake up in Barbados, I pinch myself. It's hard to believe the house is mine. (2004)

Nigel Goodwin

My personal view is that Cliff's passion and his love was the stage and the music. That drove him. Anything else was very secondary to that. He doesn't want to be on his own, though. He wants friendships. We live in a generation that doesn't allow two men, or two women, to live under the same roof without questions being asked.

Cliff

When I started out, they accused me of being a sex maniac, and then, when that didn't stick, they turned to the gay thing. Now I find it rather fun. You know, I'm an "enigma". When I looked that word up I thought, "I like this!" They don't understand me, and long may it reign. I don't intend to talk about everything in my life and you're naïve if you think that when I'm asked questions I'm going to give all the answers that you want to hear. There will be things that I take to the grave with me. (2003)

Nigel Goodwin

If he fights the accusations too much, people say "Well, there must be something there." If he says absolutely nothing, they say the same.

Hank Marvin (guitarist)

I guess there are certain things about anyone that one gets puzzled about at times. I guess what I did find a mystery is why he didn't get married. I think he would have made a good father and husband. He certainly had the opportunity. He knows why he didn't. Maybe he was right: that it wouldn't have worked out with the people involved. Maybe "mystery" is the wrong word to use. That might lead people to get the wrong end of the stick.

Tony Rivers (backing vocalist)

The thing is, if there was anything to come out in the wash about Cliff, it would have come out by now. No one can get away with big secrets. If, after all these years, he turned out to be gay I think then, first and foremost, he would be a hypocrite for daring to tell anyone else how to live.

Mike Read (DJ and friend)

People tend to be more fascinating to the public if there are many different sides to their character and they're always getting involved in different things. John Lennon was always more interesting to people than Paul McCartney because Lennon was the "bad boy of pop" whereas McCartney was perceived as the "nice boy of pop". Cliff is always perceived to be exactly as you find him: "This is me, I'm a pop singer and I'm of the Christian faith."

Cliff

I have a lot of friends. I will never ever be alone. My house is never empty. A friend of mine came and said, "This is like being in a cattery, here. People come and go all the time." And I've got three sisters who've now given me 11 nieces and nephews. (2004)

ABOVE
Cliff with some of his many nieces and nephews at the West End film premiere of Star Wars III, *May 2005*

Mike Read

He's a likeable man and most people like him. Those who don't like him don't like him because he's too likeable.

Olivia Newton-John (singer and friend)

Critics like to pull people apart. If they can't attack their music, they try to find fault with their lives. They look for the drugs, the drink and the serial affairs. The worst thing they can say about Cliff is that he's too nice – which is a compliment, really.

Graham Disbrey (teacher and Crusaders' member)

Cliff was a tremendous blessing to Gloria Hunniford when she lost her daughter, Caron Keating. Who was there the following day, all day, but Cliff? There are beautiful things like that going on that nobody knows about. He has a big heart.

ABOVE
*Cliff pictured with Gerald Coates at an event
celebrating the AIDS initiative AIDS Care
Education and Training (ACET). Coates is
a founder of ACET; Cliff is the patron*

Cliff

I like the bachelor state. I like it because I know that one thing is for certain when you get married, and that is you have to commit yourself to that. Maybe that's the reason where there are so many divorces ... I'm not being selfish; it's a choice. You can either marry or not marry. I didn't decide early on not to marry. It just happened that I reached this stage and I'm not married, but I like my life. (2004)

Ray Mackender (mentor and adviser)

I've known Cliff for a long time and I've known a lot people who have known Cliff for a long time, and we've all come to the same conclusion: we can't work it out. It's not that we're shamming or hiding something.

Cliff

There are gay people in the world. Some of them are very talented. Some of them could be great priests. Unfortunately, there have been priests who have obviously been paedophiles and have abused children. Now we have to deal with that, too. But you can't throw the baby out with the bathwater. We have a world that is full of all sorts of feelings and emotions. We take the best and make the best of it. (2005)

Gerald Coates (evangelist and spiritual mentor)

There was a time when Cliff clearly identified with what was then known as the Cobham Christian Fellowship, and which is now known as Pioneer People. He would sometimes come with Bill Latham, sometimes without. He enjoyed the worship and teaching.

Cliff

If we ignore our spirituality, we live at less than half our potential. (2000)

Olivia Newton-John

Cliff doesn't make a secret of his Christian faith and he practises it. People find it very hard to believe that someone can be so devout and believe in something so much. It's a kind of strength and I think people are intrigued to find the secret. Everyone is looking for something and Cliff has obviously found his answer so people think maybe he can help them. I think he gets a lot of that.

Cliff

For a couple of years I suffered with a kidney stone which would give me a terrible pain that was hard to locate. I could never tell if it was at the front, back or middle of my torso. One night in Portugal it became so bad I had to call a doctor. As I lay there waiting for his arrival, my fingers and my lips turned numb. I immediately thought it was my heart. I can remember thinking, "If I die now, my album will go to number one. It would have to." That was a lesson for me. I thought I might be on my death-bed and it proved to me that I didn't have any fear of this thing that I will one day have to face. Of course, I don't want to break my neck or die in terrible pain, but in general terms becoming a Christian freed me up in an area that can tie many people down. Many people spend their whole lives fearing sickness and death, even though it's the one certainty in life. Death is the one fact of life we tend not to face up to. When you become a Christian, you realize that you've started on a new life before the old one has ended.

Tony King (VP, Rocket Records)

When I worked with him, I was pleased to find that he wasn't as abstemious as I had thought he would be and that he enjoyed getting jolly. He never got drunk, but he didn't mind getting a bit jolly. I always thought he might get offended if I swore, and yet he just shrugged it off. What I liked about him was that he didn't seem to have a judgemental attitude about whatever it was that I was doing in my life. He was very accepting.

Peter Waterman (songwriter and producer)

The perception you have of Cliff before you meet him is that he wouldn't say boo to a goose. If you go to a pub with Cliff and David Bryce and order a bloody Mary and a tomato juice you'd think the tomato juice was for Cliff and the bloody Mary was for David, but it's the other way around.

Cliff

People who have never met me think that I'm a teetotal vegetarian. They're shocked when I tell them that I eat red meat and love wine. I admire vegetarians, but I couldn't see the future without a good steak. (2002)

Graham Disbrey

When we're on holiday together in Portugal, the routine is usually get up, sunbathe, swim, play tennis every day and eat out in the evening. Cliff will have coaching but the rest of us will just play on his court.

ABOVE
Cliff at his 19th-century farm house in Guia, Portugal, where he traditionally spends his summer holidays

ABOVE
The dining room at Quinto do Moinho, his
Portuguese home

Cliff

The original house I had in Portugal was alright, but it was very vulnerable. It was 200 metres from the beach and there was nothing in front. There was a 180-degree view of the sea. I'd be playing tennis and people would come up for autographs and I thought, "This is not why I came here." Then I saw this other house with a 35-acre farm, so I thought I wouldn't have a holiday house but I'd have a home. So I redecorated and refurbished it and when I come here it's like going home. It's much more comfortable and more desirable. The other place was a fantastic holiday home with a great view. All you had to do was bring an odd bit of clothing. You didn't even have to eat in. We went out every night. We just sunbathed, made tea and poured drinks. This is a fabulous home and I've met someone who is going to make wine for me. David Baverstock suggested I should plant grapevines. I told him that no one makes good wine in the Algarve and his response was that this was because they didn't know how to do it, but if I started now I'd get in a few years before the rest joined in. Sure enough, as soon as I'd planted my vineyard, hundreds of hectares were planted by locals. So, I'm hoping we've done our little bit! In fact, that's why I called the wine "Vida Nova" ["New Life"]: it seemed to give more life to my farm and new life to the wine industry in the Algarve. (2004)

Graham Disbrey

Portugal has been Cliff's primary holiday destination since the early 1960s, but he's also been to Mauritius, Madeira, America, Barbados and other places. For two years, an art dealer, David Mason, lent us his boat. For the first year we sailed round the Greek Islands and the next year we toured the Adriatic.

Cliff

I love the Algarve and I want to give something back to the area. People are surprised that I've set up a vineyard but, frankly, I'm surprised that they're surprised. Actors and singers have always branched out. I love the euphoria of being a vintner. I can put my head around the door of the kitchen and see the vineyards. It's a bit like Peter Mayles' *A Year in Provence*, except that this is *Twenty Years in the Algarve*. I want to slow down. I'm thinking of retiring and this is a project I can do for the next 20 years. Maybe this has come at the right time." (2002)

Stuart Ongley

The idea of the *Something is Goin' On* album was to get back to his roots, and Memphis and Nashville were where some of the great rock 'n' roll came from. Chris Eaton and I have worked in Nashville for years and knew the quality of writing and musicianship there, and so we had talked to Cliff and his management about doing something there for years. Eventually they thought it would be a good idea to give it a shot. It was a great experience.

Chris Eaton (songwriter)

In America, they have writers' camps where writers who don't necessarily know each other all get together to write for one particular artist. Cliff came to Nashville in January 2003 and there were about 20 writers from different genres – pop, country, gospel, blues – and they had to find out who they were writing with and then go away and come up with songs for him to record. It was very creative. Cliff loved having all these writers concentrating on writing songs for him. Some great songs came out of it. Cliff performed them with such passion as did the musicians and the result should be out in the autumn. (2004)

ABOVE
Cliff standing on a terrace at Quinto do Moinho, its vineyards stretching out behind him

Stuart Ongley

There was a lot of talk about doing something with the album in America, but really it was a Cliff album, and first and foremost it had to fit into his business. He has a career outside of America and that had to take precedence. The Nashville experience was very exciting for him; also he saw how major songwriters and producers out there respected him. He was working with some of the best songwriters in Nashville, and they were gathered together simply to write for him. He also made some magnificent music that showed people why he is Cliff Richard.

BELOW
The wine from his Portuguese vineyard is marketed as Vida Nova and Cliff maintains a close interest in its production

Cliff

I haven't given up hope. I'm going to feature songs from it heavily on tour. I thought it was one of the best albums I've made in 20 years.

Chris Eaton

Whenever Cliff comes to the States, he realizes it's easier to feed the places people already love him rather than start something new, where he'd have to dedicate himself to a new market. America is such a big place; you'd have to tour for a year to make any headway.

Cliff

I'm beginning to understand that radio in Britain, apart from Radio 2 and the gold stations, doesn't play records by people like me, regardless of whether the quality is good enough to impress a 20-year-old. We don't figure in their equation. (2006)

Tony Blackburn (DJ, Classic Gold)

It was a beautiful sunny day and I put on "Summer Holiday". Loads of people phoned in to ask for more Cliff songs, so I told listeners I'd play one every day until somebody stopped me. On Monday I got a ticking off from the head of programmes, Paul Baker, who told me this was against station policy. Why? These are good songs with proven appeal. Cliff has sold more records than The Beatles. I thought it was ludicrous that we couldn't play Cliff songs when our audience clearly wanted them. So on Tuesday I put "Summer Holiday" on again. Paul Baker emailed me saying, "You must stop playing him." For a joke, I read his message on air, tore it up and put it in the bin. Then I played "Move It", "We Don't Talk Anymore" and "The Young Ones", a Cliff hat-trick. That was when the managing director, John Baish, emailed me to say that I was being suspended. (2004)

Paul Baker (Head of Programmes, Classic Gold)

We shouldn't be playing Cliff Richard. We might carry out research on him, but for now we have a policy decision that he doesn't match our brand values. He's not on the playlist, and you must stop playing him. (June 23, 2004)

Cliff

Record sales aren't very good these days for people like me when we don't get any airplay. I'm not grumbling; I'm just stating a fact. I don't expect it any more. Things have changed. I've had my day really. Except that when inside you feel you still have something to offer – and the very fact that my album of duets just came in at number eight suggests there is something to offer – you have to find another way of presenting it. (2006)

The Independent

Blackburn is back: battle over Sir Cliff ends in victory for DJ. (June 25, 2004)

Paul Baker

We have to listen to our listeners, or they won't listen to us. It's quite obvious now that they want to hear Cliff Richard on the station, so that's what we'll do. (June 24, 2004)

Tony Blackburn

I'm really pleased to be back on air, that it's all hugs and kisses again with Classic Gold, but most of all that it's the listeners who have won this battle. I'm sure a lot of them wouldn't have rung up to ask for Cliff in the past because they wouldn't think anyone would pay attention. Now they know the power they have. The classic station that broadens its playlist will clean up. I hope that station will be Classic Gold. (June 25, 2004)

Bill Latham (mentor and friend)

Cliff became friends with Surinder Arora eight years ago when he opened two of his other hotels in Gatwick and Heathrow. Cliff respects him as a very successful hotelier and believes that the Arora International Hotel in Manchester will be a good business investment. He won't be serenading guests, but he has donated various guitars and other memorabilia. Three or four of the rooms will have Cliff Richard themes, although we haven't decided the details yet. (2004)

Cliff

The only other thing I've done outside of show business is with a friend of mine, a hotel developer. I went into partnership with him and I own part of a hotel in Manchester. It's a nice, small hotel with about 141 bedrooms and it's going really well. I have never done this sort of thing before, but think that at this stage of my life, I have to think about things to invest my money in. It was fun to get involved in the hotel because it has a great restaurant and I have a hand in designing the place. You can still be creative with something like that. (2004)

Surinder Arora (hotelier and business partner)

I met Cliff when I opened my first hotel. I turned to one of the directors at British Airways and said that I needed some help. He asked me who I wanted. Royalty? Politicians? I said, "Anyone famous. I've written to the royals and to Tony Blair and of course I've had Dear John letters back from all of them." He said, "Well, what do you think of Cliff Richard?" I told him I'd love it because when my mum used to watch Cliff on telly, she would say, "Born in India." 2007

ABOVE

Cliff in India with his friend and business partner Surinder Arora (right). The two of them became partners in a Manchester hotel that offered Cliff-themed rooms

Cliff

It makes sense for people like me to launch fragrances. Most pop singers appeal to a predominantly female audience, which likes to wear perfumes. Like wine, I don't really know how they're made, I just know that I've got a top French perfume maker. He gives me a choice of scents and I pick one. (2004)

Rory Bremner (comedian)

I think Cliff Richard tells Tony Blair what God is thinking. (2005)

Cliff

Cherie Blair came to one of my concerts. We got a request for tickets, we had a meal and a couple of times and Tony was able to join us later. Our relationship hasn't bloomed into a close friendship yet. I wouldn't dream of calling Tony up. (2006)

Cherie Blair (wife of Tony Blair)

I have been lucky enough to get to know Cliff over the years and I can say that he's a nice guy. He is also a decent one and a caring one and one who is not ashamed to say he is a Christian. (2004)

Cliff

I like Tony Blair as a person. I've found him very easy to be with. I've never, ever talked politics with him … We've talked about spiritual things. He likes talking about rock 'n' roll and what I'm doing. Occasionally he'll say "I'm off to see so-and-so tomorrow," and I try not to chase it because I don't want to talk about that with him. I feel that's part of the pressure of his life and if I'm going to befriend someone like that, it's best if I don't do that to him. (2005)

Tony Blair (former British Prime Minister)

Accompanied by my family, I spent summer holidays at a private villa in Barbados owned by Sir Cliff Richard. I have made charitable donations in lieu of the cost of this accommodation. I paid for all other expenses, including flights. (2006, *Register of Members' Interests*)

Cliff

I had watched Tony Blair wither when that war got started. I saw him on television and it seemed to me that he was suffering the results of his decision. I just felt sorry for him so I said to Cherie, "Look. I don't do this thing normally, but I just know my place on Barbados isn't going to be full of people this August and if you want to use it, then go ahead." It was just something I wanted to do for him as a human being. Certainly money didn't come into it. I don't charge any of my friends for staying at the villa. The Blairs said they would give a donation to charity.

I said fine if they were going to do that, but that was up to them. (2006)

ABOVE
Cliff's relationship with Tony Blair became controversial after the Blair family took a summer holidays in Cliff's Barbadian home

Bill Latham

The high cost of running his other properties and the fact that Cliff is spending more time in them has made him question the cost of keeping a large base here [in Weybridge]. It is empty for long periods of the year, and while he has no financial difficulties, he doesn't like to waste money. In addition, he's often complained about rattling about in such a big house. So he has put it on the market in a very discreet way. He has also decided to rent out the Barbados house when he's not there so that it can pay for its own upkeep. (2006)

Cliff

I have sold my house in St George's Hill [Weybridge] and am moving to a smaller place at Wentworth. I'm taking as much as I can from my old garden. The new garden is less than an acre and I'm going to cram everything in. But I'm looking forward to it. (2006)

BELOW
Cliff's mother died at the age of 87. Cliff was in Florida at the time, but returned for the low-key private funeral

Mail on Sunday

Sir Cliff sells up to leave Britain. (2006)

Cliff

I'm not "selling up and leaving Britain". There was a newspaper headline saying that, but in the actual story it said that I wasn't! I don't know how that happened. Journalists sometimes have agendas and I'll never be able to stop that. If the agenda is to write about me in a particular way, this will be added to the facts that I'm selling my house, possibly plan to spend more time abroad and more time in America because I haven't given up hope of breaking into the American market. (2006)

> **Dorothy Marie**
> 13 August 1920 – 17 October 2007
>
> We would like to thank all those who have sent flowers, cards, letters and messages expressing sympathy in the loss of our dear Mum.
>
> Your thoughts and support have been a great comfort to us.
>
> Thank you all.
>
> Cliff, Donna, Jacqui and Joan

Ian Anderson (member of rock group Jethro Tull)

Sir Cliff Richard's first recordings start to come out of copyright protection in just over two years' time, The Beatles in six. This means loss of royalty income not only to performers on the records but, more importantly from the industry perspective, the loss of income to the record companies, and ultimately to the UK exchequer. Our recordings are protected for 95 years in the US. Many other countries such as Australia, Singapore and Brazil protect recordings for 70 years, while India provides 60 years' protection. EU countries, including the UK, protect our recordings for just 50 years. In other words, our recordings enjoy more protection abroad than they do back home. (2006)

Cliff

I know that, as a singer, I need the songwriters, but they also need artists like me. What we want from a song is [royalties] for life, for the rest of your performing career. The fact is that if this continues to happen, artists will not be able to afford to make albums. You have to make a certain amount of money to pay for the sessions. (2006)

Olivia Newton-John

They say that the way you live shows on your face. Cliff hasn't aged in a long time, so he must be doing something right!

Cliff

What I'm finding difficult to cope with at my age – I'll be 66 this year – is that I don't know how to feel. Because I don't feel any different to how I did when I made my first record "Move It" 48 years ago. (2006)

Phil Everly (one-half of The Everly Brothers duo)

I personally like Cliff's music. I expect to see him go on forever. As long as he can go on enjoying life, he can go on enjoying rock 'n' roll. I used to hate the idea back in the fifties when people thought it was adolescent to play rock 'n' roll, that at some point you were expected to do something else. It was like you listened to rock 'n' roll when you were in high school, but then when you went to college you'd listen to folk music. When people ask me how long I can go on playing rock 'n' roll, it's the same as asking me how long I can go on being happy.

Cliff

I think I've done the things I can do and the things that I want to do. But our business is about doing things over and over again and improving them. I've done acting in musicals and on film, I've done TV and radio, I've acted on stage and in television drama. I need to keep doing things over and over again until I get them right. (2006)

Jimmy Tarbuck (comedian and actor)

He was always a nice fellow and he hasn't changed one bit. Cliff is Cliff. What you see is what you get. There isn't another side to him.

Larry Norman (singer-songwriter)

He always looks for songs that fit into his vision. He knows exactly what he wants. A lot of people underestimate his gift because he doesn't write his own songs and he's not moody. I think he has one of the best voices in pop music. He has amazing control and tone. He obviously looks after his voice; your elasticity diminishes as you get older, so to keep your range wide, you have to learn new breathing techniques: know how to relax in between notes. The songs you perform on stage tend to be as fast as they were when you were a teenager so you need to learn to rest at imperceptible stops all the way through.

Royston Ellis (author and poet)

I met Cliff again in Sri Lanka when he played a concert there on his 2007 tour. It was the first time I'd seen him since I left the set of *Wonderful Life* on the Canary Islands in 1963. It was odd meeting him again after so many years. I greeted him with a hug, but sensed that he didn't like that. However, after an hour of reminiscing, particularly about our mutual friend Tony Meehan, he relaxed and at the end there were bear-hugs all round. He made an interesting remark. He remembered that, in 1960, I had promised to have him made Duke of Redonda, since I knew the king and he'd given me a dukedom. However, that never happened. So when we were posing for a photograph he said, "Here we are, a knight and a duke!"

Cliff

The Shadows are technically retired but I'm hoping they will come together one more time so that we can celebrate 50 years together. Even if we can't make a tour I think we could do a big concert. I'd like to make a DVD of it and then everyone can see the joy of our celebration. So my fingers are crossed. As we say in show-biz, "Watch this space!"

Discography

Singles

1958
August: "Move It" #2 UK
November: "High Class Baby" #7 UK
1959
January: "Livin' Lovin' Doll" #20 UK
April: "Mean Streak" #10 UK
July: "Living Doll" #1 UK, #30 US, #37 Canada (CHUM)
October: "Travelling Light" #1 UK
1960
January: "A Voice in the Wilderness" #2 UK
March: "Fall in Love with You" #2 UK
June: "Please Don't Tease" #1 UK
September: "Nine Times Out of Ten" #3 UK
December: "I Love You" #1 UK
1961
February: "Theme for a Dream" #3 UK
March: "Gee Whiz, It's You" #4 UK
June: "A Girl Like You" #3 UK
October: "When the Girl in Your Arms Is the Girl in Your Heart" #3 UK
1962
January: "The Young Ones" #1 UK, #5 Canada (CHUM)
May: "I'm Looking Out the Window"/"Do You Want to Dance?" #2 UK
August: "It'll Be Me" #2 UK, #14 Canada (CHUM; 1963 release)
October: "Wonderful to Be Young" #16 Canada (CHUM)
November: "The Next Time"/"Bachelor Boy" #1 UK, #99 US, #2 Canada (CHUM) (US and Canada: "Bachelor Boy" only)
1963
February: "Summer Holiday" #1 UK, #1 Canada (CHUM)
May: "Lucky Lips" #4 UK, #62 US, #8 Canada (CHUM);

"Dancing Shoes" #1 Canada (CHUM)
August: "It's All in the Game" #2 UK, #25 US, #10 US Adult Contemporary, #1 Canada (CHUM)
November: "Don't Talk to Him" #2 UK, #14 Canada (CHUM)
1964
January: "I'm the Lonely One" #8 UK, #92 US, #18 Canada (CHUM)
US flip-side, I Only Have Eyes for You, bubbled under at #109
April: "Constantly" #4 UK
June: "On the Beach" #7 UK, #12 Canada (CHUM)
August: "A Matter of Moments" #12 Canada (CHUM)
October: "The Twelfth of Never" #8 UK
November: "I Could Easily Fall (in Love with You)" #6 UK, #21 Canada (CHUM)
1965
March: "The Minute You're Gone" #1 UK
June: "On My Word" #12 UK
August: "The Time in Between" #22 UK
October: "Wind Me Up (Let Me Go)" #2 UK
1966
February: "Blue Turns to Grey" #15 UK
July: "Visions" #7 UK
October: "Time Drags By" #10 UK
December: "In the Country" #6 UK
1967
March: "It's All Over" #9 UK
June: "I'll Come Runnin'" #26 UK
September: "The Day I Met Marie" #10 UK
November: "All My Love" #6 UK
1968
March: "Congratulations" #1 UK, #99 US
June: "I'll Love You Forever Today" #27 UK
September: "Marianne" #22 UK

November: "Don't Forget to Catch Me" #21 UK
1969
February: "Good Times (Better Times)" #12 UK
May: "Big Ship" #8 UK
September: "Throw Down a Line" (with Hank Marvin) #7 UK
November: "With the Eyes of a Child" #20 UK
1970
February: "The Joy of Living" (with Hank Marvin) #25 UK
May: "Goodbye Sam, Hello Samantha" #6 UK
August: "I Ain't Got Time Anymore" #21 UK
1971
January: "Sunny Honey Girl" #19 UK
March: "Silvery Rain" #27 UK
June: "Flying Machine" #37 UK
October: "Sing a Song of Freedom" #13 UK
1972
February: "Jesus" #35 UK
August: "Living in Harmony" #12 UK
November: "A Brand New Song" Did Not Chart
1973
March: "Power to All Our Friends" #4 UK
April: "Help It Along"/"Tomorrow Rising" #29 UK
November: "Take Me High" #27 UK
1974
April: "(You Keep Me) Hangin' On" #13 UK
1975
March: "It's Only Me You've Left Behind" Did Not Chart
September: "Honky-Tonk Angel" Did Not Chart
November: "Miss You Nights" #15 UK
1976
April: "Devil Woman" #9 UK, #6 US, #30 US Adult Contemporary, #3 Canada (CHUM)

July: "I Can't Ask for Any More Than You" #17 UK, #80 US
November: "Hey, Mr Dream-Maker" #31 UK
1977
February: "My Kinda Life" #15 UK
June: "When Two Worlds Drift Apart" #46 UK; "Don't Turn the Light Out" #57 US
September: "Try a Smile" #48 US Adult Contemporary
1978
January: "Yes, He Lives!" Did Not Chart
July: "Please Remember Me" Did Not Chart
November: "Can't Take the Hurt Anymore" Did Not Chart
1979
February: "Green Light" #57 UK
July: "We Don't Talk Anymore" #1 UK, #7 US, #5 US Adult Contemporary, #2 Canada (CHUM)
October: "Hot Shot" #46 UK
1980
January: "Carrie" #4 UK, #34 US
August: "Dreamin'" #8 UK, #10 US, #21 US Adult Contemporary, #7 Canada (CHUM)
October: "Suddenly" (with Olivia Newton-John) #15 UK, #20 US, #4 US Adult Contemporary
1981
January: "A Little in Love" #15 UK, #17 US, #6 US Adult Contemporary, #2 Canada (CHUM)
April: "Give a Little Bit More" #41 US, #15 Canada (CHUM)
August: "Wired for Sound" #4 UK, #71 US
November: "Daddy's Home" #2 UK, #23 US, #3 US Adult Contemporary
1982
July: "The Only Way Out" #10 UK, #64 US, 26 US Adult Contemporary

September: "Where Do We Go From Here?" #60 UK

November: "Little Town" #11 UK

1983

February: "She Means Nothing to Me" (with Phil Everly) #9 UK

April: "True Love Ways" #8 UK

May: "Drifting" (with Sheila Walsh) #64 UK

August: "Never Say Die (Give a Little Bit More)" #15 UK, #73 US, #23 US Adult Contemporary

November: "Please Don't Fall in Love" #7 UK

1984

February: "Donna" #17 US Adult Contemporary

March: "Baby You're Dynamite" /"Ocean Deep" #27 UK

September: "Two to the Power of Love" (with Janet Jackson) #83 UK

October: "Shooting from the Heart" #51 UK

1985

January: "Heart User" #46 UK

September: "She's So Beautiful" #17 UK

November: "It's in Every One of Us" #45 UK

1986

March: "Living Doll" (with "The Young Ones") #1 UK

May: "Born To Rock 'n' Roll" Did Not Chart

September: "All I Ask of You" (with Sarah Brightman) #3 UK

November: "Slow Rivers" (with Elton John) #44 UK

1987

June: "My Pretty One" #6 UK

August: "Some People" #3 UK

October: "Remember Me" #35 UK

1988

February: "Two Hearts" #34 UK

November: "Mistletoe and Wine" #1 UK

1989

May: "The Best of Me" #2 UK

August: "I Just Don't Have the Heart" #3 UK

October: "Lean On You" #17 UK

November: "Whenever God Shines His Light" (with Van Morrison) #20 UK

1990

February: "Stronger than That" #14 UK

August: "Silhouettes" #10 UK

October: "From a Distance" #11 UK

November: "Saviour's Day" #1 UK

1991

September: "More to Life" #23 UK (featured in the TV series "Trainer" on the BBC)

November: "We Should Be Together" #10 UK

1992

January: "This New Year" #30 UK

November: "I Still Believe in You" #7 UK

1993

March: "Peace in Our Time" #8 UK

June: "Human Work of Art" #24 UK

September: "Never Let Go" #32 UK

December: "Healing Love" #19 UK

1994

November: "All I Have to Do Is Dream" / "Miss You Nights" #14 UK

1995

October: "Misunderstood Man" #19 UK

November: "Had to Be" with Olivia Newton John #22 UK

1996

March: "The Wedding" (with Helen Hobson) #40 UK

October: "Be with Me Always" #52 UK

1998

October: "Can't Keep This Feeling in" #10 UK

1999

July: "The Miracle" #23 UK

November: "The Millennium Prayer" #1 UK

2001

December: "Somewhere Over the Rainbow/"What a Wonderful World" #11 UK

2002

April: "Let Me Be the One" #29 UK

2003

December: "Santa's List" #5 UK

2004

October: "Somethin' Is Goin' On" #9 UK

December: "I Cannot Give You My Love" #13 UK

2005

May: "What Car?" #12 UK

2006

December: "21st-Century Christmas"/"Move It" #2 UK

2007

October: "When I Need You"

Albums

1959 *Cliff* UK #4

1959 *Cliff Sings* UK #2

1960 *Me and My Shadows* UK #2

1961 *Listen to Cliff* UK #2

1961 *21 Today* UK #1

1961 *The Young Ones* UK #1

1962 *32 Minutes & 17 Seconds with Cliff Richard* UK #3

1963 *Summer Holiday* UK #1

1963 *Cliff's Hit Album* UK #2

1963 *When in Spain* UK #8

1963 *Wonderful Life* UK #2

1964 *Aladdin & His Wonderful Lamp* UK #13

1965 *Cliff Richard* UK #9

1965 *More Hits by Cliff* UK #20

1965 *Love Is Forever* UK #9

1966 *Finders Keepers* UK #6

1967 *Cinderella* UK #30

1967 *Good News* UK #37

1968 *Two a Penny* Did Not Chart

1968 *Established 1958* UK #30

The Best of Cliff UK #5

1969 *Sincerely Cliff* UK #24

1969 *Live at The Talk of the Town* Did Not Chart

1970 *Tracks and Grooves* UK #37

1972 *The Best of Cliff, Volume 2* UK #49

1973 *Take Me High* UK #41

1974 *Help It Along* Did Not Chart

1975 *The 31st of February Street* Did Not Chart

1976 *I'm Nearly Famous* UK #5 (Gold); US #76

1977 *Every Face Tells a Story* UK #8 (Gold)

1977 *40 Golden Greats* UK #1 (Platinum)

1978 *Small Corners* UK #33

1978 *Green Light* UK #25

1979 *Thank You Very Much* UK #5 (Gold)

1979 *Rock 'n' Roll Juvenile* UK

(Gold)#3

1980 *I'm No Hero* UK #4 (Gold); US #80

1981 *Love Songs* UK #1 (Platinum UK)

1981 *Wired for Sound* UK #4; (Gold) US #132

1982 *Now You See Me ... Now You Don't* UK #4 (Gold UK)

1983 *25 Years of Gold* AUS #1

1983 *Dressed for the Occasion* UK #7 (Gold UK)

1983 *Silver* UK #7 (Gold)

1984 *The Rock Connection* UK #43 (Silver UK)

1987 *Always Guaranteed* UK #5 (Platinum)

1988 *Private Collection: 1979-1988* UK #1 (4 wks)(Multi Platinum UK)

1989 *Stronger* UK #7 (Platinum UK)

1990 *From a Distance: The Event* UK #3 (Platinum UK)

1991 *Together with Cliff Richard* UK #10 (Platinum UK)

1993 *The Album* UK #1 (Platinum UK)

1994 *The Hit List* UK #3 (Platinum)

1995 *Songs from* Heathcliff UK #15 (Gold)

1998 *Real As I Wanna Be* UK #10 (Gold)

2000 *The Whole Story: His Greatest Hits* UK #6 (Platinum UK)

2001 *Wanted* UK #11 (Double Gold UK)

2003 *Cliff at Christmas* UK #9 (Platinum UK)

2004 *Something's Goin' On* UK #7 (Gold UK)

2005 *The Platinum Collection* UK 51

2006 *Two's Company* UK #8 (Double Gold UK)

2007 *Love: The Album*

Bibliography

Books by or about Cliff

1959 Fans Star Library (#28) 'Cliff
Richard' (London: Amalgamated
Press)
Harris, Jet and Ellis, Royston 'Driftin'
With Cliff' (London: Charles
Buchan)

1960 Richard, Cliff 'It's Great To Be
Young' (London: Souvenir Press)
Sutter, Jack 'Cliff: The Baron of Beat'
(Blackpool: Valex Products)

1961 Richard, Cliff 'Me and My Shadows'
(London: Daily Mirror Newspapers)

1964 Ferrier, Bob 'The Wonderful World
of Cliff Richard' (London: Peter
Davies)

1967 Winter, David 'New Singer
New Song' (London: Hodder &
Stoughton)

1968 Richard, Cliff 'The Way I See It'
(London: Hodder & Stoughton)

1970 Richard, Cliff 'Questions' (London:
Hodder & Stoughton)

1973 Richard, Cliff 'The Way I See It Now'
(London: Hodder & Stoughton)

1975 Tremlett, George 'The Cliff Richard
Story' (London: Futura)

1977 Richard, Cliff 'Which One's Cliff'
(London: Hodder & Stoughton)

1981 Jasper, Tony and Doncaster, Patrick
'Cliff' (London: Sidgewick &
Jackson)
St John, Kevin, 'Cliff in His Own
Words' (London: W. H. Allen)

1983 Tobler, John ' 25 Years of Cliff'
(London: Optimum)

1985 Richard, Cliff 'Jesus, You and Me'
(London: Hodder & Stoughton)
Hoffman, Dezo and Jopling, Norman

'Cliff Richard and the Shadows'
(London: Virgin)

1986 Read, Mike 'The Cliff Richard File'
(London: Houghton)

1988 Richard, Cliff 'Single Minded'
(London: Hodder & Stoughton)

1989 Wassif, Theresa 'Cliff: A Celebration'
(London: Hodder & Stoughton)
Jasper, Tony 'Survivor: A Tribute to
Cliff' (London: Marshall Pickering)

1991 Barker, Gale 'Cliff Richard (London:
Marshall Pickering)
Lewry, Peter 'The Complete
Recording Sessions 1958-1990'
(London: Blandford)

1993 Turner, Steve 'Cliff Richard: The
Biography' (Oxford, Lion)
Lewry, Peter and Goodall, Nigel
'Cliff Richard: The Complete
Chronicle' (London: Hamlyn)

1996 Lewry, Peter and Goodall, Nigel 'The
Ultimate Cliff'
(London: Simon & Schuster)

1997 Turner, Steve 'Cliff: For the Record'
(London: HarperCollins)

1999 Richard, Cliff 'Cliff Richard: A
Celebration' (London: Andre
Deutsch)

2007 Ewbank, Tim and Hildred, Stafford
'Cliff: An Intimate Portrait'
(London: Virgin)

Books that refer to Cliff's career

1961 Ellis, Royston 'The Big Beat Scene'
(London: Four Square)
Ellis, Royston 'The Shadows by
Themselves' (London: Consul)

1963 Clews, Frank 'The Golden Disc'
(London: Brown, Watson Ltd.)

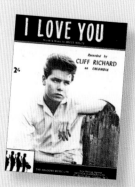

Index

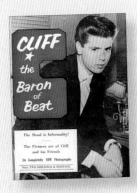